THE POLITICS OF VIRGINITY

THE POLITICS OF VIRGINITY

Abstinence in Sex Education

Alesha E. Doan and
Jean Calterone Williams

Reproductive Rights and Policy
Judith Baer, Series Editor

Westport, Connecticut
London

Library of Congress Cataloging-in-Publication Data

Doan, Alesha E., 1972–
  The politics of virginity : abstinence in sex education / Alesha E. Doan and
Jean Calterone Williams.
      p. cm. — (Reproductive rights and policy, ISSN 1558–8734)
  Includes bibliographical references and index.
  ISBN-13: 978–0–275–99009–1 (alk. paper)
  1. Sex instruction for teenagers—Political aspects—United
States.   2. Sexual abstinence—Study and teaching—Political aspects—
United States.   I. Williams, Jean Calterone, 1966–   II. Title.
  HQ35.D63   2008
    306.73'208350973–dc22   2008002467

British Library Cataloguing in Publication Data is available.

Library of Congress Catalog Card Number: 2008002467
ISBN: 978–0–275–99009–1
ISSN: 1558–8734

First published in 2008

Praeger Publishers, 88 Post Road West, Westport, CT 06881
An imprint of Greenwood Publishing Group, Inc.
www.praeger.com

Printed in the United States of America

The paper used in this book complies with the
Permanent Paper Standard issued by the National
Information Standards Organization (Z39.48–1984).

10 9 8 7 6 5 4 3 2 1

From Alesha E. Doan:
For Spencer, Cooper, and Liliana
—always remember your worth—

From Jean Calterone Williams:
For Cass and Shane

Contents

Series Foreword

"Sexual intercourse began in nineteen sixty-three," wrote the poet Philip Larkin. His precision was poetic license, but his location of the "sexual revolution" in the 1960s was accurate. At the beginning of the decade, youth were exhorted to "wait till marriage"; educational films graphically warned against the consequences of doing otherwise. Practice did not always follow precept, especially after the birth control pill gave women a reliable, convenient, and safe contraceptive. By 1970, attitudes toward nonmarital sex ranged from tolerance to acceptance to approval.

This profound change in social mores did not create a utopia of free love. "You may not" often confused "you may" with "you must." Feminists have described how the new norms, the new contraceptives, and the new abortion rights combined to put pressure on women to have sex. The new freedom was limited in scope. It excluded both homosexuals and the young, whatever their sexual preferences. Social attitudes toward homosexuals have become more liberal since the 1960s, but federal, state, and local governments continue to discourage youthful sexuality.

The new leniency never won universal approval. Many Americans continued to regard premarital chastity as a moral imperative. The size and influence of this group increased as the religious Right gained political strength in the final decades of the twentieth century. A generation ago, when the median age of women at marriage was 19, abstinence until marriage might have seemed reasonable. Now that the average age is 25 and safe sex is a possibility, the case for abstinence has weakened. But minors remain subject to control by parents, schools, and society.

More than a few adults seem to regard youthful sex like the duchess who said on her wedding night, "This is too good for the common people." Many, especially those who have frequent contact with adolescents, insist they are not "mature enough" for sex. Some empirical support for this opinion exists. Recent neurological studies suggest that the parts of the brain thought to control risk and facilitate consequential thinking do not fully develop until the mid-20s. Teens who protect themselves from pregnancy and disease are controlling risks and anticipating consequences. It is difficult for the neutral observer to avoid the conclusion that anyone who does this is mature enough to have sex. But the religious Right strives to withhold from teens knowledge that would facilitate mature behavior. One means of doing this is sex education that presents abstinence as the only acceptable method of preventing conception. This is the only instruction available in one-third of American schools. Studies show that about 90 percent of parents want their children to learn about contraception. But abstinence advocates are moralistic, not pragmatic. They want to prevent teenage sex more than they want to prevent teenage pregnancy.

The Politics of Virginity presents a masterful analysis of the origins, content, and impact of abstinence-only sex education. Alesha Doan and Jean Williams locate this controversy squarely within the context of what social scientists call morality politics. "Stealth morality policy," the authors write, "may allow an unpopular policy, or a policy supported by a well-organized minority, to be passed legislatively without having to undergo much legislative debate or public scrutiny." The abstinence lobby has been better organized, better integrated, and better prepared than the pragmatic majority. A scene I witnessed in central Texas, the hijacking of a local school board meeting by abstinence advocates, has been repeated many times, many ways, and in many places.

Doan and Williams's review of abstinence-based curricula is enlightening and troubling. Texts are chock-full of retrograde gender stereotypes, incomplete information (not to mention outright falsehoods), moralistic exhortation, scare tactics, and Biblical overtones that at best approach and at worst cross the constitutional line between religion and public education. Teen sex is "destructive" and "dysfunctional." Women cannot separate sex from relationships as men can, good girls are virgins, girls and women are responsible for preventing sexual assault, and efforts to control the consequences of sex are futile. Contraception is mentioned only in terms of failure rates, if at all. The reader may get the impression

that abstinence-only curricula educators regard pregnancy and disease as fit pun-
ishments for teenage sex.

About half of high school–age teens are sexually active. The teen pregnancy
rate has just risen for the first time in several years. These data suggest that
abstinence-based education has failed, but that depends on whether your priority
is fewer pregnancies or less sex. The fact that teen pregnancy rates fell steadily
through the 1990s and into the twenty-first century suggests that some recipients
of abstinence-based education might have taken its message to heart. And, after
all, what is so bad about postponing sexual activity for a few years? Nothing,
perhaps, if "wait" is the only message conveyed by these programs. Plenty, when
this message is combined with fear, misinformation, and bias.

Doan and Williams do not limit their study to the *macro* effects of abstinence-
only programs. Their interviews with 32 young women of diverse racial backgrounds
and sexual histories give equal attention to the *micro* effects. Some reported that
they regarded virginity as a gift and regretted having given it away. But "the idea
that teens should remain abstinent until marriage does not begin to connect with
many of these young women's lived experiences." One example of this discontinu-
ity between precept and practice is the pressure to have sex and the sexual assault
that several interviewees reported. These accounts bear out feminist caveats and
remind us of the strength and persistence of male dominance. But abstinence-only
programs offer no corrective for this abuse. Curricula that include birth control
do, by enabling young women to control the effects of what they are forced or persuaded to do. Lesson and experience did coincide, however, with respect to gender
differences in sexuality. The interviewees found that, as the texts suggested, they
attach more emotional and relational content to sex than do their partners.

So girls are reluctant to have sex, yield to their partners' desires, and have
trouble getting the information they need to control the consequences. Whatever else abstinence-only education does, it contravenes the principle of sexual
equality in both theory and practice and reinforces rather than challenges male
supremacy. *The Politics of Virginity* is an innovative, original contribution to the
study of women's reproductive rights that shows we still have a long way to go.

Judith Baer
Series Editor

Preface

In the past decade, dozens of abstinence-only organizations have sprung up across the United States. These organizations publish literature expounding on the virtues of abstinence until marriage for all unmarried individuals, both teens and adults. They write and market public school curricula to teach teens why and how to wait. They offer abstinence programs for churches, community groups, and public and parochial schools; and they hold large events around the country such as a "Day of Purity" or "The Silver Ring Thing," where teens pledge chastity until marriage. Countless Web sites sell paraphernalia embossed with abstinence-only messages to help teens keep their commitment to purity (Simon 2006). T-shirts with catchy phrases, such as "Earn your right to wear white: ABSTAIN," "Respect God, Respect Yourself, Abstain," "Virgin for Jesus," or "Abstinence makes the heart grow fonder," are readily available for purchase through the Internet.

Abstinence-only programs encourage teens and adults to abstain from sex until marriage and provide support networks, particularly for teens who want to abstain. The Christian Right helps promote an abstinence-only message by sponsoring events and publishing books to help teens honor virginity and ward off sexual desires.[1] Some of these events, books, and school curricula contain an explicitly religious message supporting abstinence, while others are more secular. For example, Focus on the Family publishes a book that is designed to offer a roadmap for maintaining virginity for young men. It is a "purity game plan for guys that promises to teach them to become warriors who are able to conquer the 'sharp-fanged, drooling monster'—lust—'that crouches at your door waiting to poison your life'" (Simon 2006, A9).

The current proliferation and success of abstinence-only programs can be credited to a measure included in the 1996 Personal Responsibility and Work Opportunity Reconciliation Act (PRWORA). Abstinence-only education was nested within this high profile welfare reform bill, suggesting that it is part of a larger plan to combat poverty. In reality, abstinence funding reaches well beyond welfare recipients. The federal government provides grants to community-based organizations that deliver abstinence-only programs as well as grants to states for abstinence-only education in the classroom.

While conservative Christians' support for abstinence-only education is not new, its scope, funding, and the idea that it can serve as a solution for poverty is a more recent tactic. Legislative success for abstinence-only proponents was followed by significantly expanded funding, signaling a new era for this particular type of education. Abstinence-only education is taught in a third of public school districts; it is the fastest growing type of sex education. The majority of teenagers in the United States receive a public school education, so abstinence-only education has significant reach (Landry, Kaeser, and Richards 1999; Vergari 2001).

Abstinence-only education, however, is out of step with public opinion. A majority of adults (approximately 82%) favor comprehensive sexuality education that encompasses both abstinence and other pregnancy prevention methods. Half of American adults oppose abstinence-only education programs (Bleakley, Hennessy, and Fishbein 2006).

To further complicate debates over sexuality education, alongside the programs, curricula, and cultural messages promoting abstinence until marriage are messages glorifying sexuality and welcoming the arrival of sexual freedom for women as well as men. Images of glamorous celebrities, unmarried and pregnant, are celebrated on the covers of popular magazines. Cohabitation rates have risen rapidly in the past few decades, with a concomitant increase in the numbers of both men and women who delay marriage. These mixed cultural messages and practices exemplify the contradictions, confusion, and competition of values surrounding issues of sexuality. Teens learn lessons about sex and sexuality from diverse sources, including families, media, and peers. Thus, the ideas represented in abstinence-only sex education are but one source of information for adolescents.

The narrow approach of abstinence-only education enforces a value system that is not reflective of the beliefs of a majority of Americans and ignores the pragmatism that characterizes many adult attitudes toward adolescent sexuality. More problematically, the lessons presented in abstinence-only education are frequently at odds with the *actual* behavior of teens. The lack of congruency between citizens' preferences, adolescent behavior, and enacted policy is puzzling.

This paradox has motivated our investigation into the politics surrounding sex education, in particular the rise of abstinence-only-until-marriage curricula in the public schools. Our research is driven by three overarching questions: (1) Why is abstinence-only education being taught in over one-third of public schools? (2) What are the implicit and explicit lessons imparted to teen women through abstinence-only teachings? (3) How do these lessons fit into young women's lives? We take different approaches to answering these questions.

To answer *why* abstinence-only education is being taught, we examine morality politics as a framework for contextualizing and understanding the formation and implications of abstinence-only policy. Morality policies are those that address moral, rather than material, issues, such as abortion or gay marriage. By analyzing the use of morality politics we argue that abstinence-only education is more than a symbolic representation of a modern cultural disagreement. Abstinence-only education represents a policy innovation in the battle for footing in the cultural and moral conflicts taking place in American politics. It is a morality policy designed to influence behavior—promoting abstinence from sexual activity for all people until heterosexual marriage. We argue this morality policy follows the contours of other morality policies but also is ushering in a new form of "stealth" morality policies that are being disguised and attached to omnibus legislation that is primarily dealing with other issues. We suggest these less visible and secretive morality policies are then being used to morph into, and regulate, other morality issues.

In turn, we use the morality politics framework to contextualize the content of abstinence-only curriculum and investigate *what* lessons these programs impart to teen women. We undertake a systematic content analysis of the four leading abstinence-only curricula, documenting the major and minor themes as well as their frequency in the curricula. The content analysis provides a systematic and balanced picture of what the curricula explicitly contains in terms of content. We follow this quantitative account with a detailed deconstruction of select passages from the curricula to investigate the lessons these programs convey to teen women.

We attempt to answer *how* abstinence-only lessons fit into young women's lives through the stories of 32 teenage women who were interviewed for this research from April 2001 to February 2002.[2] The young women interviewed were solicited from several agencies in California that work with low income or "at risk" teens, including an alternative California high school, AmeriCorp, and the Economic Opportunity Commission's Teenage Academic Parenting Program in San Luis Obispo county. Other teens came from a church youth group and from a group home for teens in foster care. All of these agencies provided access to the adolescents; however, participation was voluntary. These open-ended interviews assess respondents' experiences with and interpretations of abstinence education, in the context of their perceptions and analyses of their own sexual experiences and sexualities. The teen women interviewed included those who were sexually active, never sexually active, pregnant, and parenting.

These young women are not representative of all teenagers; in fact, they are not representative of most teens. Rather, these adolescents fit the profile of individuals targeted by the welfare reform measures: A disproportionate number of respondents are young women of color and are teenage mothers. While their experiences often diverge from the typical teenager, their stories provide meaningful and important analyses of how sex and sexuality are shaped by power differentials constructed through the matrix of gender, age, race, class, and education.

THE STRUCTURE OF THE BOOK

To explore the politics of sex education, chapter one examines abstinence-only education as a morality policy, using a morality politics framework to understand abstinence-only education. Chapter two analyzes the reform of welfare in 1996. It is this law that contains the definition of abstinence that informs abstinence-only education and is tied to several federal funding streams. We explore the politics surrounding welfare and abstinence education, linking complex issues of gender, race, and class to the changes that took place in the 1996 welfare reform. Chapter three examines the social construction of adolescent women's sexuality, pairing a deconstruction of dominant narratives of young women's sexuality with a discussion of adolescent sexual practices.

Using the first three chapters as the context to understand and assess abstinence-only education, in chapter four, the content and approach of abstinence-only curricula is examined, including the specific messages presented and methods utilized to teach abstinence. While there has been much discussion of abstinence-only education in the literature and popular media, there is a lack of systematic information on the actual content of abstinence-only curricula. Using content analysis methods, the major daily and weekly topics are identified as well as the core themes addressed in four leading abstinence-only curricula written for teens in grades 9 through 12. From the content analysis, we conclude that abstinence-only curricula reinforce traditional gender roles and gender hierarchies. At the same time, they downplay, eschew, or ignore salient issues relating to sexuality that disproportionately impact young women and completely silence sexuality that is not heterosexually compliant.

In addition to a content analysis, interviews with 32 teenage women are presented in chapter five. Teens tell gripping and poignant stories about their experiences, addressing numerous topics central to understanding gender, sexuality, and adolescence. The young women talk about pregnancy, parenting, birth control, sexual assault, and virginity, among other topics. They provide meaningful and important analyses of how sex and sexuality are shaped by power differentials constructed through interconnections among gender, age, class, and education. Though sex education policy fundamentally affects these young women, theirs are voices that are rarely heard on these issues. To give voice to some of these young women, we feature a different teen's story at the beginning of chapters one through five.

Finally, the conclusion brings together the lessons embedded in abstinence-only education, based on what is included in, and purposefully excluded from, the curricula. Pairing this with the stories of the young women interviewed, we argue that abstinence is a useful message when included with a comprehensive approach to sexuality, but as a sexual ideology used alone to educate young people, it is irresponsibly incomplete. We also revisit the larger context of abstinence education, examining its efficacy and future as a morality policy as well as the implications it suggests for future morality policy conflicts.

NOTES

1. We use the terms *New Right, Christian Right, conservative Christians*, or *religious conservatives* to refer to the larger social movement that includes a broad constellation of interest groups, think tanks, grass roots organizations, political actors, and political parties that are united in their conservative, and often Christian fundamentalist, social agenda. Some aspects of that social agenda include abstinence-only sex education, anti-abortion policies, prayer in school, and emphasizing traditional gender relationships, particularly promoting heterosexual marriage and "pro-family" reforms.

2. This is a brief description of the interviewee sample. A more thorough description of the respondents and interviewing process is contained in chapter five.

BIBLIOGRAPHY

Bleakley, Amy, Michael Hennessy, and Martin Fishbein. 2006. "Public Opinion on Sex Education in US Schools." *Archives of Pediatrics & Adolescent Medicine* 160 (November): 1151–56.

Landry, David, Lisa Kaeser, and Cory L. Richards. 1999. "Abstinence Promotion and the Provision of Information about Contraception in Public School District Sexuality Education Policies." *Family Planning Perspectives* 31 (6): 280–86.

Simon, Stephanie. 2006. "Hundreds of Teenagers Plan to Make Valentine's a 'Day of Purity.'" *Los Angeles Times* (February 13): A9.

Vergari, Sandra. 2001. "Morality Politics and the Implementation of Abstinence-Only Sex Education: A Case of Policy Compromise." In *The Public Clash of Private Values*, ed. Christopher Z. Mooney, 201–10. New York: Chatham House Publishers.

Acknowledgments

This study would not have been completed without the support and assistance of many people. We owe a great debt to the young women who agreed to be interviewed and were willing to open up their lives to us. Teachers and program coordinators at Lopez High School, San Luis Obispo AmeriCorp, and the SLO County Economic Opportunity Commission's Teenage Academic Parenting Program generously gave of their time in helping us to set up teen interviews.

We were fortunate to have had a number of hard-working and capable student research assistants who helped with various tasks such as coding curricula, transcribing interviews, and other research. In particular, we thank Amanda Alquist, Greg Worden, Brianna Swartz, Kaitlyn Alaimo, Brittany Clark, Misty Sisneros, Phil Alonso, and Meital Manzuri for their patient assistance. A grant from the Cal Poly Foundation in 2002 helped to fund a research assistant for the summer. A grant from the Institute for Policy & Social Research, University of Kansas in 2006 helped fund this research as well.

We also want to thank our editors, Hilary Claggett and Robert Hutchinson, at Praeger Press for their enthusiasm and support for this project. Judy Baer, the series editor, as well as the anonymous reviewers for this manuscript, have provided excellent critical feedback that has helped shape this project. Tom Farrell generously read multiple versions of this manuscript, and his comments and insights were among the most helpful we received. We are indebted to you all.

On a personal note, thanks to Cass Russett for his support, humor, and help throughout the course of this project. It would not have been completed without him. And finally, a special thank you to Tom Farrell and Spencer T. Doan for always being the best part of any day, and the only bright spot to a long weekend spent working.

1

Under the Radar: The Advent of Stealth Tactics in Morality Policy

I n this chapter we first hear from Yolanda, who is a teenage mother. Her story highlights the complex factors that motivate and shape adolescents' sexual decision making, and in turn, leads to an examination of how the concept of virginity fits into contemporary ideas about adolescent sexuality. This exploration indicates there are inherent limitations to promoting abstinence-only-until-marriage messages in a *post-virginal* society. Within this cultural context, abstinence-only education appears to be an awkward policy solution for preventing the unintended consequences associated with sexual activity.[1]

Why then, is abstinence-only education being taught in one-third of public schools? We propose that sex education policy can be understood within a morality policy framework in the sense that advocates are pressing a particular moral agenda through abstinence-only sex education. Specifically, Christian conservatives have been active in creating a moral agenda that calls for a return to traditional values regarding gender and sexuality. Morality policies have clear and traceable characteristics, patterns, and nuances that provide an explanation for the existence of the abstinence-only policy; morality policies tend to address such issues as gay marriage, abortion, and like policy areas where the locus of the conflict is moral, not material. Advocates of morality policies wish to create change, largely through moral persuasion and policies regulating behavior.

The introduction of abstinence-only education policy also represents a departure from the tactics most commonly used to achieve policy success in morality politics. This strategy, which we term *stealth morality policy*, mirrors omnibus legislative strategies used in nonmorality policy areas.[2] Stealth morality policy may allow an unpopular policy, or a policy supported by a well-organized minority, to be passed legislatively without having to undergo much legislative debate or public scrutiny.

YOLANDA'S STORY

When Yolanda was 14 years old she ran away from home because she was having problems with her parents. She moved in with her 14-year-old boyfriend, Mario, who lived with his parents. Yolanda's parents had never talked to her about sex. Her aunt was the only person who broached the subject with Yolanda, stressing the importance of delaying sex because of the risk of disease. Although her parents skirted "sex talks" with Yolanda, they did impress upon her their pro-life belief in the sanctity of life from conception onward.

When Yolanda moved in with Mario and his family, they did not actively decide to have sex. Rather, Yolanda says, "it just happened." Afterwards, Yolanda felt apprehensive, which gave way to relief in her decision to have sex with Mario:

> I was nervous and we did talk about it after and he said if I didn't want to have sex that we didn't have to have sex, that it wasn't a big deal to him. That he wasn't going to break up with me or nothing like that. So he made me feel safe and stuff . . . We didn't have sex for a while, then we ended up having sex again . . . I felt good that I had done something right in that I didn't do it with the wrong person. I know some girls that have done it just because of the guy making them . . . I mean, if they want to because of the guy, you can't change their opinion. I know I tried a lot with my friend that was having sex before I was and I couldn't change it. She was still gonna have sex either way.[3]

Thus, Yolanda articulates a multilayered and convoluted emotional response to her first sexual experience. Her analysis of her experience is shaped by her observations of the gendered nature of adolescent sexual activity.

Mario has been Yolanda's only sexual partner, and although she feels she chose her partner wisely, she was not prepared for the outcome of their sexual activity. After living together for a month—and sporadically using birth control pills and condoms—Yolanda became pregnant. Even though she did not want to get pregnant, Yolanda also expressed ambivalence about it. "It's not that I wanted a baby . . . I didn't care. Like really I didn't, you know, so like I didn't mean to have a baby . . . And then it turned out I was pregnant. So I couldn't do nothing about it." Given Yolanda's belief system, obtaining an abortion or placing her baby up for adoption were not options. "I don't think abortions are right. And giving up my baby—I don't think I'd even be able to do that, even to give it to my own mom."

Unlike Yolanda's ambivalence toward pregnancy, Mario wanted Yolanda to get pregnant. He pledged to stand by her and their baby and support them financially and emotionally. "He was happy. He said that he was gonna help me out and he was gonna be there when I told my parents and he told his parents. And how we were never gonna be separated." True to his word, Mario sought employment and provided emotional support to Yolanda. His age was a barrier to gainful employment but he was able to generate a marginal income helping in his grandfather's strawberry field. Mario was also with Yolanda when she told her parents that she was pregnant. Her parents were very supportive of their news: "They were happy. I mean they couldn't do nothing. It's not like they were gonna say go get an abortion because they don't like abortions. They just helped me out. They said they were gonna help me out as much as I needed their help."

Three years later, Yolanda and Mario are 17 years old, and their son is 2 years old. They are married, living with family members, and receiving emotional and financial support from both sets of parents. Mario and Yolanda are working and trying to graduate from high school. The familial support they have received has been key to maintaining their financial and emotional well being.

Even with family support, Yolanda talks about the difficulty of being a teen parent in society. During her pregnancy people often stared at her and made judgmental comments to her as well as her parents. Family friends looked down on Yolanda's parents, believing they "didn't do a good job" because she was pregnant. After her pregnancy, stares, comments, and judgments from strangers continue to be routine occurrences in her life.

> It's just their comments, "there's a baby having another baby." It's just I don't like that. And it's like they judge you just because you have a baby. Like I called the doctor a couple days ago and I told them I was seventeen and then they're all "so how old is your brother or sister?" And I said, "no, it's my son" and they're all "how old is he?" I'm all "two," and then they just go "oh, so you were how old when you got pregnant?" And I personally think it's none of their business. So that's kind of like wrong, you know? It's like none of your business. We're not asking you to take care of us.

Yolanda is firmly aware that her survival and her son's survival are linked to the support she receives from Mario and both of their families. She regards herself as fortunate to have such sound support and recognizes that many teen-age mothers who do not have similar support systems end up with very differ-ent stories. But even with a support system, Yolanda has not been shielded from society's reaction to her as a pregnant teenager, an unmarried teen mother, and even now as a married teenage mother. As Yolanda's experience indicates, her options as a teenage mother are limited and dependent upon the choices made by those around her. In Yolanda's case, the decisions made by Mario, his parents, and Yolanda's parents have created an environment where crucial resources (such as financial support, childcare, and emotional support) are available, which in turn have enabled both Yolanda and Mario to remain in school.

Yolanda's experiences with pregnancy and parenting illuminate the multidi-mensionality of adolescent sexuality, decision-making, pregnancy, and parent-hood. All of these complex issues are intertwined and coalesce in a variety of ways for individual teenagers. In talking to Yolanda, it is clear that her decision to become sexually active was not informed by any one single factor. Her parents did not discuss sex, and her aunt encouraged her to remain abstinent until marriage, but ultimately Yolanda's decision to become sexually active was motivated by a mix of factors: curiosity, ignorance, ambivalence about sex, opportunity, as well as her love toward Mario. These individual and situational factors contributed to Yolanda's unplanned pregnancy.

Teenage pregnancy and parenthood often evoke "knee jerk" reactions from people because they touch on a multitude of emotions, beliefs, and values. Most obviously, teenage pregnancy is visible evidence that adolescents are having sex-ual relationships outside of the context of marriage. For some adults, the pros-pect of adolescents engaging in sexual activity is uncomfortable or disconcerting, but for many others, it is viewed as a breach of morals and values. Beyond ques-tions of morality, unmarried childbearing creates several other costs for society. In Yolanda's case, her family was willing to bear many of the financial and emotional costs associated with teenage parenting; however, if a person's family is unwill-ing or unable to bear the costs, she may seek support from various governmental programs.

To combat unmarried teen pregnancy, policy makers and other governmen-tal and social leaders have long attempted to regulate sexual activity outside of marriage. There are multiple ways to define the issue and approach the goal of decreasing the number of unmarried teen parents. To limit teen sexual activity and childbearing, those who embrace abstinence-only education diverge consid-erably in educational methods, forms, and tactics from those who support com-prehensive sexuality education. And so advocates on both sides argue about the explicit lessons and implicit values taught in sex education and the efficacy of various sex education approaches.[4]

Historically in the United States, public policies and the discourse surrounding them often link premarital sex to immorality and tend to downplay many of the other significant issues related to unmarried pregnancy. Abstinence-only education is the latest iteration of a long-standing claim that the *best* way to eliminate childbearing outside of marriage and prevent other risks associated with premarital sex is to focus on morality. Within all these debates, competing notions of morality and divergent social constructions of sexuality, gender, race, class, and adolescence are at stake.

THE CONTEMPORARY VIRGIN

Abstinence-only education requires that young women and men abstain from all sexual activity until marriage, including any activity beyond kissing. But as Joan Jacobs Brumberg suggests, in modern society, virginity—as a concept and practice—is disappearing. "[V]irginity has become an outmoded concept. Even if a contemporary girl resists intercourse, her eyes and ears have undoubtedly been filled with graphic, sexually explicit information since an early age" (Brumberg 1997, 141). But perhaps more notable—and more distressing for abstinence-only advocates—is the relative public acceptance today of young women's sexual desires and sexual expression; we are surrounded by "the idea that sexuality is the ultimate form of self-expression" (Brumberg 1997, 143).

Sexuality is expressed, celebrated, and flaunted in many venues throughout society. Teenagers are an integral part of the performative aspects of sexuality, particularly on the Internet. Over half of all Internet blogs are authored by adolescents who volunteer information about themselves, communicate with friends, and meet other teens on the Internet (Sullivan 2005). Social networking sites rank among the most popular venues for adolescent communication; thereon, teens often compete with other bloggers by engaging in attention-seeking behavior. Provocative comments and images of teens with "their butt in the air, with their thongs sticking out" and their cleavage on display often accompany their Internet sites (Sullivan 2005, 1). In this "postmodern, post-virginal world" few people assume that most women entering into heterosexual marriage are virgins, and in practice, most are not (Brumberg 1997, 143; Finer 2007).

Yet, acceptance of female sexual self-expression is complex. Even with widespread tolerance of some aspects of adolescent sexual expression and experimentation, many adults consider teens too young and immature to understand the full context and implications of sex and sexuality. And while cultural outlets openly display adolescent women's sexuality and suggest that young women are fully sexual beings, teen women continue to face a sexual double standard that often undermines their sexual agency. The complex construction of virginity loss illustrates the tentative nature of young women's sexual agency.

Virginity loss is not experienced or interpreted in a uniform manner. For some people it is a rite of passage, for others a gift to be "given" to someone special, and for others it is a stigma, among other things (Carpenter 2005). The process through which individuals internalize and make sense of their virginity loss may in turn shape their future experiences, expectations, and interpretations of sexual activity, relationships, and self (Carpenter 2005). Based on individual perceptions, cultural messages, and experiences, many young women in this study define virginity as a gift and continue to perceive and experience sexual activity as something for teen boys that gives girls little pleasure. Young women's sexual agency can be diminished when their sexual experiences are translated into sexual identities. In many regards, contemporary adolescents live in an era where they have much more sexual autonomy; however, the perception of sexual agency is likely greater than the reality, particularly in a society where significant numbers of young women continue to endure sexual assault and pressure.

Simply taking a cursory look at a few of the contradictions facing adolescents indicates that sexual decision making is anything but simple or easy. Teens' decision making is shaped by a variety of individual and contextual factors. Gender, race, and class play a significant role in structuring, informing, and interpreting sexual experiences and choices. Policy also plays a role in shaping sexual decision making by mandating what approach to take to the subject and what set of skills need to be emphasized in the classroom. Into this incongruent and multilayered tangle of contemporary adolescent sexuality comes abstinence-only education.

ABSTINENCE IN A POST-VIRGINAL SOCIETY

Abstinence-only education is largely a one-dimensional approach for teaching sex education. The legislation authorizing the curricula and programs focuses on virginity as the socially "expected standard," not only for adolescents but also for unmarried adults, and presses for heterosexual marriage for all individuals. As the federally accepted definition of abstinence makes clear, the emphasis is on a moral definition rather than a behavioral definition of abstinence: "A mutually faithful monogamous relationship in the context of marriage is the expected standard of human sexual activity" (PRWORA 1996, 2354). Lessons about sexuality are centered on a particular moral perspective that confronts and openly criticizes today's "postvirginal" culture and teaches high school students that virginity is a "priceless treasure." The curricula often instruct teens to view sexual activity as "illicit" and "risky" and warn teens about the harmful psychological and physical affects of participating in premarital sexual activity.

In America's post-virginal society, the teachings of abstinence-only education conflict with many of the actual practices of teenagers and young adults. Today, 47 percent of high school age teens—and 62 percent of twelfth graders—engage in sexual intercourse (Centers for Disease Control and Prevention 2006; Kaiser Family Foundation 2005). The median age of first intercourse for women is 17.4 years and for men it is 17.7; however, the corresponding median age for first marriage is 25.3 and 27.1, respectively (Santelli et al. 2006). By the age of 20, around 75 percent of women have had premarital sex (Finer 2007).[5]

Many adults may not approve of adolescent sexual activity, but the majority takes a pragmatic approach to sexual education that also conflicts with abstinence-only education. Depending on the specific issue, 84 to 98 percent of parents want their children to be taught about contraception (where to get it and how to use it), pregnancy and birth, about sexually transmitted infections, and abortion (Kaiser Family Foundation 2002).[6] Over half of American adults (68.5%) support explicit instruction on how to use condoms. Irrespective of political ideology, adults overwhelmingly support comprehensive sexual education (82%), whereas around one-third support abstinence-only education (Bleakley, Hennessy, and Fishbein 2006). To make sense of this paradoxical situation, it is necessary to understand the politics surrounding morality issues and how it differs from conventional politics and policy outcomes.

LEGISLATING MORALITY IN THE POLICY PROCESS

Political disagreement is at the root of most policy conflicts. These political fights engage several organizations (that can be competing, overlapping, or working together) as well as multiple intergovernmental structures and layers of government. Public policy is a "process or a series or a pattern of governmental activities or decisions that are designed to remedy some public problem, either real or imagined" (Stewart, Hedge, and Lester 2008, 6). Public policies can broadly be categorized into three types of policies: regulatory, distributive, and redistributive (Lowi 1964).[7] Regulatory policies are generally designed to protect society by setting limits on industries providing services, such as the airlines. Policies that provide equal benefits to society (e.g., public education) can be classified as distributive policies, whereas policies that reallocate wealth among society (e.g., welfare) generally fall under the rubric of redistributive policies. The politics surrounding each of these policy arenas differ because the outcomes affect distinct constituents (Stewart et al. 2008).

Regulatory policies normally generate coalitional politics that can be characterized as competitive, prone to compromise, and often unstable. Distributive policies, where everyone stands to gain, are far more stable. They produce little disagreement and often are passed through logrolling rather than conflict. Redistributive policies contrast starkly to distributive policies in terms of the level of conflict surrounding them because there are clear winners and losers; one side gains as a result of another side's loss (Stewart et al. 2008). Although the politics characterizing each policy arena differs, all three typically deal with material outcomes.[8]

Attempts to regulate morality via political channels have been prevalent throughout American history, but the scholarship identifying morality policy as a distinctive area of study is more recent. Similar to these other policy arenas, morality policies are governed by political and environmental constraints as well as opportunities; however, they contain several exceptional characteristics (Haider-Markel and Meier 1996; Hunter 1991, 1994; Meier 1999; Mooney and Lee 1995, 2000; Sharp 1999, 2002). While scholars disagree on the exact definition of what constitutes a *morality policy*, most use the term to identify a unique group of public policies, where at least one active coalition involved in the debate focuses on an absolute right and wrong (Mooney 2000). Compared to other policy areas, the locus of these conflicts are moral, not material.

Policy conflicts involving morality issues often are inflexible because they pertain to strongly held values and belief systems that juxtapose culturally progressive and secularist beliefs against culturally traditional and religiously fundamentalist beliefs. The primary concern of morality policies is behavioral change, which is accomplished through social regulatory policy and moral persuasion (Tatalovich and Daynes 1998). The aim of most morality policies is to shape personal morality through laws regulating behaviors such as abortion practices or pornography consumption, but they also may include policies about the rightness or wrongness of governmental action, which is the case in capital punishment disputes (Mooney 2000).

Moral victories are won by gaining legal authority to redistribute values in society via policy, "to affirm, modify or replace community values, moral practices, and norms of interpersonal conduct" (Tatalovich and Daynes 1998, 1). Because morality policies address core values "rooted deeply in a person's belief system" (Mooney 2001, 4), compromise, negotiation, and coalition building play minor roles in this policy process (Meier 1999; Mooney 1999, 2001; Mooney and Lee 1995). Political compromise is perceived as simply cheapening those values being disputed, particularly when the issues relate to intimate behavior such as gay and lesbian relationships, abortion practices, unmarried pregnancies, or the message of abstinence-only until marriage (Doan 2007; Haider-Markel and Meier 1996; Lehr 2006; Meier 1999; Solinger 2000).

The degree of conflict surrounding morality conflicts is high. Value laden disputes are more intense and prone to escalation and even violence compared to "politics as usual," where economic interests typically form the core of the conflict (Doan 2007; Doan and Williams 2003; Haider-Markel and Meier 1996; Hunter 1994; Meier 1994). The salient nature of morality politics tends to foster higher levels of citizen participation. Public discourse surrounding instrumental policy issues is limited because they involve more overtly complex structures, such as globalization or the economy. The cost of participation is much lower for morality politics. Conflicts over values are more accessible for general debate because most people ascribe to a belief system and feel qualified to hold informed opinions and make political evaluations about moral issues (Hunter 1991; Meier 1994, 1999; Mooney 1999, 2000, 2001; Tatalovich and Daynes 1998). From this perspective, *solutions* should be arrived at through values and common sense, not policy expertise. In fact, the role of policy experts often is pointed to as the problem in contests over morality policies: "these experts seem to violate common sense while claiming that the problems of society and their solutions are just too complex to be grasped by the average citizen" (Watson 1997, 146).

Active participants construct and frame the parameters of morality conflicts in a way that contributes to the accessibility of these conflicts for public debate. Complex sociopolitical issues are described in elementary, nontechnical language. Over time, arguments may evolve beyond pure moral arguments against an issue, as advocates amass and marshal evidence supporting their cause, though whether the evidence is legitimate from a scientific or medical standpoint may be debated. The evidence may increase the legitimacy of the cause—and aid in framing the issue in terms other than values—but moral opposition continues to underscore these conflicts.

POLICYMAKERS' REACTION TO MORALITY POLITICS

Politicians tend to be more responsive to morality politics because they are salient and constituents can easily participate in these conflicts (Haider-Markel and Meier 1996; Meier 1994; Mooney and Lee 1995, 2000; Sharp 2005). Political actors' responsiveness, however, is nuanced. The type of morality issue under dispute tends to influence the degree of their responsiveness. Politicians usually follow the contours of public opinion and are more responsive to *pure* morality issues compared to *material* morality issues. Pure morality issues rarely have economic stakeholders involved in the conflict, whereas material morality issues generally can be characterized as conflicts involving economic stakeholders. Material morality disputes are more elite dominated compared to pure morality issues (Sharp 2005).

Morality policies can be divided further between contentious and consensus issues (Meier 1999; Mooney and Lee 2000; Sharp 1999, 2002). Consensus issues do not generate the level of conflict found in contentious morality issues because they are *sin* issues, which have one legitimate moral side. Little variation exists in the public's values regarding the particular issue (Meier 1994, 1999; Mooney and Lee 2000). For example, polygamy and suicide are sin issues. A legitimate group is not willing to advocate for policy changes that normalize these issues because the majority of Americans, 92 and 82 percent, respectively, believe polygamy and suicide are morally wrong (Carroll 2005).

Politicians follow the nuances of public opinion more closely when opinion is divided around a morality issue. The more contentious the issue, the more responsive politicians will be to their constituents' opinions on the issue. In a contentious issue, opposing sides exist in the debate, and at least one side roots its opposition in its respective sense of moral supremacy on the issue. These types of redistributive morality policies generate an incredible amount of conflict and can involve multiple political actors, elites, and general participants. Given the intensity and scope of these conflicts, they are easy to expand in a federalist structure of government both across and within various political venues (Haider-Markel and Meier 1996; Meier 1999; Mooney 2000).

In reality, morality issues are better conceptualized along a continuum between contentious and consensus politics, rather than as isolated categories, because many issues oscillate over time between consensus and contentious politics (Mooney and Lee 2000). Abortion politics illustrates the usefulness of this conceptualization. Abortion was largely a nonissue for most of the nineteenth century. It became a consensus morality issue by the early 1900s, and then morphed into a contentious morality issue, where it has remained for the past four decades (Doan 2007; Doan and Haider-Markel 2004). Sex education has followed a similar path over the past several decades (Doan and Williams 2006).

Conceptualizing the multiple dimensions of morality debates along a continuum also provides a more useful characterization of public opinion regarding many of these conflicts. Public opinion on morality issues is commonly described as a culture war, characterized by a bimodal distribution of extreme positions on the left and right of the issue. These divisions more realistically describe the highly visible and active political elites participating in the debates rather than mass public opinion. On many morality issues, the public does not consistently hold a conservative or liberal ideology. Individual opinion is more contextual and tends to fluctuate depending on the saliency of the specific issue in question (Lindaman and Haider-Markel 2002; Pew Research Center for the People and the Press 2006). At first blush, about one-third of Americans (35%) support gay marriage; however, public opinion changes dramatically in regards to civil unions for gays and lesbians. A slim majority of Americans (54%) favor it. Other contentious morality issues, such as abortion and embryonic stem cell research, exhibit similar patterns where mass opinion is not nearly as polarized as elites' opinions. These policy battles primarily are framed and constructed in terms of morality, but in reality, 66 percent of Americans favor finding "middle ground" on abortion, and 56 percent support embryonic stem cell research (Pew Research Center for the People and the Press 2006).

Similar public opinion patterns exist in regard to premarital sex. The proportion of Americans engaging in premarital sex has been relatively stable for the past 40 years, but public opinion regarding the moral wrongness of it has significantly changed. In 1969, more than 75 percent of American adults believed that engaging in premarital sex was wrong. By the 1980s, this percent dropped to roughly one-third (33–37%) and has stayed relatively unchanged into the twenty-first century (Harding and Jencks 2003; Pew Research Center for the People and the Press 2007).

TRANSLATING VALUES INTO POLICY: ABSTINENCE-ONLY AND MORALITY POLITICS

The political battle over the approach and content of sexuality education shares the same key characteristics—value conflict, simplification of issues, and saliency—found in other morality conflicts. Constructing teenage sexual activity and the subsequent risk of pregnancy and disease as a case of weakening morals begets a policy solution that simply requires a strengthening of values as a solution to the problem. Abstinence-only instruction became cast as an easy, and moral, solution for a litany of public health and social ailments: unwanted pregnancy, disease prevention, and poverty reduction. Claiming that abstinence until marriage is the only acceptable choice because it is the only moral choice leaves little room for discussion or compromise on the content of sex education. Any sexual activity outside of marriage is considered detrimental—particularly for teens—to social and psychological development and damaging to U.S. society.

Though Christian conservatives are not the first to be politically active in terms of the content of public school sex education, they have succeeded in crystallizing the issues such that sex education is widely perceived as a morality policy, and arguments about curriculum content are linked to debates over moral values. Heterosexual marriage, premarital sex, and chastity are among the moral issues at the heart of the debate: "Telling teenagers to abstain from sex until marriage is a healthy message. Instead of giving teenagers the message that unmarried sex is acceptable, as safe sex programs do, abstinence-only programs help young people develop an understanding of commitment, fidelity and intimacy that will serve them well as the foundations of healthy marital life in the future" (Kaiser Family Foundation, 2002b, 1).

Subscribing to elementary notions of cause and effect also allows abstinence proponents to highlight the simplicity and efficacy of practicing abstinence until marriage. President Bush's remarks in 2002 illustrate this concept:

> Now, let me be as candid as I can about this. Abstinence works every time when it comes to making sure somebody may not have an unwanted child or someone picks up sexually transmitted disease. And this society ought to give children the benefit of the doubt. We ought not to assume that our culture is automatically going to lead a child to defy an abstinence education program. We ought to try it. We ought to work hard; we ought to shoot for the ideal in society and not get drug down by the cynics. And so part of making sure that welfare reauthorization is going to achieve objectives is to promote family and to encourage right choices amongst American youth. (President George W. Bush 2002)

THE ROLE OF "EVIDENCE" IN MORALITY CONFLICTS

The complex issues involved in sexual health—such as gender dynamics, family background, cultural influences, and structural opportunities—are minimized or overlooked in favor of constructing the problems and solutions in a simplistic framework. Two opposing advocacy coalitions exist in the battle over how to educate adolescents about sex. Opponents of abstinence-only education primarily base their arguments on public health issues and draw on scientific studies from a variety of disciplines that link comprehensive sexuality education to positive health indicators.

The pro-abstinence-only coalition uses morality as the foundation for its support; however, advocates also rely on research to gain credibility for their side. Although the search for scientific support for abstinence-only education is relatively new, the same approach has been used by anti-abortion groups. Abstinence-only advocates seem to be following the well-established and fully developed strategy of abortion foes to marshal data for their cause. Following the legalization of abortion services, Catholic groups immediately attacked the legitimacy of the Supreme Court's *Roe v. Wade* (410 U.S. 113, 1973) decision based on their moral belief in the sanctity of life from conception to death. As the conflict has evolved, abortion opponents have produced "medical evidence" linking abortion services to depression, child abuse, and breast cancer (Center for Reproductive Rights 2004; Life Dynamics 2006). Throughout the 1990s, anti-abortion groups and advocates increasingly denounced abortion based on this "medical evidence." The "medical evidence" has been severely criticized by many organizations and individuals in the medical community; however, these studies continue to be cited by anti-abortion organizations, politicians, and individuals.

A similar trend is occurring in the abstinence-only education debate. The attempt to find scientific corroboration for abstinence-only programs lends credibility to the cause and equips advocates with a mechanism for challenging and dismissing their opponents' scientific support. Abstinence advocates have generated many studies based on often questionable scientific data, supporting the efficacy of abstinence-only programs for limiting the transmission of sexual disease. Others make dubious and scientifically inaccurate claims about the ineffectiveness of condoms for preventing pregnancy and transmission of STIs, particularly HIV (Irvine 2002, 117).

For example, Dr. Joe McIlhaney founded the Medical Institute for Sexual Health in 1992 to rein in the "first-hand full effects of the sexual revolution" (Batchelder, 2006). Dr. McIlhaney is interested in influencing sexual behavior through both cultural and policy changes. Based on the Institute's years of research, it has concluded that "waiting to have sex until you are in a faithful, life-long relationship (such as marriage) is the only certain way to avoid being infected sexually" (Medical Institute for Sexual Health 2008). This "finding" has been used to support abstinence-only instruction in the public schools. Yet, as multiple studies show, the preponderance of impartial scientific evidence suggests that abstinence-only programs and curricula do little to influence or change teens' sexual decisions.[9]

Advocates for abstinence-only education, however, often dismiss reputable scientific research that contradicts their agenda. In 2006, a researcher from Harvard University published a study in the *American Journal of Public Health* calling into question the efficacy of abstinence-only until marriage pledges. She found that 53 percent of adolescents who made virginity pledges denied taking those pledges when asked about it the following year. Many of the teens that denied ever taking pledges had become sexually active (Rosenbaum 2006). Although the findings were based on 13,000 teenagers in grades 7 through 12 and appeared in a peer reviewed journal, Leslee Unruh, president of Abstinence Clearinghouse in Sioux Falls, South Dakota, dismissed the study as "junk science" that was riddled with problems because the data was collected 10 years ago. Unruh described Rosenbaum's study as a "politically motivated attack" because "these [abstinence] programs work . . . We see it all the time" (Boodman 2006, 2).

Though abstinence advocates like McIlhaney and Unruh may engage in debates over scientific studies and dispute evidence when it does not corroborate their position, the core conflict in this debate remains the one over fundamental values. Denny Pattyn, founder of Silver Ring Thing, which is an abstinence-only program that received federal funding in the past, stated, "we teach abstinence because it's the truth. We don't analyze ourselves based on reducing the risk" (Boodman 2006, 2).

ALTERNATIVE VENUES FOR MORALITY POLICY

While elite discourse is often bitterly divided on the topic, there is a high level of consensus among citizens' opinions. Similar to other morality issues, such as abortion and embryonic stem cell research, Americans tend to make trade-offs between morality and pragmatism when it comes to teens and sex. A substantial percent of Americans believe young women and young men should wait until they are married before having sexual intercourse (47% and 44%, respectively), yet most (nearly 9 out of 10) do not believe teens, irrespective of gender, will abstain until marriage (Kaiser Family Foundation 2004). Pragmatism overrides morality for most Americans: 93 percent believe sex education should be taught in the public schools. Regarding the substance of sex education curriculum, 46 percent of the public favor comprehensive education with an abstinence message, and another 36 percent do not believe abstinence is the most important message to impart on teens; rather, responsible decision-making concerning sexual health should be the focus (Kaiser Family Foundation 2004).

The lack of congruency between abstinence-only education policy and public opinion is an oddity with respect to morality politics. The dynamic nature of morality politics tends to generate a "hyper-responsiveness where policymakers strive to mirror the preferences of their constituents very closely" (Mooney 2000, 175). In the case of abstinence-only education, this congruence between constituent preferences and policy outcome is largely absent. Despite the wedge between policy and public opinion, abstinence-only education is being taught in one-third of public schools, and it is the fastest growing curricula used to educate adolescents.

Answering the question of *why* abstinence-only education is taught, in the face of such a policy-constituent preference divide, can be answered by investigating the origination of the policy. Most morality policy occurs at the state level where policymakers more easily can reflect the values of their constituents, thus keeping parity between policy and citizen preferences. Abstinence-only education, however, was passed at the federal level, pushed by a well-organized and politically sophisticated Christian conservative coalition.

Even though proponents of abstinence-only education have been active for several decades, 1996 was a turning point for abstinence-only education. Congress passed the Personal Responsibility and Work Opportunity Reconciliation Act

(PRWORA), which was an elaborate, complex, and high profile welfare reform bill. Within this reform, Title V was quietly folded into federal welfare policy at the end of the legislative process. This provision provided a five-year, $250 million grant for abstinence-only sex education and ushered in a new period of legislative success for abstinence-only proponents. It was followed by significantly expanded funding, signaling a new era for this particular type of education.

Federal intervention into morality conflicts is unusual but not unique. The Supreme Court has been far more active than Congress in introducing policy shocks that lead to incongruent policy-citizen preferences in rulings governing morality issues such as abortion (*Roe v. Wade* [1973]), capital punishment (*Furman v. Georgia* [1972]), and pornography (*Miller v. California* [1973]). Less often, Congress has played a role through legislation, such as the Indian Gaming Regulatory Act (IGRA) of 1988 (Mooney 2000).[10]

While federal intervention into morality issues has occurred in the past, we suggest that Title V represents an innovation in morality politics. Unlike the transparency of past federal interventions into morality policies, Title V was quietly included in welfare legislation and justified through a loose connection to poverty prevention. The practice of bundling largely unrelated provisions into a single piece of legislation has become a common strategy for contemporary policymakers in nonmorality policy issues. We suggest that the inclusion of the abstinence-only provision into welfare reform signifies the beginning of a new morality politics strategy borrowed from omnibus legislating tactics used in other policy areas. We refer to this practice as *stealth morality policy*.

LEGISLATIVE STRATEGIES: THE TACTICAL USE OF OMNIBUS BILLS

Omnibus legislating has become a common tactic used by lawmakers to increase the productivity of Congress (Krutz 2000). Omnibus legislation refers to the practice of packaging numerous, disparate policy issues into one massive bill. Congressional scholar Barbara Sinclair defines omnibus legislation as, "[l]egislation that addresses numerous and not necessarily related subjects, issues, and programs, and therefore is usually highly complex and long" (1997, 64). Although a similar legislative strategy has been used in the past (e.g., including riders to expedite controversial proposals), the contemporary omnibus bills assembled in Congress are far more expansive and include a diverse mix of substantive—and unrelated—issues that result in significant policy changes.

Omnibus legislating has become a useful technique for passing bills in a complex political environment, often marked by fragmentation, divided government, and congressional gridlock (Krutz 2000, 2001). This legislative tactic is viewed as a practical way to reduce uncertainty in Congress through building coalitions that accomplish policy goals. Others take a less sanguine view. Omnibus legislating has been roundly criticized by scholars and politicians for, among other things, reducing member participation in the legislative process. Indeed, most members-at-large are unaware of the details included in an omnibus package. This is generally attributable to the sheer size and density of these bills (Krutz 2000).

While normative implications of omnibus legislating are up for debate, several practical interests—both institutional and individual—are served through these massive bills. Institutionally, omnibus bills provide a conduit for advancing a party's policy agenda and affecting policy outcomes. The locus of attention in an omnibus bill typically has widespread support from legislators. By focusing attention onto the positive and widely supported aspects of an omnibus bill, party leaders are able to deflect, downplay, or ignore the more controversial (and less supported) provisions included in the legislation; it is a coalition-building tool. A presidential veto is less likely under these conditions because a president may be willing to overlook provisions he finds unattractive in order to sign a prominent and widely supported bill into law (Krutz 2001; Sinclair 1997).

Members of Congress individually benefit from omnibus legislating in two primary ways: It aids in their bids for reelection and helps them enact policies they care about (Fenno 1973; Mayhew 1974). Job retention is the primary goal for members, and one way to remain elected is by delivering tangible benefits to their constituents. Omnibus legislation provides a mechanism for including particularized benefits, especially for members of the majority party, without attracting too much negative attention. Securing pork-barrel items for rank and file party members increases their prospects of reelection and their party's prospects for retaining majority status.

Omnibus legislating also presents a maneuvering tactic for members, who would like to see their policy agendas advanced. The institutional structure and environment in Congress creates barriers for members seeking to advance their policy goals. Members have a difficult time attracting attention to their "pet" policy initiatives, let alone getting them to advance forward through legislative channels. Omnibus legislation presents an opportunity to circumvent these traditional challenges.

NEW TACTICS FOR OLD BATTLES: STEALTH LEGISLATION AND ABSTINENCE-ONLY

Title V was a little noticed measure included in a massive bill intended to overhaul and "end welfare as we know it" (Clinton 1993). Abstinence-only education is similar to other morality policies in that there are clear and traceable political ramifications. This is a political battle where the winners gain power to create and implement policy and access funding to further their moral agenda. But abstinence-only also represents a departure from the ways in which morality politics usually is fought.

We suggest that omnibus legislative tactics are being applied to morality politics. Using a stealth morality policy strategy enabled policymakers discretely to insert an unpopular policy initiative into a prominent bill that had widespread popular and political support and was signed by a Democratic president. For Congressional members who rely on the political support of the Christian right, abstinence-only education was a tangible policy victory for their constituents. But the reach of abstinence-only education spans beyond particularized benefits for evangelical Christians.

Participation in abstinence-only education is voluntary; states are not federally mandated to comply with this policy. The monies made available to the states through the abstinence-only grant, however, are too lucrative for most to pass up. Even though this morality policy is out of step with many states' political culture, only a handful have rejected this policy (Kaiser Family Foundation 2007). Some states that accepted abstinence-only funds have tried to mitigate the impact of abstinence-only education in their states by working with abstinence opponents and bureaucracies in an attempt to bring some parity between their constituents' preferences and policy (Arsneault 2001; Mooney 2000). But this has been a precarious arrangement and one that is more difficult to do under the new language of the reauthorization bill.

Since 1996, abstinence-only funding has increased steadily and the legislation has been reauthorized and rewritten with a clearer message of morality. The reach of this morality policy has transcended the classroom. Monies made available through this provision have also helped finance other contentious morality issues that are only loosely related to abstinence-only education, such as abortion. Millions of federal abstinence-only funds have been funneled to pro-life crisis pregnancy centers across the country (Lin and Dailard 2002).

Sex education policy can be understood within a morality policy framework in the sense that abstinence-only advocates are pressing a particular moral agenda through abstinence-only sex education. In most regards, abstinence-only education has followed the trajectory of other morality policies, but the nature of its policy origin departs from other morality policies in an important way. Morality policy debates are visible, salient, and predominately waged at the state level; these characteristics were largely absent in the authorization of Title V, which defined and funded abstinence-only education.

We contend that abstinence-only education represents an innovation in an old battle over the best way to educate adolescents about sexual health and decision making. Including "under the radar" morality policies into larger legislation appears to be a fairly successful strategy in advancing a conservative moral agenda. The reach of this policy goes well beyond particularized benefits to select constituents, and we suggest it may be ushering in a new period of stealth morality policy tactics.

CHAPTER SUMMARY

Individual factors as well as structural factors help shape adolescents' sexual decision making; it is a multifaceted process. Teens learn lessons about sex and sexuality from diverse sources, including families, media, and peers. Thus, the ideas represented in abstinence-only sex education are but one source of information for adolescents that tends to reinforce one category of existing cultural messages about young women's sexuality.

As a morality policy, abstinence-only shares characteristics with other morality policies that are absent in nonmorality policy debates: They are value based, technically unsophisticated, and highly salient. These characteristics create a unique political environment that is not found in other areas. The origination, development, and implementation of morality policies follow general patterns, which help to account for why these types of policies come into existence. Using a morality policy framework, we have attempted to initially answer why abstinence-only education is being taught in one-third of public schools. We also suggest that the tactics used to pass this policy may be indicative of a stealth strategy, where morality policy is slipped into omnibus legislation, raising many questions about the future direction of morality policy battles.

In chapter two, we continue to answer why abstinence education is the prevailing policy by investigating the inclusion of Title V, Section 510 into the 1996 welfare reform bill. Title V articulates a narrow definition of abstinence that subsequently has been used for three programs that fund abstinence-only instruction. We trace the evolution of the measure through its reauthorization, noting how gender, race, and class are intimately tied to the politics surrounding welfare policy. This exploration provides insight and some supporting evidence of a stealth strategy in crafting abstinence-only legislation into welfare legislation. Then we turn to a more comprehensive examination and assessment of existing research regarding the efficacy and success of abstinence-only education.

NOTES

1. The three primary types of sexuality education are comprehensive sexuality education, abstinence-based (sometimes called abstinence-plus) education, and abstinence-only education. All teach abstinence from sexual activity as a healthy choice for teens. Comprehensive sexuality education addresses wide-ranging information on sexual health, contraceptives, sexual activity, and relationships. Abstinence-based and abstinence-only programs are

narrower in their coverage of sexuality and sexual activity, contraceptives, and the like. While abstinence-based programs contain some information on contraceptives, abstinence-only education does not provide contraceptive information, except in terms of failure rates and dangerous side effects. Abstinence-only instruction teaches teens that all premarital sexual activity, for both teens and adults and including most premarital sexual acts in addition to intercourse, are unhealthy physically and psychologically.

2. Thanks to an anonymous reviewer of this book for pointing out the importance of the stealth morality policy framework.

3. Unless noted otherwise, all interviews in this book were conducted by the authors between April 2001 and February 2002.

4. As Kristin Luker notes in her book on the battle over sex education in the schools, "[F]ights about sex are also fights about gender, about power and trust and hierarchy, about human nature, and, not surprisingly, about what sex really is and what it means in human life" (Luker 2006, 7).

5. Recent data indicates that the majority of both sexes participate in premarital sex, and the proportion has not significantly changed in the past 40 years (Finer 2007).

6. We use the terms *sexually transmitted infections* and *sexually transmitted diseases* to refer to the same set of infections, including chlamydia, gonorrhea, syphilis, HPV, and herpes. Though we prefer and more often use the term sexually transmitted infections (STI), both are used interchangeably in the vernacular and in the literature.

7. Lowi's three category policy typology has been criticized by many scholars. Some contend that various policies are hard to classify as either distributive or redistributive, and they change over time (i.e., start off as one type of policy and morph into another). Many others have critiqued the typology as being overly simplified and failing to capture the complexity involved in the policy process. Even with these criticisms noted, Lowi's typology remains a useful conceptual tool (Stewart et al. 2008).

8. This is a simplified overview of the policy process that is intended to introduce the reader to the range of public policies that exist in American politics and illustrate how these policy disputes differ from morality policy disputes. A comprehensive examination of all public policies is well beyond the scope of this book. (For a more thorough description of the public policy process see Stewart et al. 2008 and Peters 2007.)

9. In chapter two, the findings and conclusions of many of these studies will be explored in more detail.

10. The IGRA essentially authorized gambling on Native American lands.

BIBLIOGRAPHY

Arsneault, Shelly. 2001. "Values and Virtue: The Politics of Abstinence-Only Sex Education." *American Review of Public Administration* 31 (4): 436–54.

Batchelder, Myra. 2006. "An 'Institute' of Ideology." Available at: www.plannedparent hood.org/issues-action/sex-education/ideology-institute-6241.htm.

Bleakley, Amy, Michael Hennessy, and Martin Fishbein. 2006. "Public Opinion on Sex Education in US Schools." *Archives of Pediatrics & Adolescent Medicine* 160 (November): 1151–56.

Boodman, Sandra G. 2006. "Virginity Pledges Can't Be Taken on Faith." *Washington Post* (May 16): B6.

Brumberg, Joan Jacobs. 1997. *The Body Project: An Intimate History of American Girls*. New York: Random House.

Bush, George W. 2002. "President Discusses Welfare Reform and Job Training." White House Release (February 27). Available at: http://www.whitehouse.gov/news/releases/2002.

Carpenter, Laura M. 2005. *Virginity Lost*. New York: New York University Press.

Carroll, Joseph. 2005. "Society's Moral Boundaries Expand Somewhat This Year." *The Gallup Poll* (May 16). Available at: http://www.poll.gallup.com. Subscription required.

Center for Reproductive Rights. 2004. "Yet Another Anti-Abortion Scare Tactic: False Claims of Breast Cancer Link." Available at: http://www.reproductiverights.org/pub_fac_abortiondom.html.

Centers for Disease Control and Prevention. 2006. "Healthy Youth! Sexual Behaviors." Available at: http://www.cdc.gov/HealthyYouth/sexualbehaviors.

Clinton, Bill. 1993. "State of the Union Address." Washington, D.C.

Doan, Alesha E. 2007. *Opposition and Intimidation: The Abortion Wars and Strategies of Political Harassment*. Ann Arbor: University of Michigan Press.

Doan, Alesha E., and Donald Haider-Markel. 2004. "The Abortion Movement." In *Encyclopedia of American Social Movements*, ed. Immanuel Ness, 378–86. New York: M.E. Sharpe.

Doan, Alesha E., and Jean Williams. 2003. "Good Girls or Dirty Ho's? The Social Construction of Sex Education Policy." Presented at the annual meetings of the Midwest Political Science Association, Chicago, April.

Doan, Alesha E., and Jean Williams. 2006. "Sex Education." In *Social Issues: An Encyclopedia of Controversies, History, and Debates*, ed. James Ciment, 1520–31. New York: M.E. Sharpe.

Fenno, Richard. 1973. *Congressmen in Committee*. Reprinted by Institute of Governmental Studies, University of California at Berkeley.

Finer, Lawrence B. 2007. "Trends in Premarital Sex in the United States, 1954–2003." *Public Health Reports* 122 (January–February): 73–78.

Haider-Markel, Donald P., and Kenneth J. Meier. 1996. "The Politics of Gay and Lesbian Rights: Expanding the Scope of Conflict." *Journal of Politics* 58 (May): 332–49.

Harding, David J., and Christopher Jencks. 2003. "Changing Attitudes Toward Premarital Sex: Cohort, Period, and Aging Effects." *Public Opinion Quarterly* 67: 211–26.

Hunter, James Davidson. 1991. *Culture Wars: The Struggle to Define America*. New York: Basic Books.

Hunter, James Davidson. 1994. *Before the Shooting Begins: Searching for Democracy in America's Culture War*. New York: Free Press.

Irvine, Janice. 2004. *Talk About Sex: The Battle over Sex Education in the United States*. Berkeley: University of California Press.

Kaiser Family Foundation. 2002a. *Kaiser Weekly Reproductive Health Reports* (February 26). Available at: http://www.kff.org.

Kaiser Family Foundation. 2002b. "Kaiser Daily Women's Health Policy." *Daily Reports* (May 1): 1. Available at: http://www.kaisernetwork.org/Daily_reports/rep_index.cfm?DR_ID=10912.

Kaiser Family Foundation. 2004. "Sex Education in America." *Public Opinion and Media Research Program*. Available at: http://www.kff.org/youthhivstds/3048-index.cfm.

Kaiser Family Foundation. 2005. "U.S. Teen Sexual Activity" (January). Available at: http://www.kff.org/youthhivstds/3040-02.cfm.

Kaiser Family Foundation. 2007. Advocacy Group Launches Ads Urging Massachusetts Gov. Patrick to Accept Federal Abstinence-Only Sex Education Grant." *State Politics and Policy* (September 7). Available at: http://www.kaisernetwork.org/daily_reports.

Krutz, Glen S. 2000. "Getting around Gridlock: The Effect of Omnibus Utilization on Legislative Productivity." *Legislative Studies Quarterly* 25 (4): 533–49.

Krutz, Glen S. 2001. "Tactical Maneuvering on Omnibus Bills in Congress." *American Journal of Political Science* 45 (1): 210–33.

Landry, David, Lisa Kaeser, and Cory L. Richards. 1999. "Abstinence Promotion and the Provision of Information About Contraception in Public School District Sexuality Education Policies." *Family Planning Perspectives* 31 (6): 280–86.

Lehr, Valerie. 2006. "Sexual Agency in Risk Society." Conference Paper Delivered at the 2006 Annual Meeting of the Midwest Political Science Association, Chicago, April.

Life Dynamics. 2006. "Death Camps." Available at: http://www.lifedynamics.com/Death Camps/DeathCamps.cfm.

Lin, Vitoria, and Cynthia Dailard. 2002. "Crisis Pregnancy Centers Seek to Increase Political Clout, Secure Government Subsidy." *The Guttmacher Report on Public Policy* (November 2).

Lindaman, Kara, and Donald P. Haider-Markel. 2002. "Issue Evolution, Political Parties, and the Culture Wars." *Political Research Quarterly* 55 (1): 91–110.

Lowi, Theodore. 1964. "American Business, Public Policy, Case Studies, and Political Theory." *World Politics* (July 16): 677–715.

Luker, Kristin. 2006. *When Sex Goes to School: Warring Views on Sex—And Sex Education—Since the Sixties*. New York: W. W. Norton & Company.

Mayhew, David R. 1974. *Congress: The Electoral Connection*. New Haven, CT: Yale University Press.

Medical Institute for Sexual Health. 2008. "The Facts About Sexually Transmitted Infections (STIs)." Available at: http://www.medinstitute.org/content.php?namestifacts.

Meier, Kenneth J. 1994. *The Politics of Sin: Drugs, Alcohol, and Public Policy*. New York: M.E. Sharpe.

Meier, Kenneth J. 1999. "Symposium: The Politics of Morality Policy—Drugs, Sex, Rock, and Roll: A Theory of Morality Politics." *The Journal of Policy Studies* 27 (4): 681–95.

Mooney, Christopher. 1999. "The Politics of Morality Policy: Symposium Editor's Introduction." *Policy Studies Journal* 27 (4): 675–80.

Mooney, Christopher. 2000. "The Decline of Federalism and the Rise of Morality-Policy Conflict in the United States." *Publius* 30 (1/2): 171–89.

Mooney, Christopher. 2001. *The Public Clash of Private Values: The Politics of Morality Policy*. New York: Chatham House Publishers.

Mooney, Christopher, and Mei-Hsien Lee. 1995. "Legislating Morality in the American States: The Case of Pre-*Roe* Abortion Regulation Reform." *American Journal of Political Science* 39: 599–627.

Mooney, Christopher, and Mei-Hsien Lee. 2000. "The Influence of Values on Consensus and Contentious Morality Policy: U.S. Death Penalty Reform, 1965–82." *The Journal of Politics* 62 (1): 223–39.

Peters, Guy B. 2007. *American Public Policy: Promise and Performance*, 7th ed. Washington, D.C.: CQ Press.

Personal Responsibility and Work Opportunities Reconciliation Act of 1996 (PRWORA). Public Law 104–193, Title I, August 22, 1996.

Pew Research Center for the People and the Press. 2006. "Pragmatic Americans Liberal and Conservative on Social Issues: Most Want Middle Ground." *Survey Reports* (August 3). Available at: http://people-press.org/reports.

Pew Research Center for the People and the Press. 2007. "As Marriage and Parenthood Drift Apart, Public is Concerned about Social Impact." *Survey Reports* (July 1). Available at: http://people-press.org/reports.

Rosenbaum, Janet. 2006. "Reborn a Virgin: Adolescents' Retracting of Virginity Pledges and Sexual Histories." *American Journal of Public Health* 96 (6): 1098–1103.

Santelli, John, Mary A. Ott, Maureen Lyon, Jennifer Rogers, and Daniel Summers. 2006. "Abstinence-Only Education Policies and programs: A Position Paper of the Society for Adolescent Medicine." *Journal of Adolescent Health* 38: 83–87.

Sharp, Elaine B. 1999. *Culture Wars and Local Politics*. Lawrence: University Press of Kansas.

Sharp, Elaine B. 2002. "Culture, Institutions, and Urban Officials' Responses to Morality Issues." *Political Research Quarterly* 55 (4): 861–83.

Sharp, Elaine B. 2005. *Morality Politics in American Cities*. Lawrence: University of Kansas Press.

Sinclair, Barbara. 1997. *Unorthodox Lawmaking: New Legislative Processes in the U.S. Congress*. Washington, D.C.: Congressional Quarterly.

Solinger Rickie. 2000. *Wake Up Little Susie: Single Pregnancy and Race before Roe v. Wade*. New York: Routledge.

Stewart, Joseph, Jr., David M. Hedge, and James P. Lester. 2008. *Public Policy: An Evolutionary Approach*, 3rd ed. Boston: Thomson Wadsworth.

Sullivan, Bob. 2005. "Kids, Blogs and too Much Information." *MSNBC* (April 29). Available at: http://www.MSNBC.com.

Tatalovich, Raymond, and Byron W. Daynes. 1998. "Conclusion: Social Regulatory Policy Process." In *Moral Controversies in American Politics: Cases in Social Regulatory Policy*, ed. Raymond Tatalovich and Byron Daynes, 258–70. New York: M.E. Sharpe.

Vergari, Sandra. 2001. "Morality Politics and the Implementation of Abstinence-Only Sex Education: A Case of Policy Compromise." In *The Public Clash of Private Values*, ed. Christopher Z. Mooney, 201–12. New York: Chatham House Publishers.

Watson, Justin. 1997. *The Christian Coalition: Dreams of Restoration, Demands for Recognition*. New York: St. Martin's Press.

COURT CASES CITED

Furman v. Georgia, 408 U.S. 238 (1972).

Miller v. California, 413 U.S. 15 (1973).

Roe v. Wade, 410 U.S. 113 (1973).

2

Tightening the Sexuality Noose:
Title V and Abstinence-Only Education

To more thoroughly answer *why* abstinence-only education is being taught in public schools, chapter two traces the development of its inclusion in the 1996 welfare reform bill. Through this exploration we offer some evidence supporting the use of stealth legislative tactics to deliver a morality policy victory to a narrow constituency—Christian conservatives. The inclusion of an abstinence-only provision represents a significant policy victory for advocates because it affirms and codifies a particular moral agenda and also provides material support for their agenda.

Several related issues are addressed in this chapter, beginning with social conservatives' involvement in abstinence-only education, which has its roots in the Reagan Administration. Changes in the political environment and the opening of new political opportunities contributed to the welfare reform of 1996. The history and politics of welfare reform will be examined, with attention given to the gendered and racialized elements that have been inextricably woven into welfare politics. As a special focus of welfare reform, unmarried teen pregnancy and childbearing were highlighted in the debates over why and how to reform welfare. To abstinence-only advocates, teen pregnancy represents the nadir at which teenage sexual activity, irresponsible parenting, and poverty converge.

Then we turn to a detailed look at Title V as well as two other federal programs that provide funding for abstinence-only education: the Adolescent Family Life Act (AFLA) and Community-Based Abstinence Education (CBAE).[1] Chapter two ends with a look at the growth in abstinence-only education and programs and an examination of the major studies assessing abstinence-only education.

DIANE'S STORY

Diane is an 18-year-old senior in high school. She became pregnant in ninth grade and had a baby at age 15; her boyfriend was slightly younger than she. She had never had sex education in school because her mother asked that Diane be excluded from the class; Diane's mother preferred that she not have information "to keep me from growing up. She was afraid." Before she became pregnant, Diane did not receive any education about sexuality, pregnancy, or birth control from her school, her parents, or any other source besides her peers. During the interview, Diane first describes an absolute lack of knowledge about birth control at the time she became pregnant, including "condoms . . . birth control pills and stuff," stating that she and her boyfriend never used contraception. Later in the interview, Diane asserts that she and her boyfriend did use condoms consistently, but "that three percent [failure rate] had to be me," as an explanation for her pregnancy. Regardless, her pregnancy was unintentional.

Diane moved in with the father of her baby when she was 15 years old and 7 months pregnant, and they married 2 years later. To help support the family, Diane's husband dropped out of high school and currently works as a roofer for $1,500 per month. Diane balanced her high school studies with a job in a motel but lost the job recently. Living with, and later marriage to, the father of her baby meant living in poverty for Diane; in particular, she has struggled to remain stably housed. When she first moved in with the father of her child, because the couple could not afford anything larger, he and Diane moved into a studio apartment even though by law they were required to rent a larger apartment. When the landlord discovered that three people were living in the studio apartment, she evicted them. Diane and her family then lived in a motel for two years, all the while searching for affordable housing, and have just recently moved into another studio apartment.

Diane's economic difficulties were made worse by the problems she experienced trying to get government assistance. Diane tried to obtain housing assistance but was unsuccessful:

> It's been really rough so I went and applied for emergency housing, because I was in a motel for two years. . . . And of course I didn't qualify. I have two vehicles. . . . And because my car is worth $4,000 and my husband's is

worth $1,500 [we do not qualify for help] . . . but he needs his to go to work, and I need mine to come here [to school].

For social conservatives, Diane's story represents much that is failing in American society. Diane is a teenager who had premarital sex, resulting in an unplanned pregnancy and birth outside the context of heterosexual marriage. Her life illustrates the convergence between immorality, illegitimacy, and dependency on governmental aid. Echoing this belief during a welfare reform hearing, members of the Christian Coalition testified about the harm stemming from illegitimacy, identifying it as "the single most important social problem today largely because it contributes to many other social problems such as crime, drugs, poverty, illiteracy, welfare and homelessness" (Heidi H. Stirrup, quoted from 2003, 482).

Peering closer into Diane's life reveals a different story; marriage to the father of her child did not provide a route out of poverty, or an easy pathway to successful parenting and educational achievements. Rather, Diane and her husband were already poor before they met. Since their marriage, their low income status has not changed. They have oscillated between temporary housing and homelessness, struggling to parent their child together, and trying to achieve a high school education for at least one of them.

The lack of sexuality education in Diane's life is one contributing factor to her unplanned pregnancy—a pregnancy that both opponents and advocates of abstinence-only education agree is avoidable. While both sides agree teen pregnancy is undesirable, their respective plans for preventing it radically diverge. Diane's mother removed her from the sex education offered at school because she was "afraid" that the exposure would expedite Diane's maturity and interest in sex. Her mother's concerns underscore the point of departure for advocates of abstinence-only education. They believe that sex education can be taught to adolescents without exposing them to graphic details about sex and instilling in teens an appreciation of the responsibilities—and inherent morality involved—in sexual relationships.

THE CHRISTIAN RIGHT AND SEX EDUCATION

Providing teenagers with sex education in the public schools is a relatively recent phenomenon, dating back to events that occurred in the 1960s, when birth control pills were approved for consumption in the United States.[2] The advent of the pill along with the liberalization of contraception and abortion laws contributed to an impressive decline in unwanted pregnancies among adult women in the 1960s and 1970s (Luker 1996; U.S. Department of Health, Education, and Welfare 1979). Teen pregnancy, however, was on the rise in the early 1970s, particularly births to unwed mothers (U.S. Department of Health and Human

Services [HHS] 1984). The Senate Human Resources Committee reported in the 1970s that approximately 1 million teens became pregnant each year, resulting in nearly 600,000 live births (CQ Congress Collection 1981; Guttmacher Institute 2006). The abortion rate for teens was also high in 1976: Over one-third of abortions were obtained by adolescents.

Lawmakers turned their attention to pregnancy prevention among this subpopulation. Congress passed the Family Planning Services and Population Research Act (PL 91-572) in 1970. This Act established an office of Population Affairs in the Department of Health, Education, and Welfare and added Title X to the Public Health Service Act. Title X provided funds for family planning services, training, information, and education programs (CQ Congress Collection 1981). Building onto the effort to combat teen pregnancy, Senator Edward Kennedy (D-MA) spearheaded the Adolescent Health Services and Pregnancy Prevention Care Act in 1978 (PL 95-626). This Act intended to reduce teen pregnancy by increasing access to federally funded contraception and abortion services (Arsneault 2001).

Federal efforts to combat teen pregnancy centered on a "clinical approach" to family planning—increasing access to subsidized contraception. Planned Parenthood and other family planning clinics received funding through Title X to help deliver services to indigent women as well as teenagers. Beyond clinical services, the federal government played a very limited role in prescribing educational programs for public schools.[3] Despite the government's "hands off" approach to sex education programs, most public schools implemented sexual education into the classroom. The main focus of most sex education was teaching physical and sexual development, sexually transmitted disease prevention, and contraceptive use (Darroch, Landry, and Singh 2000; Landry, Kaeser, and Richards 1999).

Almost since its introduction, teaching sex education in the classroom, coupled with the legislatively prescribed remedies for reducing teen pregnancy, has provoked debate. The explicit teaching of sexuality in public schools has been opposed vehemently by the Christian Right, who largely ascribe to an alternative set of values and morals governing human behavior. Evangelical Christians (or born-again Christians) generally hold different views toward sex and sexuality compared to the larger population. This particular population of conservative Christians is much more inclined than the general population to believe premarital sex and sexual arousal are immoral activities (81% and 56% of Evangelical Christians, compared to 33% and 31% of the general public, respectively; Kaiser Family Foundation 2004). They are also more likely to believe premarital sexual activity leads to harmful psychological and emotional consequences for the unwed compared to other Americans (78% versus 46%, respectively; Kaiser Family Foundation 2004).

Emerging on the political scene in the 1970s, the Christian Right's conservative "pro-family" agenda "linked opposition to a range of social justice issues and couched them as a defense of the American family against the incursions of feminism, gay rights, and sex education" (Irvine 2002, 66). The Christian Right viewed sex education as liberals' attempt to "undermine all parental authority . . . subvert all Christian morality . . . [by] promoting sexual perversion, homosexuality, pornography, abortion, family destruction, population control." Furthermore, explicit sex education is viewed as "anti-life" and "anti-family" (McKeegan 1992, 41–42). Several conservative Christian groups contend that teaching "raw sex" in public schools violates parental rights: The home is viewed as the appropriate venue for discussions and teachings about sexuality. Certain groups went so far as to claim that sexuality education in the classroom was tantamount to child abuse (Rose 2005).

Nearing the end of the 1970s and during the 1980s, it became increasingly clear to conservative groups that their push to eliminate sexuality education in the public schools was futile. For example, by 1988, 93 percent of seventh to eleventh grade public school teachers taught in schools that offered sex education (Darroch et al. 2000; Landry et al. 1999). Rather than concede defeat, Christian conservatives adopted a new strategy: restructuring the *content* of sex education (Rose 2005). Christian groups—namely, the Eagle Forum, Focus on the Family, Concerned Women for America, and Citizens for Excellence in Education—focused their resources and time on rallying grassroots support against comprehensive sex education and replacing it with abstinence-only education (Rose 2005). As Carmen Pate, vice president of communications for Concerned Women for America (CWA), explains:

> Our fight and our voice was simply that if you're going to be talking about sex education in schools—which we don't think should be done, we think we should be empowering our parents to teach kids about sex—but if it is going to be in the schools, then it needs to be abstinence-only. (Vergari 2001, 204–5)

Conservatives believed that Title X family planning programs created a "contraceptive mentality" that promoted sexual activity among teens (LeClair 2006). Critics opposed federal funding for Title X because it unjustly favored, and provided money for, a clinical approach to sexuality education. Activists lobbied lawmakers for an alternative that emphasized values and was family centered. By the end of the decade, the Christian Right had gained significant allies and support for their social and political agenda (McKeegan 1992; Watson 1997).

Senator Orrin Hatch (R-UT) and Senator Jeremiah Denton (R-AL) were essential partners in securing an important policy victory for Christian conservatives. They engineered the 1981 Adolescent Family Life Act (AFLA; PL 97-35) to replace the Adolescent Health Services and Pregnancy Prevention Care Act of 1978. Senators Hatch and Denton wanted to supplant the earlier 1978 Pregnancy Prevention Act with a new one focusing on the prevention of adolescent sexual relations through "chastity" and "self-discipline" (Dailard 2006; Donovan 1984; McFarlane and Meier 2001).

Senator Hatch gained the support of Democratic Senator Kennedy—who was responsible for the 1978 Act—by including a statute that designated the bulk of the money (two-thirds) to support services for pregnant and parenting teens (LeClair 2006). Through this compromise, Senator Hatch along with Senator Denton was able to quietly include the AFLA in the Omnibus Budget Reconciliation Act of 1981. The AFLA was signed into law as Title XX of the Public Health Service Act without drawing hearings or floor votes in the U.S. Congress (LeClair 2006; SIECUS 2005b). This was an important step in gaining liberal concessions to a largely conservative policy agenda.

The AFLA became the first federally funded, and sanctioned, sex education legislation, opening the door for funding abstinence-only education. The legislation is designed "to find effective means, within the context of the family, of reaching adolescents before they become sexually active in order to maximize the guidance and support available to parents and other family members, to promote self-discipline and other prudent approaches to the problem of adolescent premarital sexual relations" (Adolescent Family Life Act of 1981, 579–80).

Aside from a few dedicated lawmakers, Congress has never provided broad support for the AFLA, evidenced by the decrease in appropriations for the program from 1981 to 1996. The AFLA probably has survived reauthorization because the program never has been subjected to a vote in Congress (Daley 1997). Even with the limitations on funding alternative "family value based" prevention programs, the AFLA resulted in the subsidized development of abstinence-only curricula during the Reagan Administration. Over the next 15 years, approximately 7 million dollars of "seed" monies were annually available for the creation of "family central" pregnancy prevention programs that emphasized abstinence and adoption as an alternative to abortion (Dailard 2006; Rose 2005). Advocates view this period as a crucial stage in the development of abstinence-only programs. One writer for *Conservative Digest* succinctly described the purpose of the AFLA: "the Adolescent Family Life Act was written expressly for the purpose of diverting [federal] money that would otherwise go to Planned Parenthood into groups with traditional values. This noble purpose has certainly been fulfilled here" (quoted in Rose 2005, 10).

THE ROAD TO WELFARE REFORM

While the Christian Right fought sex education, they concurrently focused their "pro-family" agenda on welfare, which was viewed as a liberal social policy that undermined the traditional family by contributing to the rise in female, single-headed households. Some evidence indicates that the Christian Right contributed to Republican politicians' ability to successfully press for welfare reform. For example, Fording (2003) examines states' efforts to reform welfare before the 1996 federal reform through adoption of federal waivers to require that welfare recipients work and/or to impose time limits. He finds that Republican governors played a significant role in whether a state successfully participated in welfare reform, but only in states where the Christian Right had "a strong presence in the state. This suggests that the battle over welfare reform has been to some extent a battle over moral values, and that the aggressiveness of the Republican party on this issue has perhaps been motivated by the mobilization of the Christian Right" (Fording 2003, 87).

Social conservatives viewed welfare as providing young women a means of circumventing both marriage and work by having children and collecting government aid. According to Pat Robertson, founder of the Christian Coalition, "it doesn't take a rocket scientist to deduce that this [welfare] system promotes illegitimacy, discourages stable families, and promotes dependency" (Watson 1997, 146; Viguerie 1981). For the Christian Right, the welfare system reflected the larger social problems in America, specifically, declining moral values. The decline in values was reflected most obviously in premarital sexual activity, especially teenage sexual activity resulting in teenage pregnancy: "Pre-marital sex and adultery . . . are much more serious threats to our society than homosexuality. They lead to over half a million illegitimate births a year" (Viguerie 1981, 160). Thus, the policy solution was to "cut off the money" for welfare and simultaneously provide resources for unmarried pregnancy prevention through the promotion of abstinence-only education (Watson 1997, 146).

Linking welfare and sex education in its "pro-family" movement proved a useful strategy for the Christian Right. Janice Irvine describes the efforts of the Christian Right to build support in the 1990s: "The Christian Right's mobilizations against comprehensive sexuality education attracted a diverse constituency of Christian evangelicals and fundamentalists, conservative Catholics, along with some Muslims, and conservative Jews. Indeed, the movement's power is that it can draw even nominally religious individuals and further build its strength" (Irvine 2002, 129). Inclusion of the abstinence-only section in welfare reform represents the convergence of value distribution with public policy; it is a significant morality policy gain for the Christian Right at the federal level.

In addition to concentrating on federal legislation, the movement directed its efforts to the local level throughout the 1990s. Many of the decisions about whether or not to teach sex education, which sex education curricula to use, and what to include and not include in classroom discussions, are decisions made at the local level, often by school boards. The Christian Right attempted to gain power through school board elections, using covert candidates who were Christian conservatives that ran for office without identifying themselves as part of a larger Christian conservative movement (Irvine 2002). Normally, they did not publicize their agendas to revamp sex education in the public schools, among other goals, until after an election was decided. A similar tactic was used when social conservatives introduced a stealth provision into welfare reform legislation, drawing very little attention from lawmakers or the public.

ELECTORAL CHANGES

Throughout his 1992 presidential campaign, Bill Clinton highlighted welfare reform as one of his key issues, promising to "end welfare as we know it." His pledge largely was shelved the first two years of his presidency as his administration focused on health care reform. On June 14, 1994, President Clinton unveiled a detailed proposal centered around moving people off of welfare and into the job market, a strategy he shepherded while he was the Governor of Arkansas (CQ Congress Collection 1997). Moderate Republicans also introduced their version of welfare reform legislation, but neither version made it out of Congress in 1994.

Lawmakers' attention was turning to the 1994 midterm elections, where the electoral winds were starting to shift. Sensing their first opportunity to win a majority in the House of Representatives since 1952, Republicans opted to present a united front on the campaign trail. They crafted the "Contract with America," which was signed by over 300 incumbents and challengers. The Contract outlined, and promised to bring to the floor within the first 100 days of Congress, 10 specific issues. Welfare reform was the third issue on the list. During the campaign season, the stage was being set for how welfare reform would come to be debated through ads such as the one appearing in *TV Guide* that stated, "Welfare Reform: The government should encourage people to work, *not* to have children out of wedlock" (Arsneault 2001).

After winning a majority in the House, true to their promise, Republicans introduced welfare reform legislation on the first day of the 104th Congress. Unlike President Clinton's costlier version that focused on job training and assistance such as child care, the Republicans' version sought to reduce federal spending through a variety of radical measures, including time limits, work requirements, family caps, and prohibiting the allocation of welfare checks to children born to unwed teenage mothers and current welfare recipients (CQ Congress Collection 1997). Reflecting social conservatives' agenda, the proposed welfare legislation steered away from an emphasis on education and job training for welfare recipients and proposed to reduce welfare dependence by reducing illegitimacy and strengthening the family (Arsneault 2001).

Analyzing hearings and debates in the 102nd, 103rd, and 104th Congresses exemplifies how lawmakers and expert witnesses used rhetoric comparing traditional nuclear families to welfare families to construct the latter as dysfunctional (Gring-Pemble 2003). Much of the debate cast welfare as the root cause of dysfunctional families. Representative Marge Roukema (R-NJ) characterized welfare as a system that "promotes unhealthy, unproductive, dysfunctional families that sentence children to a lifetime of economic, social, and emotional deprivation" (*Congressional Record,* March 21, 1995, quoted in Gring-Pemble 2003, 481).

From this vein, the logical answer was to "compassionately" eliminate the "causal" pathway to dysfunction by radically overhauling the welfare system. Examining the floor debates related to the 1996 welfare reform, Stryker and Wald (2007) conclude that a new definition of compassion emerged and became central to reconceptualizing welfare. Talking on the floor on March 21, 1995, Representative Gerald B. H. Solomon (R-NY) stated, "I ask my colleagues today now what is compassionate about continuing failed welfare programs that encourage a second, and third and fourth generation of welfare dependency? I say to my colleagues, 'You know, and I know, the answer is nothing.'" A couple of days later, on March 23, Representative Andrea Seastrand (R-CA) reiterated her colleague's sentiments. "We are ending a welfare system that is not compassionate and replacing it with hope and opportunity. We are ending a failed system and encouraging personal responsibility" (Stryker and Wald 2007, 61).

The rhetoric surrounding welfare reform debates overwhelmingly focused on, and projected, images of family dysfunction and dependency—including teen pregnancy—and argued for a new definition of compassion. These themes structured the floor debates leading up to the final passage of the bill. During these lengthy debates, abstinence-only education was never presented to Congress, or the general public, as a solution to illegitimacy, poverty, or welfare abuse (Gring-Pemble 2003; Stryker and Wald 2007). But ultimately, the restructuring of welfare presented an opportunity for social conservatives to use stealth tactics at the federal level and greatly expanded the reach of morality policy.

STEALTH TACTICS

During the reauthorization of the Elementary and Secondary Education Act in 1994, Representative John Doolittle (R-CA), a well-established social conservative, proposed an amendment that would "limit the content of HIV-prevention and sexuality education in school-based programs" (LeClair 2006, 296; CQ Congress Collection 1995). Doolittle's amendment was a precursor to abstinence-only education. It contained a similar definition of abstinence-only education that is used in Title V. His amendment failed in the House, and rather than mandate a version of abstinence education, the language was drastically modified to emphasize local communities' authority to choose their own program content for education (Daley 1997; LeClair 2006).

Conservative groups were deeply troubled by this concession and quickly learned two important lessons they could apply in the future. First, they could not intervene in state and local curricula decisions due to federal laws prohibiting this activity (Daley 1997). Second, opponents realized their proposals were either seriously modified or defeated when subjected to debate in Congress and by the general public. The logical solution was to circumvent the federal laws by restricting, and shaping, education programs through health policy and funding. To be successful, this plan needed to be linked to an existing "problem" on Congress's policy agenda and executed without drawing Congressional or public debate (Daley 1997; Vergari 2001).

Two years later, the conditions were ripe for revisiting a version of Doolittle's amendment under the radar of broad political and public scrutiny. Attention to and support for welfare reform by elites increased appreciably; elites' attention in turn influenced public opinion (Schneider and Jacoby 2005). "A stream of critiques of AFDC from both Republican and Democratic politicians contributed both to a marked increase in the prominence of welfare reform issues and to increasing dissatisfaction with the current system" (Weaver 2000, 171–72). By the summer of 1996, a majority of citizens polled considered America's moral decline more serious than any economic problems facing the country.

After two years of a divided government and gridlock, the political climate was changing. Public support was favoring the goals of Congressional Republicans, and reelection was looming large for President Clinton, who had yet to fulfill his campaign promise of reforming welfare. This political environment created an opportunity for including a loosely related morality policy provision into the massive and complex welfare reform legislation. "The final maneuver in legislating welfare reform flowed from the converging electoral interest between a Democratic president seeking a second term and Congressional Republican leaders struggling to retain control of Congress after only two years at the helm" (Heclo 2001, 193).

As lawmakers were moving closer to a resolution, a small group of core, social conservatives began to champion legislation for abstinence-only education that was tangentially related to the larger goals of welfare reform. Initially introduced by Senators Lauch Faircloth (R-NC) and Rick Santorum (R-PA) in September 1995, the legislation introduced a definition of abstinence education and proposed moving $200 million from existing Maternal and Child Health Block Grant services into funding for abstinence-only education. Conservative groups such as the Heritage Foundation helped craft the language of the bill (Daley 1997). The sponsors of the bill used the Christian Right's "pro-family" rhetoric and logic—linking premarital sex to pregnancy to poverty—to justify including it into welfare legislation. Senator Faircloth reasoned:

Most welfare reform proposals try to pick up the pieces after an out-of-wedlock birth has occurred. It is much more effective to prevent young women from getting pregnant in the first place. And teaching young people to abstain from sexual activity is one of the best ways to accomplish that. (Vergari 2001, 204)

After receiving substantial criticism from other senators as well as from maternal and child health advocates, Faircloth and Santorum's legislation did not receive much support and went nowhere.

Abstinence-only education was dropped but then quietly reappeared right before the bill was passed. During the final version of welfare reform, which is typically used for corrections and technical revisions, two Congressmen from Oklahoma, Ernest Istook and Tom Coburn, approached Speaker Newt Gingrich about abstinence-only education. Without a Congressional floor debate or a separate vote, and absent any open public debate, Speaker Gingrich was persuaded to include federal funding for an abstinence-only-until-marriage program (Title V) into the miscellaneous provisions of the welfare reform bill (Daley 1997; LeClair 2006). Title V authorized $50 million annually from 1998 through 2002 for abstinence-only education (CQ Congress Collection 1997).

THE PERSONAL RESPONSIBILITY AND WORK OPPORTUNITY RECONCILIATION ACT

After vetoing two earlier and more punitive versions of welfare reform, President Clinton signed the Personal Responsibility and Work Opportunity Reconciliation Act (PRWORA) into law on August 22, 1996. Explaining his decision, President Clinton remarked:

I will sign this bill, first and foremost, because the current system is broken; second, because Congress has made many of the changes I sought; and third, because even though serious problems remain in the *non-welfare reform provisions of the bill*, this is the best chance we will have for a long time to complete the work of ending welfare as we know it, by moving people from welfare to work, demanding responsibility, and doing better by children. (Stryker and Wald 2007, 37, emphasis mine)

When President Clinton signed the bill, religious conservatives gained an innovative and significant morality policy victory (CQ Congress Collection 1997).

The Personal Responsibility and Work Opportunity Reconciliation Act of 1996 (PRWORA) repealed the entitlement status of Aid to Families with Dependent Children (AFDC), replacing the previous program's unlimited federal funds with a block grant, Temporary Assistance for Needy Families (TANF). Grounded in a neoconservative critique of the welfare system, the law focused in particular on unmarried pregnancy, arguing that because "marriage is the foundation of a successful society" (PRWORA 1996, 2110), unmarried women—teens and adults—who bear children "out-of-wedlock" undermine both their children's chances for success and the American social fabric (Mills 1996).

The TANF block grant begins by stating four general purposes of the program. These include the goal of ending "dependence of needy parents on government benefits by promoting job preparation, work, and marriage," preventing and reducing the number of pregnancies to unmarried women, and encouraging "the formation and maintenance of two-parent families" (PRWORA 1996, 2113). As the statement of purposes makes clear, the goal is not to end poverty; rather, it is to move women off the welfare rolls as quickly and efficiently as possible. The program also strives to advance a cultural shift: to promote heterosexual marriage and end the trend toward increasing numbers of children born to unmarried couples, and to undercut the growing public support for such historically nontraditional family formations.

The portion of welfare reform that specifically targets teens focuses on creating disincentives for teens to become parents, and if they already are parents, makes it difficult to obtain welfare benefits. First, to be eligible for cash benefits, teens must live with a parent or guardian and finish high school.[4] The provision requiring teens to live with their parents is designed to cut the welfare rolls by making it less likely that a teen will qualify for benefits, because her parents' or guardian's income is considered for eligibility purposes. And welfare receipt no longer provides a path to living independently of one's parents. Consonant with the program's purposes, marriage to the father of the child will supposedly appear a more promising method of living independently.

Statutory rape provisions in the reform encourage states to pursue more diligently older men who impregnate young women, based on state laws that are already on the books. This aspect of the law perceives teen mothers at least in part as victims of older male "predators" (PRWORA 1996, 2111). This provision provides a counterargument to the more dominant perception (in the law's purposes) that teen women's sexuality needs to be inhibited and controlled.

Finally, the law provides funding for abstinence-only education as a method to decrease unmarried pregnancy without a concomitant increase in abortion. Though the law does not expressly refer to teens as the only targets of abstinence-only education, they have been the primary recipients through schools and community groups. States apply for federal funds and may use them for state programs, or distribute monies to schools, community groups, and the like; recipients of the funds either can create new programs or expand existing abstinence programs.

LINKING DEPENDENCY TO WELFARE

The elite discourse that helped shape the public's understanding of welfare reform suggests that much of the impetus for welfare reform was generated by concerns about dependency, and the proposed remedies are reflective of this link. Historically, the word *dependency* described the economic relationship between a worker and his or her employer; a worker is dependent on the employer for his or her wages. Over time, the word has moved away from describing solely economic relationships and currently is used to explain socioeconomic relationships (Fraser and Gordon 1994). Children are viewed as dependent on their parents for their survival; likewise a woman who does not work for a wage outside of the house is dependent on her husband. Dependency in both children and housewives historically was not perceived as problematic because children need care and housewives performed two valued tasks: raising children and maintaining the home. Individuals who do not fit into either of these categories also are viewed as dependent; however, their dependency increasingly has become perceived and constructed—politically and socially—as problematic.

For those mothers who rely on governmental aid, their dependency has come to be understood as a burden to society. Throughout the 1980s and 1990s, conservative, and to some degree liberal, politicians claimed that children whose mothers received welfare payments were at a high risk of learning welfare dependency from their mothers. Politicians argued that children will grow up believing that dependence on the state is normal, as is living without a permanent male figure in the household, and will thus fail to learn important middle-class values such as the value of work and the ability to delay gratification, both financially and sexually. Growing up in this environment will perpetuate the cycle. As children whose families receive welfare approach adolescence, they will likely be promiscuous, resist marriage, have children at an early age and outside the context of heterosexual marriage, and avoid a paying job outside of the home because they have supposedly learned that the state will take care of them—indefinitely.

These historical, and gendered, links persist in contemporary politics. Throughout floor debates and hearings over welfare reform, politicians explicitly connected illegitimacy, dependency, and irresponsibility to welfare. Representative Charlie Norwood (R-GA) passionately questions:

> Could the welfare system be any more destructive to the family than it is? It has made fathers trivial . . . Why do children need fathers in today's

America? The food on their table comes from food stamps. The roof over their head comes from public housing. When you need a doctor, there's always Medicaid. And of course the clothes on their backs come by way of a welfare check. We are replacing the financial importance of fathers with the power of the Federal Government to take from one man's labor and give to others. (*Congressional Record,* March 23, 1995, p. H3716, quoted in Gring-Pemble 2003, 483)

Mirroring his colleague's sentiments, Representative David McIntosh (R-IN) contended that the "welfare system . . . creates incentives for women to leave their husbands in order to receive benefits, it penalized families that stick together, and it ultimately undermines the family as an institution in our society" (*Congressional Record,* March 23, 1995, p. H3687, quoted in Gring-Pemble 2003, 483). Later, Senator Trent Lott (R-MS) summed up the discourse by concluding, "There is already a national consensus that illegitimacy is the key factor that drives the growth of welfare. It is the single most powerful force pushing women and children into poverty" (*Congressional Record,* September 7, 1995, p. S12794, quoted in Gring-Pemble 2003, 481).

Much of the debate over "ending welfare as we know it" ignored the fact that most women received welfare benefits because of poverty, generally persistent poverty that is intergenerational because of the differences in educational, occupational, and housing opportunities available to the rich and poor. Women's poverty additionally is associated with their traditional responsibility for the care of children and lower wages. The gendered nature of poverty, and the growth of women's poverty as a percentage of the poor, is striking, yet was not central to the dominant policy discussion of dependency and the perceived divergence between the "deserving" and "undeserving" poor.

In 1995, as debates about welfare reform continued, 14.3 million women and children (9.6 million children in 5 million families) received welfare benefits through Aid to Families with Dependent Children (U.S. House of Representatives 1996). Contrary to stereotypes about women on welfare having many children, the average family size (including a parent) for those receiving welfare payments in 1995 was 2.8 (U.S. House of Representatives 1996). Also contrary to public opinion about the generosity of welfare payments, the average monthly cash grant in 1995 was $377 per month: "The average monthly benefit measured in 1995 dollars, fell from $713 in 1970 to $377 in 1995, a 47 percent drop" (U.S. House of Representatives 1996). Even adding in the value of monthly food stamps, the average monthly AFDC payment amounted to approximately $8,124 per year, significantly below the 1995 poverty line of $12,278 for a parent and two children (U.S. Census Bureau 1995).

Despite the true picture of poverty in the country, the debate also recycled numerous constructions of welfare and welfare recipients that have been present in various forms—and exploited for different means—for decades. Particularly, the fears of dependency and the racialized aspects of the welfare debate can be traced at least to the 1910s with the inception of Mothers' Pensions and to the 1930s with the passage of the Social Security Act.

RACE AND WELFARE

The concept of *dependency* has long been racialized when it is connected to welfare. Gilens (1999), for example, shows that whites overestimate the number of blacks on welfare relative to whites, and thus tend to associate Aid to Families with Dependent Children (AFDC) and Temporary Assistance for Needy Families (TANF) with blacks. Further, "white attitudes toward welfare policy are strongly related to white stereotypes of blacks" (Fording 2003, 78; Gilens 1999), in particular, the belief that blacks lack a strong work ethic. In states with a large Latino population, such as California, this association likely increasingly includes Latinas as well. Soss, Schram, Vartanian, and O'Brien support this contention by demonstrating that state adoption of strict time limits and the family cap under welfare reform "was unrelated to any factor other than racial composition [of the AFDC caseload]" (2001, 390). That is, states with higher percentages of African American and Latina welfare recipients were more likely to employ stringent and punitive methods to move people off the welfare rolls.

Federal and state measures to reduce welfare use are partially responsible for a 50 percent reduction in caseloads since 1996. But similar to state policy adoption, research has suggested that race plays a role in the success of welfare exit strategies at the local level (Parisi et al. 2006). Conditions such as poor economic opportunities, poor social resources, and chronic unemployment structure a person's ability to move off of welfare. Compared to whites, disproportionate numbers of African Americans live in depressed regions, primarily inner cities, which are less likely to support individual efforts to exit TANF. Their access to job training and educational opportunities also is complicated by racial discrimination (Brown 2003; Parisi et al. 2006).

Race is also important in understanding the aspects of welfare reform that focus particularly on teenagers. While the majority of teen pregnancies are accounted for by white teenagers, this number obscures the differences in pregnancy rates when race is considered. The pregnancy rate for teenagers varies considerably. In 2000, among black teenagers the pregnancy rate was 151 pregnancies per 1,000 women aged 15–19, 132 per 1,000 Latino teens, and 56.9 per 1,000 white teenagers (Fields 2005, 557). Such differences in pregnancy rates, in concert with the findings by Gilens (1999), Soss et al. (2001), and others, suggest that welfare reformers concentrate on teenage pregnancy (at least in part) in an attempt to control the reproductive decisions of black and Latina young women.

Cementing the link between race and illegitimacy, Representative Philip Crane, a Republican from Illinois, commented and made future projections about the implications of African American women's reproductive decisions for society:

> Back in the midtwenties in New York, 85% of black families were still together and they looked after their children. And today they are project- ing that by the year 2000 in our major cities, 85% of black children are going to be illegitimates if these trends aren't reversed. You bring a child up in a handicapped circumstance like that with no future and the dete- rioration of our educational system where he is illiterate, he has nothing to look forward to, and he has the enticement of gangs and drugs and so forth. (House Committee on Ways and Means, January 11, 1995, quoted in Gring-Pemble 2003, 485)

Black women, in particular, are socially constructed as having an "excessive and corrupted sexuality" (Fields 2005, 549), which extends to the construction of African American teens as sexually experienced and uncontrollable. When racial stereotypes dovetail with perceptions of welfare "abuse" and "dependency," it is often young black women who get defined as "welfare queens." Thus, as the culture of poverty thesis would have it, African American teens' sexual expe- rience and inability to delay gratification is expressed in early pregnancy and unmarried childbearing.

Recent ethnographic research that monitored policy debates on abstinence- only education helps to demonstrate the links between constructions of race, fears of teen pregnancy that shaped welfare reform, and sex education. In particular, Fields (2005) completed research in North Carolina that documents the impor- tance of race in understanding sex education debates. Fields analyzed meeting notes, interviews, and school board debates concerning a North Carolina state law mandating abstinence-only sex education. She argues that in North Carolina, discussion about the importance of abstinence-only curricula reflected the notion that "unwed teen pregnancy [is] a Black cultural trait that is infiltrating white America" (quoted in Fields 2005, 562); consequently, it was seen as the responsi- bility of educators to protect "innocent" (white) students from what could be the infectious and deviant behavior of sexually open or advanced (nonwhite) teens.

Thus, as Fields argues, "The sexuality of African American women and girls is a central concern in contemporary debates over the companion issues of abstinence- only sex education and welfare reform" (2005, 549). Welfare and abstinence-only sex education are wed in law through PRWORA because of the perceived need to protect white American teens while controlling racially "other" teens, who are constructed as both hypersexual and likely to become welfare dependent.

TITLE V GUIDELINES AND FUNDING

The historical gendered and racialized understandings of dependency and welfare continue to inform contemporary policy and play a role in the underlying aim of abstinence-only education. Title V defines abstinence education as follows:

For purposes of this section, the term "abstinence education" means an educational or motivational program which—

(A) has as its exclusive purpose, teaching the social, psychological, and health gains to be realized by abstaining from sexual activity;

(B) teaches abstinence from sexual activity outside marriage as the expected standard for all school age children;

(C) teaches that abstinence from sexual activity is the only certain way to avoid out-of-wedlock pregnancy, sexually transmitted diseases, and other associated health problems;

(D) teaches that a mutually faithful monogamous relationship in the context of marriage is the expected standard of human sexual activity;

(E) teaches that sexual activity outside of the context of marriage is likely to have harmful psychological and physical effects;

(F) teaches that bearing children out-of-wedlock is likely to have harmful consequences for the child, the child's parents, and society;

(G) teaches young people how to reject sexual advances and how alcohol and drug use increases vulnerability to sexual advances; and

(H) teaches the importance of attaining self-sufficiency before engaging in sexual activity.

Abstinence, as defined by Title V, is connected to physical, social, and psychological health; the definition of abstinence contains the warning that premarital sex can be both psychologically harmful and lead to STIs and pregnancy. Abstinence is pressed on both teens and adults who remain unmarried, assuming a heterosexual audience when it mandates that a "mutually faithful monogamous relationship in the context of marriage is the expected standard of human sexual activity" (PRWORA 1996, 2354). Most abstinence-only programs also attempt to influence teen culture by arguing that premarital sex reflects and further promotes irresponsibility and devalues commitment and marriage in general.

While states are not mandated to participate in abstinence-only education and programs, the federal government has created three streams of funding to entice their participation. Abstinence-only education and programs are funded through: Title V, the AFLA, and CBAE. The amount of funding available varies by source, which is summed up in Table 2.1.

The AFLA, enacted in 1981, is the original source of abstinence-only education monies; it also provides the smallest amount of funding. Through formula grants to states, the AFLA promotes abstinence-only education, particularly directed at teen mothers. Initially used as seed money for developing abstinence-only curricula, the reach of AFLA has grown. Beginning in 1997, "funds for AFLA were explicitly tied to the more stringent eight-point definition of 'abstinence education' found in Title V" (SIECUS 2006a).

A second and much larger source of funding is allocated through Section 510 of Title V. This legislation authorized $250 million to states for abstinence education through a five-year block grant. States have to match $3 of their own money to receive $4 from the federal government, and the state's matching funds can be in-kind contributions from state, local, or private sources, making this a lucrative source of federal grant money (Vergari 2001). The state matching requirement means that as much as $87.5 million has been available each year for abstinence-only education (Trenholm et al. 2007, 2).[5] Congress reauthorized the funding in 2002, making Title V funds available to states beyond the initial five-year period.

States originally had some flexibility in choosing which aspects of Title V's concept of abstinence to emphasize in their programs. Several state and local

Table 2.1
Federal Funding for Abstinence-Only Education, Fiscal Years 1997–2006

Program[a]	*Funding (Millions $)*
Adolescent Family Life Act (AFLA)	125
Welfare Reform, Title V	
Federal	500
State	375
Community Based Abstinence Education (CBAE)	484
Total Funding	1,484

[a] AFLA was enacted in 1981; Title V was enacted in 1996; and CBAE was enacted in 2001.
Source: Table adapted from McFarlane, 2006.

bureaucracies, working in concert with each other, mitigated the impact of abstinence-only education and programs by implementing watered down versions of the legislation (Arsneault 2001; Mooney 2000; Vergari 2001). For example, in fiscal year 1998, 30 states applied for abstinence-only education grants to fund media campaigns; another 5 intended to use their grants for mentoring or after-school programs (Vergari 2001).

States' actions were highly scrutinized by abstinence-only advocates. Focus on the Family publicized their dissatisfaction with the manner in which states were using abstinence-only grants. House Representatives Thomas Bliley (R-VA) and Bill Archer (R-TX) both expressed their frustration with states' implementation of the grants, accusing them of skirting the full requirements of the grant (Vergari 2001). The National Coalition for Abstinence Education (NCAE) started using "report cards" to grade states' performances in implementing Title V monies. Only 5 states received an "A" from NCAE, and 11 earned a failing grade. According to the NCAE's report card system, states receiving failing grades were "in clear violation of some aspect of the spirit as well as the letter of the law (NCAE 1998, 2). In 1998, testifying in the U.S. House of Representatives before the Committee on Commerce, the NCAE reported:

> There has been a concerted attempt by some in the public health establishment to water down, and in some cases to even violate, the intent of the law. This subversive effort has been successful in too many states. The potential and importance of the abstinence law is too exciting for Congress to allow anything short of full national commitment to the sexual health of our children. (Arsneault 2001, 466)

Heeding these criticisms, during George W. Bush's presidential campaign, he promised to increase funding for abstinence programs to similar levels as those programs funding contraceptive services for adolescents (McFarlane 2006). Upon assuming office in 2000, President G. W. Bush advocated for a third abstinence program, Community-Based Abstinence Education (CBAE). Congress authorized CBAE and initially funded the program at $20 million for fiscal year 2001.

This program bypasses state intervention by providing money directly to community organizations, including faith-based organizations. Community-Based Abstinence Education is the strictest abstinence-only program and has experienced the steepest rise in funding since 2001 (see Table 2.2). It mandates that grantees comply with the Title V, Section 510 definition of abstinence (Trenholm et al. 2007). Additionally, in 2006, CBAE funding began to emphasize more strongly the endorsement of both "marriage" and "moral purity" (SIECUS 2006b). The Administration for Children and Families, which is housed in the U.S.

Table 2.2
Growth in Funding for Community Based Abstinence Education (CBAE)

Fiscal Year	Funding for CBAE (Millions $)	Total Funding for Abstinence (Millions $)
2001	20	80
2002	40	100
2003	55	117
2004	75	138
2005	103	166
2006	115	176
2007	137[a]	200[b]

[a] Presidential request. The House Appropriations and Senate Appropriations Committees approved $113 million for FY 2007.

[b] Presidential request. The House Appropriations and Senate Appropriations Committees approved $176 million for FY 2007.

Source: Table adapted from McFarlane 2006.

Department of Health and Human Services, added a new section—containing 3,000 additional words—to the funding announcement for CBAE programs (SIECUS 2006b), shifting the program "from promoting abstinence among teens as a way to reduce 'risky behavior' to promoting abstinence because it 'improves preparation for a stable marriage'" (SIECUS 2006a).

The change in CBAE's language was complimented by similar changes in the language of Title V. Reacting to the states' circumvention of Title V guidelines, Congress passed legislation in 2007 requiring that all state programs in receipt of Title V dollars abide by all eight points defining abstinence-only education. Thus, *each* of the eight points in the abstinence definition had to be addressed if a program were to receive funding. Additionally, the rules on how to teach abstinence have become more stringent: "states must provide 'assurances' that funded curricula and materials 'do not promote contraception and/or condom use'" (SIECUS 2006a).

STATES' REJECTION OF TITLE V MONEY

The new requirements mandating a more rigorous adherence to all of the eight points of the Title V abstinence definition, and the mounting evidence that abstinence-only programs do not decrease teen sexuality activity, prompted several states to refuse Title V funding. California was the only state never to accept Title V funding, based partially on its own experiment with a state-funded abstinence-only program, Education Now and Babies Later (ENABL), in place from 1992 to 1996. Program evaluations did not indicate a decrease in sexual activity among teens, nor were there changes in teen pregnancy or STIs, prompting California to end the program in 1996 (SIECUS 2006a). California was joined in refusing Title V funds by Maine in 2005, followed by New Jersey, Wisconsin, Ohio, and Massachusetts. These states rejected Title V funding for various reasons, citing the lack of flexibility in the requirements to the lack of proof that abstinence-only education impacts teen sexual activity (SIECUS 2006a).

Other states have responded to shortcomings of abstinence-only education by largely restricting the use of Title V funds. For example, after fielding numerous complaints about the medical inaccuracies of abstinence-only curricula, New Mexico's Department of Health restricted Title V abstinence-only-until-marriage funding to grades six and younger (SIECUS 2005c). In a press release issued on April 8, 2005, the secretary of the Department of Health stated,

> The most effective way to protect kids is to discourage them from engaging in sexual activity. However, the reality is some adolescents do engage in sexual behavior. To be cognizant of the fact and do nothing about it is unconscionable. We want to make sure all of New Mexico's children know how to protect themselves if they become sexually active. (SIECUS 2005c)

Even if states reject Title V funding, significant funding remains available (SIECUS 2006a).[6] CBAE provides the largest portion of abstinence-only funds. Because organizations apply directly to the federal government, their state's rejection of Title V funds has little bearing on their ability to secure CBAE funds. California is a case in point. In fiscal year 2006, CBAE provided over $5 million to organizations and schools in the state for abstinence-only curricula and programs. An additional $1.2 million in AFLA funds put California's abstinence-only funding at over $6.4 million, a figure well over the abstinence-only funding (including Title V funds) in all but six states. Thus, to view states that do not apply for Title V funding as if they were devoid of abstinence-only programs is quite misleading.

Additionally, even if individual states decline to apply for Title V funds from the federal government, the federal government's support of abstinence-only curricula continues to be felt in all states. Even though the federal government cannot write its own curricula or tell public schools which of the existing curricula they must use, it still has significant influence over programs at the local level through funding guidelines. According to SIECUS, an organization that attempts to closely track the use of abstinence-only curricula and programs, such influence even extends beyond the actual funded programs:

Although the federal government cannot require or control the content of sexuality education that is not supported by federal funds, many states and communities see the availability of federal money as a "stamp of approval" for an abstinence-only-until-marriage approach. In addition, the substantial federal investment in these programs has drastically increased the number of abstinence-only-until-marriage curricula and materials that are available to schools and community-based programs. In this way the federal government has been very influential in affecting how sexuality education is delivered in local schools and communities. (SIECUS 2005a)

In these ways, the federal government has been able to initiate something of a sea change in sex education policy since 1996.

SUPPLEMENTING MORALITY POLICY AT THE STATE AND LOCAL LEVEL

Federal laws and guidelines tied to abstinence-only funds provide only part of the story because of state and local government's dominant input into sex education decisions. States can require public schools to teach sex education, and they can set guidelines regarding what should or should not be taught. In 2005, some states mandated that sex education curricula must *stress* abstinence, while others indicated that curricula had to *cover* abstinence. Twenty states' laws included direction on how to teach contraception, and a few states banned schools from providing information about abortion to students (SIECUS 2006a).

Most of the control, however, is at the local level with school boards. In addition to school boards, School Health Advisory Committees, superintendents, principals, teachers, and other school administrators also often have input into how sex education will be taught (SIECUS 2005a). According to SIECUS, it is therefore quite difficult to quantify the number of school districts using abstinence-only curricula:

When it comes down to it, we often see that a state will have one policy and school districts will simply ignore it. Or the school district will have a policy, but it is unenforceable on the individual schools. We have even seen schools where one sex-ed teacher will bring in a guest speaker who promotes an abstinence-only message, while the other teacher brings in someone from Planned Parenthood. The only numbers that we have ready access to is how much federal money flows out, and who receives it. After that, the money can go anywhere. Also, many speakers will come in for free, or state money will be used, so we lose the trail there, too. . . . We don't have an accurate picture of what the nation really looks like in terms of what is being taught in the classroom. (Personal communication with author, July 12, 2007)

Thus, the reach of abstinence-only education is probably more extensive than suggested by current reports. This is particularly true of CBAE funds, which are significantly more difficult to track than Title V funds because of the looser administrative process for CBAE grants (Personal communication with author, July 12, 2007).

VARIATIONS IN SEX EDUCATION CURRICULA

The abstinence-only movement has grown significantly to include hundreds of organizations that range from those that write curricula, such as Teen Aid and Choosing the Best, to think tanks such as Focus on the Family and others that support abstinence-only education through workshops, speaking engagements, and pursuing scientific and medical support for claims about the efficacy of abstinence-only education.[7] In addition to authoring public school curricula, some organizations writing curricula also create programs specifically for use by parochial schools, churches, and other religiously affiliated groups. For example, Colleen Mast, who composed *Sex Respect* (for public schools), also wrote *Love and Life: A Christian Sexual Morality Guide for Teens* (2005). *Love and Life* employs explicitly religious language and lessons throughout the curriculum. Though *Love and Life* differs from *Sex Respect* in the overt way it makes use of biblical teachings to promote abstinence, *Sex Respect* has some of the same kinds of lessons, secularized for a public school audience.

Among the more secularized programs, three types of sexuality education dominate public school curricula: comprehensive sexuality education, abstinence-based (also referred to as abstinence-plus or abstinence-centered), and abstinence-only programs. As of 1999, 51 percent of school districts teaching sexuality education had an abstinence-based policy, whereas 35 percent had an abstinence-only policy. Among districts teaching abstinence-only, there is a regional component at play. Southern school districts rely on abstinence-only education at a higher proportion (55%) than the rest of the country, and while a causal link has not been established, birthrates in the South are significantly higher than the national average (Guttmacher Institute 2002). Comprehensive sexuality education is the least common and only taught in 14 percent of school districts teaching a sexual health curriculum. Thirty-three percent of school districts had no sex education policy (Landry et al. 1999). Most sex education policies are relatively new; 53 percent were adopted after 1995 (Landry et al. 1999).

These three types of sexuality education policies cover different issues and emphasize diverse causes and consequences of adolescent sexual behavior. Comprehensive sexuality education teaches a broad curriculum that incorporates sexual development and physiology, reproductive health, including pregnancy and sexually transmitted infections (STIs) and HIV/AIDS, abstinence and other birth control methods, and interpersonal relationships. Thus, abstinence is encouraged within the context of extensive discussion of human sexuality and sexual behavior. Similarly, abstinence-based and abstinence-only programs deal with physiology and reproductive health issues. In contrast to comprehensive sexuality education, however, abstinence-based and abstinence-only education take more limited approaches to human sexuality and downplay information on contraception. Abstinence-only education either bans communication about contraception or allows it only in the framework of contraceptive failure rates (Landry et al. 1999; U.S. General Accounting Office 1998). Abstinence-based education, on the other hand, contains some discussion of contraceptive methods and the use of condoms and other barrier methods to prevent STIs.

The content of sex education classes also varies depending on the grade level of students. In fifth and sixth grade classrooms, sex education tends to cover the physiological changes involved in puberty and information about how HIV is transmitted. Sex education of any kind is taught in only approximately 50 percent of fifth and sixth grade classrooms. Though educators at these grades recommend teaching a broader curriculum, including contraception, abortion, sexual abuse, and sexual orientation, they report feeling unsupported by their communities (Landry, Singh, and Darroch 2000). In grades 7 through 12, sex education becomes more common, with approximately 65 percent of students receiving instruction before they graduate from high school. Many high school instructors teach a broader curriculum than those teaching fifth and sixth grade, but a 1999 study also showed an increase in the number who taught in abstinence-only programs; thus, teachers were less likely to cover contraception in depth compared to the early 1990s (Wilson 2000).

There are approximately 12 to 15 abstinence-only curricula that have received regular federal funding or have garnered significant attention at the federal level through studies and analyses (Devaney et al. 2002; Maynard et al. 2005; U.S. House of Representatives 2004). These include the four curricula that we analyze: *Sex Respect, Teen Aid, Sex Can Wait,* and *Choosing the Best*. In addition, *Heritage Keepers, Worth the Wait,* A. C. Green's *Game Plan, WAIT Training, Why kNOw, Navigator, True Love Waits, ReCapturing the Vision/Vessels of Honor,* and *Facing Reality* are important abstinence-only curricula. SIECUS named *Choosing the Best* and A. C. Green's *Game Plan* as two of the most popular and widely used abstinence-only curricula in 2005 (SIECUS 2006a).[8]

ASSESSMENT OF ABSTINENCE-ONLY CURRICULA

There are several types of studies that assess the claims, approaches, and outcomes of abstinence-only curricula. These include statewide evaluations, longitudinal studies of teen behavior, and analyses of the curricula's content and messages. Empirical studies assessing the efficacy of abstinence-only curricula suggest that it is riddled with problems, ranging from a lack of medically appropriate information to outright incorrect information.

Advocates for Youth summarized statewide evaluations of 11 abstinence-only programs in 2004. These state evaluations attempted to determine the impacts of the programs they had in use. Advocates for Youth reported that states found that abstinence-only education programs were "most successful at improving participants' attitudes towards abstinence and were least likely to positively affect participants' sexual behaviors" (Hauser 2004, 2). Six of the state evaluations assessed programs' impact on short-term changes in sexual behavior; three of the programs showed no impact on sexual behavior, two programs showed increases in sexual behavior, and one program reported mixed results (Hauser 2004, 2). Similarly, of the five long-term evaluations that states undertook, "no evaluation demonstrated any impact on reducing teens' sexual behavior at follow-up, three to 17 months after the program ended" (Hauser 2004, 3). To date, there is a lack of evidence demonstrating that abstinence-only curricula is effective in changing adolescent sexual behaviors (Devaney et al. 2002; Kirby 2001; Landry et al. 1999; Rabasca 1999; SIECUS 2001; Trenholm et al. 2007). Thus, abstinence-only advocates generally have been unable to prove their key claim, that abstinence-only programs decrease teen sexual activity.

Similar to state evaluations, in 2007, Mathematica Policy Research published its report on one of the most important scientific studies to be completed to date. Mathematica researchers undertook a longitudinal study of abstinence-only programs in order to assess the effects of abstinence-only education on adolescent sexual behavior. Participants in four abstinence programs were compared to students in control groups that were not exposed to the abstinence-only programs and were surveyed over the course of four to six years (Maynard et al. 2005; Trenholm et al. 2007). The first-year impact analysis did not show a decrease in sexual activity for the youth enrolled in the abstinence-only programs. The youth exposed to abstinence programs reported "views more supportive of abstinence and less supportive of teen sex than would have been the case had they not had access to the abstinence education programs" (Maynard et al. 2005, xxi). Changes in attitudes did not extend to changes in behavior, however; there was little difference between the study and control groups. Mathematica researchers posited that because the four programs targeted students in elementary and junior high school, most of the students were younger than the average age of sexual initiation (around age 17), so it was not clear whether the programs would impact sexual activity in the future (Maynard et al. 2005).

To test this question, Mathematica researchers completed a follow-up study four to six years later, with youth who had participated in their original survey.

By this time, the average participant age was 16.5 years, and most students had completed their abstinence-only programs. Mathematica indicated again that there were no differences among the students who had received abstinence-only instruction and those who had not on important measures of sexual behavior. "[Y]outh in the program group were no more likely than control group youth to have abstained from sex and, among those who reported having had sex, they had similar numbers of sexual partners and had initiated sex at the same mean age" (Trenholm et al. 2007, xvii). Approximately 51 percent of both the students in the programs and those who had not received abstinence-only instruction had had sexual intercourse, and both groups reported a mean age of first sex as 14.9 years. Of those who had sex, "one quarter of all youth in both groups had sex with three or more partners, and about one in six had sex with four or more partners" (Trenholm et al. 2007, xviii). Finally, groups were almost identical in their reported use of condoms; 17 percent of both groups occasionally used condoms and 4 percent of both groups never used condoms (Trenholm et al. 2007).

While the Mathematica study focused on the effectiveness of abstinence-only education in modifying teens' sexual behavior, the Waxman Report takes a different analytical approach to analyzing abstinence-only curricula, focusing on the specific content of curricula. The report was requested by Congressional Representative Henry Waxman and written by The U.S. House of Representative's Committee on Government Reform. The Waxman Report cites numerous examples of "false, misleading, or distorted information about reproductive health in abstinence-only curricula," including "false information about the effectiveness of contraceptives . . . [and] risks of abortion" (U.S. House of Representatives 2004, i). Though the Centers for Disease Control and Prevention have clearly stated that condom use is "highly effective in preventing the transmission of HIV" (U.S. House of Representatives 2004, 8), several of the curricula analyzed for the report erroneously claimed that condoms were not highly protective against HIV infection. Likewise, abstinence-only curricula often "exaggerate condom failure rates in preventing pregnancy," basically giving students the message that condoms are not useful in protecting them from pregnancy or STIs (U.S. House of Representatives 2004, 11).

The Waxman Report also criticizes abstinence-only curricula for its "blurring" of science and religion, such as claiming that life begins at conception; for its numerous "scientific errors"; and for treating "stereotypes about girls and boys as scientific fact" (U.S. House of Representatives 2004, 16). These aspects of the curricula often are intertwined, particularly those that blur science and religion and pass on gender stereotypes as if they were biological fact. For example, curricula state that girls are less concerned about achievement than boys, are more interested in the success of their relationships than in their futures, and that girls "are weak and need protection" from men (U.S. House of Representatives 2004, 17).

These few studies comprise the most methodologically sound statewide or national evidence regarding abstinence-only curricula, but numerous other, smaller studies also exist. Sociologists Bearman and Brückner have done research on a specific aspect of abstinence-only programs, the virginity pledge. Virginity pledges are used by programs like Silver Ring Thing and by some public school curricula to encourage teens—and provide them with tangible evidence of their promises—to delay sexual activity until marriage. Initially sponsored by the Southern Baptist Church in 1993 (outside the context of public school sex education), some 2.5 million teens took pledges by 2001 (Bearman and Brückner 2001).

Using data from the National Longitudinal Study of Adolescent Health, Bearman and Brückner found that taking a virginity pledge, "decreases the risk of intercourse substantially and independently. Pledgers' relative risk of sexual initiation is estimated to be 34% lower than nonpledgers" (Bearman and Brückner 2001, 883), after controlling for characteristics such as religiosity, race, and class. According to this study, virginity pledges can delay first intercourse up to 18 months for 15 to 17 year olds. Interestingly, this delay is strongest in contexts where teen pledgers are relatively few in number. Perhaps being in the minority enables pledgers to adopt an alternative group identity, in keeping with Bearman and Brückner's sense that the push toward making virginity pledges is a social movement. And it is important to note that a substantial percentage of pledgers still had sexual intercourse before marriage; 88 percent of pledgers had sexual intercourse before marriage, as compared to 99 percent of nonpledgers (Brückner and Bearman 2005, 275).

In a follow up article, Brückner and Bearman report that virginity pledges are not effective in reducing STI rates among teens; they compared infection rates for Human Papilloma Virus, Chlamydia, Gonorrhea, and Trichomoniasis. Pledgers and nonpledgers had similar rates of infection, despite the fact that Brückner and Bearman found that pledgers had sexual intercourse for the first time later than did nonpledgers, and that female pledgers were likely to marry earlier than nonpledgers (Brückner and Bearman 2005, 275). They posit that teens who take virginity pledges may be less likely to use condoms when they do initiate sexual activity, and that they are less likely to be tested for STIs than nonpledgers. Other studies have confirmed these findings (Dailard 2006).

A perhaps secondary impact of abstinence-only education—in educational programs and cultural messages—is the redefinition of what it means to be sexually active by adolescents, particularly among virginity pledgers. Some evidence suggests that among pledgers the focus on vaginal virginity may be contributing to a higher level of their participating in oral and anal sexual activity as a means of "preserving" vaginal virginity (Dailard 2006).

In the face of a lack of significant scientific evidence supporting abstinence-only education, studies suggest that comprehensive sexuality curricula can delay the age of initial intercourse as well as improve the likelihood that once sexually active, teens will use contraception (Darroch et al. 2000; Kirby 2001; Kirby et al. 1994; Landry et al. 1999). In Kirby's (2001) review of over 250 methodologically sound studies on sex education programs, he found that many of the arguments propagated by abstinence-only supporters are untrue. For example, Kirby says of comprehensive sexuality education:

> A large body of evaluation research clearly shows that sex and HIV education programs included in this review do not increase sexual activity—they do not hasten the onset of sex, increase the frequency of sex, nor increase the number of sexual partners. To the contrary, some sex and HIV education programs delay the onset of sex, reduce the frequency of sex, or reduce the number of sexual partners. (Kirby 2001, 8)

He also found that some comprehensive sexuality education curricula led to increased use of condoms and other contraceptives.

LEGAL CHALLENGES TO ABSTINENCE-ONLY PROGRAMS

In addition to the lack of research showing positive results associated with abstinence-only education, and the problems associated with specific lessons in these curricula, there have been several legal challenges regarding the way that abstinence-only funding has blurred the lines between church and state. In 1987, the American Civil Liberties Union (ACLU) filed a suit in federal court alleging that the AFLA was violating the separation of church and state. The district judge agreed and found the AFLA unconstitutional; however, the Supreme Court reversed the decision in 1988 and remanded the case to a lower court. Ultimately, the case was settled out of court in 1993 with four stipulations. Organizations and programs using AFLA funds must: "(1) not include religious references, (2) be medically accurate, (3) respect the 'principle of self-determination' regarding contraceptive referral for teenagers, and (4) not allow grantees to use church sanctuaries for their programs or to give presentations in parochial schools during school hours" (LeClair 2006, 296).

Despite the AFLA settlement, the constitutionality of funding abstinence-only programs is far from resolved. Several other legal challenges over the religious misuse of funding have been mounted more recently. In 2002, the ACLU mounted a legal challenge to Louisiana's abstinence-only programs, citing numerous violations of the separation between church and state. For example, federal funds were granted to Rapides Station Community Ministries to engage in such activities as a "back-to-school 'Youth Revival' where the Reverend Roger Layton 'proclaim[ed] God's Word with power as to why we should live pure and Holy. He made it clear that abstinence is the only way. . . . Some promise[d] to become members of the Abstinence Club at their school'" (*ACLU v. Foster* 2002, 5). Thus, federal funding was being used to specifically advance a particular religious perspective.

A theater group called Just Say "Whoa" also received national attention as one of the groups targeted by the ACLU suit against the state of Louisiana. Just Say "Whoa" performed skits for sex education classes in Louisiana junior and senior high schools. Describing its "format [as] hard hitting, truth-based, entertaining, and Christ centered," Just Say "Whoa" asserted, "Our belief is that sexual activity outside the commitment of marriage is offensive to the Lord we serve" (*ACLU v. Foster* 2002, 9). In one skit called "Damaged Goods," "Kandace" states, "One thing I've learned is that . . . *everyone* is damaged goods. We all sin and make mistakes. Some have bigger consequences than others, but they all cost Jesus His life. We don't have to stay damaged goods" (*ACLU v. Foster* 2002, 10).

In response to the ACLU's case, the Just Say "Whoa" players, along with other grant recipients in Louisiana, were forced to remove overt references to the Bible and God in their materials, but the revised message—and even the language—differs little as compared to the original. For example, "Damaged Goods" was renamed "You Think So?" and minimally rewritten to remove the words "Jesus" and "sin," but otherwise remains intact (Louisiana Governor's Program on Abstinence 2003).

Another well-known abstinence-only program designed for use in public schools to accompany a sex education curriculum is Silver Ring Thing, mentioned previously, which derives its name from the silver rings it passes out to students willing to take virginity pledges at the end of Silver Ring Thing's abstinence-only performance (SIECUS 2004). The organization received federal abstinence-only funding until the ACLU sued the Department of Health and Human Services (HHS) for funding organizations with an explicitly religious message; the suit resulted in HHS withdrawing federal funds from Silver Ring Thing, though the organization continues to operate with private funds (SIECUS 2006a).

Silver Ring Thing's message is that complete abstinence from sexual activity until heterosexual marriage is the sole method for maintaining physical and emotional health; contraception is not discussed (SIECUS 2004). As Silver Ring Thing states, abstinence from sexual activity is wrapped up with Evangelical Christian faith: "The mission is to saturate the United States with a generation of young people who have taken a vow of sexual abstinence until marriage and put on the silver ring. This mission can only be achieved by offering a personal relationship with Jesus Christ as the best way to live a sexually pure life" (Silver Ring Thing 2004). The mission extends beyond the United States, as the organization is attempting to make forays abroad to share its message.

REAUTHORIZATION OF WELFARE REFORM

The legal challenges notwithstanding, the House of Representatives passed H.R. 473, the Personal Responsibility, Work and Family Protection Bill, in May 2002. This bill renewed funding for abstinence-only programs at $50 million a year for the following five years (Rose 2005). Many representatives opposed the renewal of funds for abstinence programs, citing the use of inaccurate medical information in abstinence-only literature and asserting that programs rely on "terror tactics" in promoting abstinence. Political supporters of the bill retorted that forming a consensus on what constitutes "medically accurate" information is impossible: The bill ultimately passed by a vote of 229 to 197 (Rose 2005; U.S. House of Representatives 2004).

Abstinence-only education and programs have received a fivefold increase in federal appropriations, but funding may be leveling, or even decreasing. After the 2006 midterm elections, Democrats won a slim majority in both chambers of Congress. In June 2007, the Senate appropriations committee proposed the first cut in spending for abstinence-only funding. Title V was given a three-month extension by Congress. Debate continues to surround Title V, and the U.S. House of Representatives proposed adding new language into the provision to require medical accuracy, provide states with flexibility on content, and fund programs proven effective in decreasing teen pregnancy, STD, and HIV/AIDS rates (SIECUS 2007a). The provision passed the House by a 225 to 204 vote, but the Senate has yet to decide on Title V reauthorization.

CHAPTER SUMMARY

The language of PRWORA clearly demonstrates the intent of curbing welfare use by targeting current and potential welfare recipients. Contemporary policy largely has been crafted for these target groups through gendered and racialized understandings of dependency, single parenthood, and pregnancy. These social constructions of race, class, and gender have been employed in various forms and resonated with both the political elite and general public in multiple ways, for decades. Christian conservatives have been successful in this context, pressing for changes to sex education and in developing abstinence-only programs funded with federal dollars.

We have attempted to lend evidence to the contention that Title V was included as a stealth morality policy as part of a large and complex bill intended to radically reform the welfare system. Under the initial guise of preventing unmarried pregnancy and subsequent poverty, the authors of the bill instituted a stealth morality policy as part of a massive and complex redistributive policy. And as we argue, abstinence-only curricula and programs, in turn, help to considerably shape and further advance a conservative Christian agenda. By reaching so many teens, abstinence-only programs are in the forefront of providing Christian conservatives with an audience for its belief systems and the possibility that it can gain further ground both politically and culturally.

The focus on abstinence within a welfare reform law may be read as an attempt to instill middle-class values of delayed childbearing in young girls caught in the culture of poverty, which assumes that young, poor women are promiscuous. But, as we look closer at issues surrounding, and related to, teen sexuality in the remainder of this book, this perception of teens—in particular poor teens—is sorely inaccurate. Adolescents' sexual decision making is far more complex than indicated by many of the simplistic, socially constructed characterizations of them and their behavior.

NOTES

1. Before Fiscal Year 2005, CBAE was called Special Projects of Regional and National Significance-Community-Based Abstinence Education (SPRANS-CBAE).

2. Advocates for sexuality education existed well before the 1960s. Toward the end of the 1900s, social reformers criticized the "conspiracy of silence" surrounding sexuality, reinforcing the social taboo against open and accurate discussions of sex-related issues. New scientific discoveries about venereal diseases provided the impetus for public sexuality education because advocates were able to focus on the physical consequences of sexually transmitted infections from a "scientific" perspective (Burnham 1973; Moran 2000; Odem 1995). Social hygienists attempted to educate the public about the dangers of disease and prostitution by publishing pamphlets and giving public lectures on these topics. In 1913, Ella Flagg Young, while superintendent of Chicago schools, boldly proposed providing high school students with three lectures given by a physician about the biological, physiological, and hygiene issues associated with sexual activity (Moran 2000). Although the students favored making the lectures part of the regular curriculum, they ended due to parental opposition. A few years later in 1916, the first book concerned with establishing sex education in public schools was published. Similar to other educational efforts directed at adolescents, it did not receive much support. Mindful of the controversy, the U.S. Public Health Service only allocated money to hygiene departments in colleges because it was less controversial (Moran 2000).

3. Public education is decentralized and designed to allow local communities to determine the appropriate curricula for their respective communities. The federal government is prohibited from interfering in state and local decisions about curriculum standards

through four statues: The Department of Education Organization Act (Section 103a), the Elementary and Secondary Education Act (Section 14512), Goals 2000 (Section 319b), and the General Education Provisions Act (Section 438; Advocates for Youth & Sexuality Information & Education Council of the U.S. 2001).

State and local communities determine whether or not sexuality education should be taught in their schools. While statutes prohibit the federal government from prescribing curriculum, it does not prevent the federal government from using other incentives—primarily through monetary incentives and penalties—to shape curriculum content. In this historical context, the government's more recent role in providing financial incentives for states to teach abstinence-only curricula is even more remarkable and reflects the influence of social conservatives on the national policy agenda (LeClair 2006).

4. Despite the reauthorization of the welfare bill six years after it initially passed in 1996, there has been scant research examining the impact of the provisions on teenagers' behavior. Adolescent pregnancy was one focal point of the 1996 debate but played a much less visible role in 2002 (Offner 2005). The minor role of adolescent pregnancy may have been a result of the significant decrease in the number of teens receiving cash benefits: Since 1996, there has been a 60 percent decline in the allocation of cash benefits to teens. Very few studies have examined the relationship between welfare provisions and teen behavior, and the existing studies have some notable limitations. Using the March Current Population Survey for the years 1989 to 2001, Offner (2005) provides a look at this relationship. He finds some evidence linking the provisions to a decrease (among 16- and 17-year-old girls) in school drop out rates for young women who have children compared to those young women who are childless. Offner also finds some evidence of a reduction in the number of out-of-wedlock births: a decline from 8.5 percent in 1989 to 5.8 percent in 2001. While Offner attributes these findings to the welfare provisions implemented in 1996, further studies are necessary to more firmly determine the causal path of these relationships. For example, he finds a reduction in illegitimate pregnancies in his research; however, a substantial body of research suggests that teen pregnancy rates had been declining *prior* to the 1996 welfare reform.

5. Of a total of $69 million in Title V abstinence-only education funds that were spent in fiscal year 1999 (primarily Title V Section 510 and AFLA monies), public entities expended $33 million, private entities $28 million, and faith-based entities $7 million. Thus, faith-based groups spent approximately 10 percent of Title V dollars. Almost all of this money was used to fund activities related to public school instruction (Sonfield and Gold 2001).

6. Total funding for all abstinence-only programs has risen quite rapidly and steeply, from $96.5 million in 1998 when Title V funding initially became available, to $218 million in 2006 (SIECUS 2006a). President Bush proposed increasing abstinence-only education funding 15 percent over the allocation for fiscal year 2007, which would bring the total funding to $204 million for fiscal year 2008 (SIECUS 2007b). President Bush has indicated elsewhere that he would like to increase abstinence-only education funding to $270 million by 2008 (Ertelt 2005).

7. For example, in 2002 alone, Mathematica Policy Research reported that 700 abstinence-only programs received Title V funding (Devaney et al. 2002, 8).

8. Although A. C. Green's *Game Plan* is cited as one of the most popular texts used, it is written and recommended primarily for middle school (grades 7–9), which precluded its use in the content analysis contained in chapter four (Project Reality 2007).

BIBLIOGRAPHY

Advocates for Youth & Sexuality Information & Education Council of the U.S. 2001. "Toward a Sexually Healthy America: Roadblocks Imposed by the Federal Government's Abstinence-Only-Until-Marriage Education Program." Available at: http://www.advocatesforyouth.org/publications/abstinenceonly.pdf.

Arsneault, Shelly. 2001. "Values and Virtue: The Politics of Abstinence-Only Sex Education." *American Review of Public Administration* 31 (4): 436–54.

Bearman, Peter S., and Hannah Brückner. 2001. "Promising the Future: Virginity Pledges and First Intercourse." *American Journal of Sociology* 106 (4): 859–912.

Brown, Michael K. 2003. "Ghettos, Fiscal Federalism, and Welfare Reform." In *Race and the Politics of Welfare Reform*, ed. Sanford E. Schram, Joe Soss, and Richard C. Fording, 47–71. Ann Arbor: The University of Michigan Press.

Brückner, Hannah, and Peter Bearman. 2005. "After the promise: The STD Consequences of Adolescent Virginity Pledges." *Journal of Adolescent Health* 36: 271–78.

Burnham, John C. 1973. "The Progressive Era Revolution in American Attitudes Toward Sex." *The Journal of American History* 59 (4): 885–908.

CQ Congress Collection. 1981. "Family Planning, SIDS, 1978 Legislative Chronology." In *Congress and the Nation, 1977–1980*, vol. 5. Washington, D.C.: CQ Press. Accessed September 15, 2007. Available at: http://library.cqpress.com/congress/catn77-0010173044. Document ID: catn77-0010173044.

CQ Congress Collection. 1995. "Elementary and Secondary Education Reauthorization/ Sex Education (in H.R.) HR 6." In *Congressional Roll Call 1994*. Washington, D.C.: CQ Press. Accessed September 13, 2007. Available at: http://library.cqpress.com/congress/rc1994-196-9304-570959. Document ID: rc1994-196-9304-570959.

CQ Congress Collection. 1997. "Welfare Reform, 1995–1996 Legislative Chronology." In *Congress and the Nation, 1993–1996*, vol. 9. Washington, D.C.: CQ Press. Accessed September 13, 2007. Available at: http://library.cqpress.com/congress/catn93-0000141468. Document ID: catn93-0000141468.

Dailard, Cynthia. 2006. "Legislating against Arousal: The Growing Divide Between Federal Policy and Teenage Sexual Behavior." *Guttmacher Policy Review* 9 (3, Summer): 1–4. Available at: http://www.guttmacher.org/pubs/gpr/09/3/index.html.

Daley, Daniel. 1997. "Exclusive Purpose: Abstinence-Only Proponents Create Federal Entitlement in Welfare Reform." Report 24:4. New York: Sexuality Information and Education Council of the United States.

Darroch, Jacqueline E., David J. Landry, and Susheela Singh. 2000. "Changing Emphases in Sexuality Education in U.S. Public Secondary Schools, 1988–1999." *Family Planning Perspectives* 32: 204–11, 265.

Devaney, Barbara, Amy Johnson, Rebecca Maynard, and Chris Trenholm. 2002. "The Evaluation of Abstinence Education Programs Funded under Title V Section 510: Interim Report." Princeton, NJ: Mathematica Policy Research, Inc.

Donovan, Patricia. 1984. "The Adolescent Family Life Act and the Promotion of Religious Doctrine." *Family Planning Perspectives* 16: 221–27.

Ertelt, Steven. 2005. "Planned Parenthood Blasts President Bush for Increasing Abstinence Funds." (February 8). Available at: http://www.lifenews.com/nat1183.html.

Fields, Jessica. 2005. "'Children Having Children': Race, Innocence, and Sexuality Education." *Social Problems* 52 (4): 549–71.

Fording, Richard C. 2003. "'Laboratories of Democracy' or Symbolic Politics?: The Racial Origins of Welfare Reform." In *Race and the Politics of Welfare Reform*, ed. Sanford E. Schram, Joe Soss, and Richard C. Fording, 72–100. Ann Arbor: The University of Michigan Press.

Fraser, Nancy, and Linda Gordon. 1994. "A Genealogy of Dependency: Tracing a Keyword of the U.S. Welfare State." *Signs* 19 (2): 309–36.

Gilens, Martin. 1999. *Why Americans Hate Welfare: Race, Media, and the Politics of Antipoverty Policy*. New Haven, CT: Yale University Press.

Gring-Pemble, Lisa M. 2003. "Legislating a "Normal, Classic Family": The Rhetorical Construction of Families in American Welfare Policy." *Political Communication* 20 (4): 473–98.

Guttmacher Institute. 2002. "Sexuality Education." *Facts in Brief*. Available at: http://www.guttmacher.org/pubs/factsheet_121399.html.

Guttmacher Institute. 2006. "U.S. Teenage Pregnancy Statistics: Overall Trends, and State-by-State Information." Available at: http://www.guttmacher.org/pubs/teen_preg_stats.html.

Hauser, Debra. 2004. *Five Years of Abstinence-Only-Until-Marriage Education: Assessing the Impact*. Washington, D.C.: Advocates For Youth.

Heclo, Hugh. 2001 "The Politics of Welfare Reform." In *The New World of Welfare*, ed. Rebecca M. Blank and Ron Haskins, 169–200. Washington, D.C.: Brookings Institution Press.

Irvine, Janice. 2002. *Talk About Sex: The Battles over Sex Education in the United States*. Berkley: University of California Press.

Kaiser Family Foundation. 2004. "Sex Education in America." *Public Opinion and Media Research Program*. Available at: http://www.kff.org/youthhivstds/3048-index.cfm.

Kirby, Douglas. 2001. *Emerging Answers: Research Findings on Programs to Reduce Teen Pregnancy*, summary. Washington, D.C.: National Campaign to Prevent Teen Pregnancy.

Kirby, Douglas, L. Short, J. Collins, D. Rugg, L. Kolbe, M. Howard, et al. 1994. "School-Based Programs to Reduce Sexual Risk Behaviors: A Review of Effectiveness." *Public Health Reports* 19 (3).

Landry, David J., Susheela Singh, and Jacqueline E. Darroch. 2000. "Sexuality Education in Fifth and Sixth Grades in U.S. Public Schools, 1999." *Family Planning Perspectives* 32 (5): 212–19.

Landry, David, Lisa Kaeser, and Cory L. Richards. 1999. "Abstinence Promotion and the Provision of Information About Contraception in Public School District Sexuality Education Policies." *Family Planning Perspectives* 31 (6): 280–86.

LeClair, Danielle. 2006. "Let's Talk about Sex Honestly: Why Federal Abstinence-Only-until-Marriage Education Programs Discriminate against Girls, Are Bad Public Policy, and Should Be Overturned." *Wisconsin Women's Law Journal* 29 (291): 291–323.

Louisiana Governor's Program on Abstinence. 2003. Available at: http://www.abstinencedu.com.

Luker, Kristin. 1996. *Dubious Conceptions: The Politics of Teenage Pregnancy*. Cambridge, MA: Harvard University Press.

Maynard, Rebecca A., Christopher Trenholm, Barbara Devaney, Amy Johnson, Melissa Clark, John Homrighausen, et al. 2005. "First-Year Impacts of Four Title V, Section 510 Abstinence Education Programs." Princeton, NJ: Mathematica Policy Research, Inc.

McFarlane, Deborah R. 2006. "Reproductive Health Policies in President Bush's Second Term: Old Battles and New Fronts in the United States and Internationally." *Journal of Public Health Policy* 27 (4):405–26.

McFarlane Deborah R., and Kenneth J. Meier. 2001. *The Politics of Fertility Control*. New York: Chatham House Publishers.

McKeegan, Michele. 1992. *Abortion Politics: Mutiny in the Ranks of the Right*. New York: The Free Press.

Mills, Frederick B. 1996. "The Ideology of Welfare Reform: Deconstructing Stigma." *Social Work* 41 (4).

Mooney, Christopher. 2000. "The Decline of Federalism and the Rise of Morality-Policy Conflict in the United States." *Publius* 30 (1/2): 171–89.

Moran, Jeffrey P. 2000. *Teaching Sex: The Shaping of Adolescence in the 20th Century*. Cambridge, MA: Harvard University Press.

National Coalition for Abstinence Education (NCAE). 1998. *NCAE Title V Report Card Grading Guidelines*. Colorado Springs: Author.

Odem, Mary E. 1995. *Delinquent Daughters: Protecting and Policing Adolescent Female Sexuality in the United States, 1885–1920*. Chapel Hill: University of North Carolina Press.

Offner, Paul. 2005. "Welfare Reform and Teenage Girls." *Social Science Quarterly* 86 (2): 306–22.

Paden, Catherine, and Benjamin I. Page. 2003. "Congress Invokes Public Opinion on Welfare Reform." *American Politics Research* 31 (6): 670–79.

Parisi, Domenico, Diane K. McLaughlin, Steven Michael Grice, and Michael Taquino. 2006. "Exiting TANF: Individual and Local Factors and Their Differential Influence Across Racial Groups." *Social Science Quarterly* 87 (1): 76–90.

Personal Responsibility and Work Opportunity Reconciliation Act of 1996 (PRWORA). Public Law 104–193, Title I, August 22, 1996.

Project Reality. 2007. "Game Plan." Available at: http://projectreality.org/about.

Rabasca, Lisa. 1999. "Not Enough Evidence to Support 'Abstinence-Only.'" *APA Monitor Online* 30 (11).

Rose, Susan. 2005. "Going Too Far? Sex, Sin and Social Policy." *Social Forces* 84 (2): 1207–32.

Schneider, Saundra K., and William G. Jacoby. 2005. "Elite Discourse and American Public Opinion: The Case of Welfare Spending." *Political Research Quarterly* 58 (3): 367–79.

Sonfield, Adam, and Rachel Benson Gold. 2001. "States' Implementation of the Section 510 Abstinence Education Program, FY 1999." *Family Planning Perspectives* 33 (4): 166–71.

SIECUS. 2001. "Exclusive Purpose: Abstinence-Only Proponents Create Federal Entitlement in Welfare Reform." *SIECUS Report Articles* 24 (4).

SIECUS. 2004. "Making the Connection—News and Views on Sexuality: Education, Health and Rights." *SIECUS Report Articles* 3 (2).

SIECUS. 2005a. "Sexuality Education Policy: Who Makes Decisions?" Available at: http://www.communityactionkit.org/pdfs/Getting_Ready_To_Advocate/Education_Policy.html.

SIECUS. 2005b. "A Brief Explanation of Federal Abstinence-Only-Until-Marriage Funding." Available at: http://www.siecus.org/policy/states/2005/explanation.html.

SIECUS. 2005c. "Sexuality Education and Abstinence-Only-Until-Marriage Programs in the States: An Overview." *Policy and Advocacy*. Available at: http://www.siecus.org/policy/states.

SIECUS. 2006a. "SIECUS State Profiles: A Portrait of Sexuality Education and Abstinence-Only-Until-Marriage Programs in the States." Available at: http://www.siecus.org/policy/states/index.html.

SIECUS. 2006b. "It Gets Worse: A Revamped Federal Abstinence-Only Program Goes Extreme." *Special Report*. Available at: http://www.siecus.org/media/index.html.

SIECUS. 2007a. "Title V Abstinence-Only Funding Proposal to Reauthorize with Important Fixes." Press Release (August 2). Available at: http://www.siecus.org/media/press.

SIECUS. 2007b. "Fiscal Year 2007 Appropriations Completed as Fiscal Year 2008 Budget Released: Congress Approves Fiscal Year 2007 Spending Bill." Policy Updates (February). Available at: http://www.siecus.org/policy/PUpdates.

The Silver Ring Thing. 2004. "It's Time: Silver Ring Thing Newsletter." The John Guest Team. Available at: http://www.silverringthing.com/newsletters.asp.

Soss, Joe, Sanford F. Schram, Thomas P. Vartanian, and Erin O'Brien. 2001. "Setting the Terms of Relief: Explaining State Policy Choices in the Devolution Revolution." *American Journal of Political Science*, 45 (2, April).

Stryker, Robin, and Pamela Wald. 2007. "Redefining Compassion to Reform Welfare: How supporters of 1990s Federal Welfare Reform Aimed for the Moral High Ground." Presented at the 19th Annual International Meeting of Socio-Economics, Copenhagen Business School, June 28–30.

Trenholm, Christopher, Barbara Devaney, Ken Fortson, Lisa Quay, Justin Wheeler, and Melissa Clark. 2007. *Impacts of Four Title V, Section 510 Abstinence Education Programs: Final Report*. Princeton, NJ: Mathematica Policy Research, Inc.

U.S. Census Bureau. 1995. Poverty Thresholds. Available at: http://www.census.gov/hhes/www/poverty/threshld.

U.S. Department of Health and Human Services. 1984. "Trends in Teenage Childbearing United States 1970–1981." DHHS Publication No. (PHS) 84-1919 (September). Available at: http://www.cdc.gov/nchs/data/series/sr_21/sr21_041.pdf.

U.S. Department of Health, Education, and Welfare. 1979. "Patterns of Aggregate and Individual Changes in Contraceptive Practice United States 1965–1975." DHEW Publication No. (PHS) 79-1404 (June).

U.S. General Accounting Office. 1998. "Teen Pregnancy: State and Federal Efforts to Implement Prevention Programs and Measure Their Effectiveness." Health, Education, and Human Services Division (November) GAO/HEHS-99-4. Available at: http://www.gao.gov/archive/1999/he99004.pdf.

U.S. House of Representatives, Committee on Government Reform-Minority Staff. 2004. "The Content of Federally Funded Abstinence-Only Education Programs." Prepared for Rep. Henry A. Waxman. Available at: http://www.oversight.house.gov/documents/20041201102153-50247.pdf.

U.S. House of Representatives, Committee on Ways and Means. 1996. *Green Book*. Washington, D.C.: U.S. Government Printing Office, 104–14.

Vergari, Sandra. 2001. "Morality Politics and the Implementation of Abstinence-Only Sex Education: A Case of Policy Compromise." In *The Public Clash of Private Values*, ed. Christopher Z. Mooney, 201–12. New York: Chatham House Publishers.

Viguerie, Richard A. 1981. *The New Right: We're Ready to Lead*. Falls Church, VA: The Viguerie Company.

Watson, Justin. 1997. *The Christian Coalition: Dreams of Restoration, Demands for Recognition*. New York: St. Martin's Press.

Weaver, Kent. 2000. *Ending Welfare As We Know It*. Washington, D.C.: Brookings Institution Press.

Wilson, Susan N. 2000. "Sexuality Education: Our Current Status and an Agenda for 2010." *Family Planning Perspectives* 32 (5): 204–11, 265.

CASES CITED

ACLU v. Foster, 2002 WL 1733651 (E.D.La.)

PUBLIC LAWS CITED

Adolescent Family Life Act of 1981, Pub. L. No. 97-35, 95 Stat. 357.

Adolescent Health Services and Pregnancy Prevention and Care Act of 1978, Pub. L. 95-626, Tit. VI, 92 Stat. 3595–3601.

Personal Responsibility and Work Opportunity Reconciliation Act (PRWORA) of 1996, Pub. L. no. 104-193, 110 Stat. 2105.

Public Health Service Act of 1970, Pub. L. no. 91-572, 84 Stat. 1504.

3

"Good Girls" or "Dirty Whores"? Images and Behaviors of Adolescent Women

To contextualize the contemporary debate over abstinence-only education, this chapter will deconstruct and analyze dominant social constructions of gender and sexuality, with a specific focus on adolescent women's sexuality. Multiple cultural understandings of young women's sexuality—some that have endured since the Victorian Era—are at play at any one time in public discourse. Competing definitions of young women depict them at times as innocent and childlike and at other times as sexually knowledgeable and deviant. Factors such as race and class often fuel these disparate portrayals.

We contrast various constructions of adolescent sexuality against numerous statistics about adolescent sexual behavior over the past several decades. Sexual practices are influenced by complex psychological, social, and institutional factors that are not reflected in a simplistic or one-dimensional construction of adolescence. Through this exploration, a fuller, more multilayered picture of adolescent women's sexuality will be painted.

This background provides a context for the analyses in chapters four and five, where we analyze abstinence-only curricula and teen interviews, respectively. Constructions of sexuality offer a framework for interpreting myriad lessons about young women as sexual beings that permeate the abstinence-only curricula. Likewise, constructions of sexuality juxtaposed with the data on teen sexual behavior, both presented in this chapter, provide important background information for understanding teen interview responses.

LAURA'S STORY

Laura has been in and out of group homes, foster care, and most recently a maternity home since she was 12 years old. When Laura was 11, her mother and stepfather moved to northern California with her younger sister and brother to be closer to her stepfather's family. Laura remained in central California with her father. After her dad lost his job, they relocated to Arkansas where Laura spent most of her time unsupervised. She became sexually active at the age of 11 with her 15-year-old boyfriend. Laura has mixed emotions about the experience. To the extent that Laura conceptualizes virginity as a special gift, to be "given" but once, she regrets the experience: "I wish . . . I regret it. I can't say I regret it 'cause it taught me a lot, but if I could go back . . . to when I was 11, and change everything, I would do that. I'd still be a virgin today. 'Cause I think it's something that's very special. I wish I wouldn't have lost my virginity."

Since becoming sexually active, Laura believes she has had between 15 to 20 sexual partners, but she willingly had sex with only 6 of them. Laura has been pressured into many sexual relationships and was sexually assaulted several times between the ages of 11 and 15. Lacking the resources to cope with her initiation into sexual activity, she started drinking alcohol and smoking marijuana shortly after becoming sexualized and ventured into heavier drugs, such as crank, after being assaulted. Laura moved back to California to live with her father's brother and his wife. After about a month she was put in a placement home. Laura was 13 at the time.

Laura developed post traumatic stress disorder (PTSD) stemming from her experiences with sexual violence.[1] She has received some therapy for PTSD and is currently in a psychological space where she can begin to talk about her victimization.

> I used to not be able to hear the word slut—ever . . . I've gone through enough therapy I can talk about it to a certain extent. It still hurts, it's hard . . . I still have a hard time sleeping by myself in a room. I get scared. Like last night, my roommate's gone, and I haven't slept alone in about five years, since I was eleven I haven't slept alone. So it really scares me when I'm alone. And I had to sleep with the hall light on and my door wide open all night. And I got up a couple of times and knocked on my foster mom's door just because I'd hear something. It scared me.

Laura has experienced many forms of victimization in her life that continue to affect her and the choices that she makes.

Today, as a 15 year old, Laura is 8 months pregnant. She says of her 20-year-old boyfriend: "He wanted me to get pregnant. He had told me he wanted me to have a baby. He planned it, I didn't." Laura tried to persuade her boyfriend to use condoms but he refused telling her "no, no, no, it's okay. I'll take care of you," so she resigned herself, adopting an apathetic attitude toward sex and pregnancy. "I was just like, if it happens it happens, I guess. I wasn't very happy about it when I first found out but he was . . . When I found out I was pregnant, I laughed. I didn't know whether to cry or be happy so I just laughed. I just laughed hysterically . . . It really scared me." Laura does not believe in aborting an unwanted pregnancy, and over time she started to embrace her pregnancy. After Laura had her first ultrasound, her feelings about her pregnancy started to change: "I saw his heart beat and it kind of changed everything. And it still was really scary, but it made things a little bit more real, and like okay, this is gonna happen. And I'm just gonna have to deal with it."

Laura is trying to finish high school, find a better living situation (a place other than a group home that would be more suitable for a mother and newborn), and find a way to support her new family. She is trying to accomplish all of this while taking classes and monitoring the end of her pregnancy because she is at risk for premature labor. Laura's relationship with her boyfriend is strained because he has multiple issues that she does not want to deal with in addition to caring for a newborn:

> There's not much of a relationship. He wants to have a relationship but I'm kind of at a point where I have to figure my own stuff out first. And he needs . . . he doesn't really take too good care of his other son. He doesn't see him . . . I want him to figure that out for himself first. . . . I think he needs to go back to school. I think he only finished ninth or eighth grade. . . . And he needs to get a job, which he's working on right now. He's working on getting a job, but I really think he needs to go back to school. And he needs to stop being put in jail, which he's always in jail for something: fighting, drugs, something. I mean he's already stopped his drugs, he did stop that. But he still has drinks a lot.

Pregnancy has forced Laura to confront her own substance abuse. She was using crank before she found out she was pregnant. The day she found out she was pregnant Laura stopped using crank, alcohol, nicotine, and even caffeine. She plans on staying clean after her baby is born.

In school, Laura received some sex education but it was not very helpful for her. "I think it was [helpful] to a lot of kids in class who were virgins, but I wasn't at the time. So it kind of didn't do me any good. I had already experienced what I had experienced, and nothing's gonna change it." Based on her experiences and those of her peers, Laura argues that to reduce teen pregnancy, schools should provide education on abstinence, birth control, and finally, educate teens about the responsibilities involved in raising a child:

> Sex ed people say things about parents letting their kids do stuff. Kids are gonna do it. Whether their parents tell them it's okay or not. Kids are gonna do it. You're gonna sneak out. I mean if you tell them no, they're just gonna rebel. I don't care what kind of education you give them, if they want to do it they're gonna do it. You can lock them in their rooms [but], they're gonna find a way out. You have to educate them as well as you can, hopefully they'll get it. And hopefully it's not too late. And give them birth control, give them condoms. . . . If they want to become pregnant, throw a baby in their arms and have them take care of it for a day or two. They won't want to be pregnant any more. If a teenager came up to me and talked to me about it I would say, "okay do you have a job? How are you gonna support the baby? Are you responsible enough? Would you rather go with your friends and party or do you think you can stay home and take care of a baby? Are you gonna mind getting up in the middle of the night? Do you mind dirty diapers? What are your goals? Is the baby gonna interfere with that? Where's the father gonna be? Is he gonna be supportive?"

Laura is a strong, determined young woman who is facing many obstacles in her life. When asked what it's like to be a teenager, she tells us, "don't underestimate. We get underestimated a lot. 'You can't do it. You can't raise a kid. You don't know what you're doing.' . . . They can do it. I mean, I'm taking responsibility and I've seen a lot of girls in my class take a lot of responsibility. We can do it. We do know how to raise kids." Laura construes her history as a story of survival, one that is in many ways just beginning. Though her story also could be read as one of considerable victimization, Laura does not interpret it that way.

For advocates of abstinence-only education—and for the Christian Right more generally—Laura's life might provide an example of the overly sexualized and unrestrained society that they criticize. In this context, she may be defined by Christian conservatives as a victim. In particular, she may be seen as a victim of social changes that make "committed relationships, men who would marry women whom they made pregnant, men who would take responsibility for the children they fathered, even marriage itself—scarcer and scarcer" (Luker 2006, 10). On the other hand, Laura's choices, particularly her early sexual activity, pregnancy, and multiple partners, might well place her among what *Sexuality, Commitment and Family* calls the "sexually dysfunctional faction of students," whose presence in the classroom threatens to undermine the lessons of abstinence-only education (Teen Aid, 1998, insert, 15). In this light, she is less a victim and more a threat to the chastity and morality of other teenagers.

Laura's story is important for this study in view of the range of experiences she has had. This chapter will consider how such experiences do and do not reflect teen lives more generally, and how such experiences may be interpreted through various social constructions of adolescent sexuality. Laura's story, however, is not representative of all teen women's experiences, as it presents some of the extremes of adolescent sexual experience. She has had multiple sexual partners, was sexually assaulted several times, was pregnant, and had sexual intercourse for the first time at a young age. Though Laura's narrative is not every teen's story, her life experiences nonetheless provide an instructive context for examining adolescent sexuality. Though the percentage of high school age teens that are sexually active has been declining since 1991, 47 percent of high school students reported having sexual intercourse in 2005 (Centers for Disease Control and Prevention 2006b), and 63 percent of high school seniors reported having sexual intercourse in 2005 (Centers for Disease Control and Prevention, 2006a). Six percent of high school students had sex before the age of 13. Further, teens are among the groups most vulnerable to sexual assault: Results from the National Violence against Women Survey reported that of women who had been raped in their lifetimes, 54 percent were under the age of 18 at the time of the rape (Tjaden and Thoennes 2000).

Perhaps more importantly, Laura is the teenager reformers initially had in mind when crafting welfare reform in 1996; she is young and poor, receives government support, is pregnant, and is not married. She is an adolescent making life decisions with little aid from adults. Constructions of adolescent sexuality that dominated discussions about welfare reform reflect Laura's experiences and some of the decisions that she has made in her young life. It is these constructions of sexuality—contrasted with data that reflects teen sexual activity and decision making—to which we turn our attention in this chapter.

THE SOCIAL CONSTRUCTION OF ADOLESCENTS' SEXUALITY AND GENDER

This study uses a social construction approach to understand adolescent sexuality, arguing that meanings for both gender and sexuality are constructed, or defined, through cultural norms and social institutions (Rubin 1984; Vance 1991). While gender refers to social and cultural aspects of femininity and masculinity, sexuality represents sexual practices and sexual identity and the ways sexual practices and identity are culturally and socially defined and interpreted. Sexuality and gender often are constructed in terms of one another, and in that sense, their meanings are interwoven. The social constructions of masculinity and femininity are both dependent upon and help to shape the meanings of sexuality; likewise, the interpretation of sexuality helps to structure understandings of gender. Additionally, constructions of gender and sexuality vary with race, ethnicity, class, and age: "A social construction approach views sexual desires and practices as existing within social contexts in which power structures are present. Sites of power differences, such as age, gender, class, and ethnicity, must be examined to fully understand the structural field in which sexuality is being enacted" (Asencio 2002, 2).

Such a perspective runs counter to the notion that gender and sexuality primarily are biologically based categories. If gender and sexuality are biologically based, then apparent differences between young women and men in terms of their aspirations, talents, intelligence, emotional capacity, interest in sex, and so on are based on their differing genetic makeup and are not heavily influenced by culture and environment. As we will show, this is the standpoint taken by most abstinence-only curricula. Lessons suggest, for example, that gender and sexuality are biologically assigned, and thus girls and boys, women and men, are inherently very different from one another. As *Sex Respect,* an abstinence-only curriculum, maintains, gender and sexuality are "part of us from the very beginning of life. . . . Although men and women equally deserve respect, they were not made exactly the same emotionally, physically and psychologically" (Mast 2001, 6).

In the face of such arguments about the inherent divergence between the genders, feminist scientists and theorists have argued that much of the so-called scientific knowledge about women's and men's biological differences actually should be understood as theories, where both research questions and findings are influenced by cultural norms regarding gender: "In the study of gender (like sexuality and race) it is inherently impossible for any individual to do unbiased research" (Fausto-Sterling 1992, 10). Cultural expectations and beliefs about gender differences shape scientific research in the same ways that they impact other practices and institutions.

Because of the influence of cultural norms and expectations on research into biological aspects of gender and sexuality, Anne Fausto-Sterling, among others, argues:

Biology may in some manner condition behavior, but behavior in turn can alter one's physiology. This new vision challenges the hunt for fundamental biological causes at its very heart, stating unequivocally that the search itself is based on a false understanding of biology. The question "What fraction of our behavior is biologically based," is impossible—even in theory—to answer, and unanswerable questions drop out of the realm of science altogether, entering instead that of philosophy and morality. (1992, 8)

The alternative position, that gender and sexuality are socially constructed, argues that the meanings of gender and sexuality are culturally based and change historically. As Judith Butler states, gender and sexuality are best understood as "the effects of institutions, practices, discourses with multiple and diffuse points of origin" (1990, ix). Sexuality and gender are categories of identity made real by social institutions—such as family, religion, and education—and cultural practices associated with birth, socialization of children, social and workplace codes of conduct and interactions, and the like.

Adolescents' sexuality also is socially and culturally constructed in a variety of ways. At any one time, several definitions and understandings of young women's sexuality exist simultaneously, even if they contradict one another. Although many different constructions of teens are at play, only the dominant ones most directly related to the sex education debate will be deconstructed.

ADOLESCENT SEXUALITY AS CRISIS

Young women's sexuality often is cast as a "problem" to be studied and understood (Asencio 2002). How the problem is defined varies with how subpopulations of teen women are socially constructed and with the social constructions of teens that predominate at any given time. In the context of defining adolescent sexuality as a problem, in the past several decades a number of *crises* of teen sexuality have been identified, ranging from concerns about teen pregnancy to fears that innocent teens will be exposed to sexual information and pressures while still too naïve to handle the information.

Adolescent sexuality may be defined as "in crisis" when the wider culture threatens to sully young women's innocence. Here, adolescent women may be constructed like children, as relatively pure youngsters in need of protection. When teen women are constructed as childlike, the impetus is to protect them from sexual activity, but it is also their lack of knowledge that must be protected. "Children have been defined as pure and nonsexual, and part of the force of the term 'children having children' is the juxtaposition of children with childbearing. The time of childhood and young adults is meant to be asexual" (Lesko 2001, 138). Therefore, it is argued, some sexual material should be censored from music, videos, and other cultural outlets favored by teens, as well as school curricula.

This construction of purity and naïveté historically has been reserved for the middle and upper-middle classes, particularly for whites.[2] When evidence that teen women may not be wholly innocent surfaces—evidence that often is based on anecdotal accounts rather than scientific fact—a moral "panic" tends to characterize the discourse surrounding adolescent sexuality. The increased funding of abstinence-only programs coincides with media reports documenting the prevalence of oral sex, "hook-ups," and "friends with benefits" among the affluent white (and primarily suburban) classes (Dailard 2006). These descriptions of middle-class teens' behavior call into question the idea that white, elite adolescents are pure and innocent, fueling panic and a sense that teen sexuality is in crisis.

Teen sexuality also has been perceived as a problem to be fixed in the context of teenage pregnancy (Thompson 1995).[3] In the 1980s and 1990s, concerns over unmarried teen pregnancy led social scientists, religious leaders, and others to focus on all young women's sexuality as a crisis to be battled and newly proscribed. In this sense, the sexuality of adolescent women as a whole is sometimes constructed similarly to low-income women of color, through reference to teens' unrestrained sexuality. The ongoing panic over teen pregnancy has yielded a limited view and stunted discourse about adolescent sexuality. Even though teen sexuality encompasses multiple issues, societal attention remains fixated on teen pregnancy where complicated issues relating to race and class are folded into the debate (Luker 1996; Solinger 2000). When probed more deeply, it is unclear whether the concern is related to parental age or parental marital status (Luker 1996), or concerns over the behavior and choices of low-income black teens (Luttrell 2003).

For women of color, sexual behavior and pregnancy outcomes are scrutinized in the context of racial stereotypes that preclude the characterization of teens of color as innocent. Similar to white teen mothers, minority teenage mothers disrupt society's temporal understanding of human sexual development. However, unlike their counterparts, women of color also disrupt society's racialized sense of progress—understood as modern, Westernized development. As Nancy Lesko argues, "Central to successive psychological prescriptions for adolescents to lead to proper human development and the progress of the race was the postponement of sex, for unrestrained sexuality was the hallmark of "savages." . . . When New Right critics label school-aged mothers as the source of family and social deterioration, it clearly communicates a sense of backwardness for them as individuals and for society" (2001, 137).

Stereotypes of pregnant teenagers of color rely on and further reify a view of teen women of color as primitive, oversexualized, immoral, and irresponsible (Kaplan 1997). The dominant construction of their sexuality suggests that outside controlling forces must keep such deviant and unrestrained sexuality in check. The focus on young women of color as uncontrolled has converged most often on teen pregnancy as an intractable problem of black and Latina teens: "In terms of the dominant image that gets evoked, the 'pregnant teenager' is seen as a black, urban, poor female who is more than likely herself the daughter of a teenage mother. She is probably failing at school, has low self-esteem, sees no future for herself, and now must deal with the untimely end of her youth"

(Luttrell 2003, 4). The construction of the teenage parent as a low-income African American girl deeply affects views of low-income adolescents of color, as teen pregnancy tends to dominate discussions about teen sexuality.

In conjunction with these conceptualizations of teen sexuality is the relative position of adolescents in contemporary society: Teens are both visible and invisible. They are visible to the extent that they are easily vilified as contributing to societal ills and held up as negative examples of what life "choices" to avoid (Harris 2004). If teens are not being constructed in terms of their potential threat to the operations of daily life (e.g., criminal activity or sexual recklessness), they are largely invisible in society.

ADOLESCENT SEXUALITY: SPECTACLE AND DISPLAY

While on one hand, a dominant social construction of teen women casts them as innocent, and therefore sexual information must be shrouded in secrecy, on the other hand, sexuality is everywhere in U.S. culture. Particularly young female sexuality is on display for titillation, comment, and judgment; pop culture—movies, music videos, advertising—displays young women's sexuality relentlessly. Popular cultural outlets often present an oversexed, sexually free woman who exists for male pleasure. In this sense, adolescent women are constructed not as naïve and childlike, but as fully sexual temptresses and overtly ready for and knowledgeable about sex.

Given the scarcity of facts and lack of discussion in schools about "why sex happens" or "sexual intercourse itself"—as young women put it—they often learn about their sexuality from peers and from television, movies, books, and advertising. Sexual scenes on television shows have almost doubled since 1998. The vast majority of prime time shows (77%) contain sexual content, averaging 5.9 sexual scenes per hour, but only 11 percent of the shows containing sexual content make any references to sexual risks or responsibilities (Kaiser Family Foundation 2005a).

The hypersexualized media image of young women has affected cultural views of adolescents. As the end of the twentieth century arrived, teens increasingly were constructed as potentially dangerous, and danger was firmly linked to sexuality. Teenagers were too sexual (Levine 2002). This portrayal of adolescents has roots in the early 1800s, when teens started to be characterized as a group that is ruled by reckless desire and raging hormones. Teens' emotional volatility was attributed to physiological changes taking place, indicating that they were beyond social intervention and incapable of making rational or intelligent decisions (Lesko 2001; Levine 2002; Luker 1996). More recently these characterizations of teens have contributed to a "sexual politics of fear" where teen sexuality is seen as risky, harmful, and immoral (Levine 2002). Teens exist in a society filled with mixed messages—both institutional and cultural—about their sexuality, sexual decision making, and responsibility. Sexual freedom and liberty are institutionally vilified in abstinence-only curricula that encourage teens to abstain from intercourse until heterosexual marriage, but then glorified in many other aspects of Westernized cultures (Driscoll 2002).

CONTROL AND REPRESSION

Teens' daily choices and activities are subjected to familial and bureaucratic control; in this vein, they have limited autonomy (Lesko 2001). This limited autonomy is particularly salient with regard to sexuality. As Valerie Lehr notes: "Although they may see greater possibilities reflected in the culture that surrounds them, they continue to spend much time in institutional settings that can actively attempt to define such alternatives as immoral and the young people who might wish to define agency through making sexual choices as acting with premature (and unnatural) autonomy" (2006, 5). Abstinence-only is a policy that ultimately aims to curb female autonomy and individual sexuality by building on the social construction of teenagers as a class of people in need of protection or control and on traditional concepts of gender differences that cast female sexuality as a problem to be addressed.

Controlling sexual behavior historically has been a concern for those interested in the moral health of the nation. A closer examination of the politics of sexuality, however, suggests that moral regulation of sexuality masks other social issues that are tied into sexual behavior (Brodie 1994; Burnham 1973; Morone 2003). For most of American history, societies have suppressed individual interests in favor of communal interests for survival purposes. Illicit sexuality (i.e., sex outside of marriage and for nonprocreative ends) has been associated with pursuing individual interests at a cost to communal interests (Freedman 1982, 203–4; Walters 1976). Evidence of female autonomy, in particular sexual autonomy, has been met with opposition in the form of legal punishment, societal wrath, and repressive sexual ideology.

Moral objections to sexual improprieties appear to be the driving force in perpetuating conservative sexual ideologies (Degler 1974; Freedman 1982; Gordon 2002). Unregulated sexuality is linked to other social issues and concerns such as poverty, social control, racism, and reproduction. In the 1800s, the higher fertility rate among the poor was pointed to as visible proof of their sexual recklessness and inferior values, which served to reinforce the prevailing ideology linking sexual control to economic success and, by implication, sexual desire to economic failure (Roberts 1999; Rosenberg 1973). These sexual–economic linkages continue to be ascribed to in modern times; sexual control and purity are associated with "good morals" and economic success in a newer version (abstinence-only education) of an older, Victorian sexual ideology.

A disjuncture has existed between the social construction of sexuality and actual sexual behavior occurring in societies throughout history (Degler 1974; Doan 2007). Much like their predecessors, political actors and institutions are trying to establish abstinence until marriage as the prevalent view and practice governing sexual behavior and change the culture's sexual permissiveness. Yet, in some ways, the perception of sexual promiscuity driving abstinence-only policy is at odds with the reality of the behavior it is attempting to regulate.

SEXUAL ACTIVITY, PREGNANCY, AND ABORTION

Historical changes in the emphasis and character of sex education have been linked to transformations in the larger culture vis-à-vis sexuality. The growing liberalization toward sexuality in the 1960s prompted the government to reverse its policies regulating sexual behavior and move toward publicly educating adolescents about sex. At the same time, a more progressive sexual culture was institutionalized through such Supreme Court decisions as *Griswold v. Connecticut* (381 U.S. 479, 1965), which upheld married women's right to use birth control; *Eisenstadt v. Baird* (405 U.S. 438, 1972), which extended the decision in *Griswold* to unmarried women; and *Roe v. Wade* (410 U.S. 113, 1973), which legalized abortion. When married and unmarried women gained access to the pill, specifically, sexual decision making, sexual pleasure, marriage, and procreation became more distinct from one another (Luker 2006). Scholars have suggested, moreover, that the availability of the pill is largely responsible for women's entry into law, medicine, and other professions in larger numbers beginning in the 1960s and 1970s, breaking down traditional gender stereotypes and broadening women's roles in society (Luker 2006).

Changes in institutional policies and public opinion developed together, eventually altering and challenging the prevailing social construction of gender roles, sexuality, and the family. From 1960 to today, marriage, parenthood, and sexual activity rates have altered significantly. Specifically, since the 1960s and 1970s, a rapid increase in premarital sex and cohabitation rates have combined with a rise in the numbers of men and women who delay marriage. In 1960, 28 percent of women ages 20 to 24 and 53 percent of men ages 20 to 24 had never married, whereas in 1995, 74 percent of women and 86 percent of men in this age group had never married (McGlen and O'Connor 1998). By 2000, the proportion of women ages 20 to 24 who had never married remained well over 70 percent, and among women ages 30 to 34, the figure tripled from 6 percent in 1970 to 22 percent in 2000 (U.S. Census Bureau 2001a). Relatedly, the number and percentage of heterosexual couples cohabitating saw a fourfold increased from 1970 to the 1990s. They currently represent 5.2 percent of all households, which demonstrates a continual upward trend from 3.5 percent in 1990 (U.S. Census Bureau 2001b).

For many young people, traditional ideas about family have given way to more fluid conceptualizations of what it means to be a family and what is morally acceptable behavior as it relates to family. Among teens aged 13 to 17, the majority believe cohabitation prior to marriage or in place of marriage is acceptable (Lyons 2004a). Social taboos surrounding divorce, premarital sex, and unmarried pregnancy have also diminished. The majority of adolescents believe divorce (66%) and premarital sex (57%) are morally acceptable. A sizable group of teens (42%) believe it is morally acceptable to have children outside of marriage (Lyons 2003; McGlen and O'Connor 1998).

Teenagers' liberalized views about behavior mirror the changing patterns in their sexual activity. Adolescent sexual activity has followed a similar trajectory to that of adult sexual activity since the 1960s. Teens are much more likely to be sexually active today than in 1960, though teen sexual activity has been declining since 1991. For most teens, first sexual activity occurs during the high school years, but some adolescents have sex even younger: 16 percent of seventh and eighth graders report that they have had intercourse (Dailard 2001). By the time adolescents leave their teen years, the majority—over 70 percent of 19 year olds—have had sex (Guttmacher Institute 2006; Haffner 1995). Among sexually active teens, 14 percent reported having four or more sexual partners: Males (18%) are more likely than females (11%) to have multiple partners (Centers for Disease Control and Prevention 2006b; Kaiser Family Foundation 2005b).

Although teen sexual activity has increased over the past several decades, there is little difference in the age of sexual initiation and frequency of sexual activity for American teenagers relative to teens in comparable developed countries such as Canada, Great Britain, France, or Sweden (Guttmacher Institute 2001). American adolescents differ in that they are more inclined to become sexually active before the age of 15 and are more likely to enter into sporadic sexual relationships for a shorter period of time compared to their cohorts in other countries. These factors contribute to a higher propensity for having multiple sexual partners in a given year for American teens (Guttmacher Institute 2001).

The most pronounced difference between the United States and other developed countries is the teen pregnancy rate. American teens have one of the highest rates of pregnancy among developed countries. Teen pregnancy rates have fluctuated substantially over the past 25 years and remain high (Guttmacher Institute 2006). From 1980 to 1987, teen pregnancies declined by 4 percent then increased 10 percent by 1990, representing the highest teen pregnancy rate since 1972. During the 1990s, the teen pregnancy rate declined as quickly as it had increased in the preceding two decades (see Figure 3.1; Boonstra 2002). By 2002, the teenage

Figure 3.1
Fertility Rates among All Teens Aged 15–19 Years

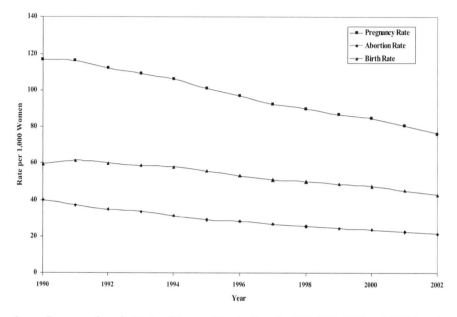

Source: Data come from the National Survey of Family Growth, 1982, 1988, 1995, and 2002. http://www.cdc.gov/nchs/nsfg.htm.

pregnancy rate was lower than at any time since it was first measured in the 1970s (Boonstra 2002; Ventura et al. 2006).

Decreases have occurred across all racial and ethnic groups, but as Figure 3.2 demonstrates, significant variation exists across these groups. African Americans experienced the sharpest decline in teen pregnancy during the 1990s, although their pregnancy rate remains much higher (154 per 1,000 females aged 15–19) relative to other groups. Latinas' pregnancy rate (140 per 1,000) is lower than black teens, but remains substantially higher than the national rate (Kaiser Family Foundation 2005b).

For sexually active teens, pregnancy rates have decreased, and in turn, birth rates have declined. Figure 3.3 displays the downward trends in births to teens aged 15 to 19 years old. Again, birth rates, stratified by race and ethnicity, show an interesting pattern. Throughout the 1990s, the birth rate for black teens declined and dipped below the birth rate for Latinas around the middle of the decade. While birth rates have been trending downward for all racial/ethnic groups, births to unmarried women—both teens and adults—have been moving in the opposite direction. In 1960, approximately 15 percent of teenage women who gave birth

Figure 3.2
Pregnancy Rates among Teens Aged 15–19 Years

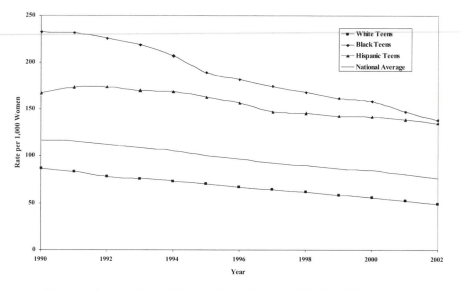

Source: Data come from the National Survey of Family Growth, 1982, 1988, 1995, and 2002. http://www.cdc.gov/nchs/nsfg.htm.

were unmarried. By 1978, that figure had climbed to 50 percent (Moran 2000), and by 1999, to 78 percent (Guttmacher Institute 1999). The upward trend continued in 2004, where more than four out of five teen births were to unwed women (Hamilton et al. 2005).

Preliminary data (based on 99% of all births in the United States in 2006) released by the CDC's National Center for Health Statistics indicated that there was an upward trend in teen birth rates in 2006. Until 2006, the teen birth rate had been declining for 14 years. Overall teen births increased by 3 percent in 2006; however, this figure varied by both racial/ethnic and age groups. Among African American teens, the increase was the steepest (a 5% increase over 2005), for Latina teens there was a 2 percent increase over the 2005 rates. White and American Indian teens also experienced an increase in birth rates. Asian teenagers were the only group that continued to see a decline in their teen birth rates. In terms of age, teens aged 18–19 saw the largest increase (4%) followed by teens aged 15–17 (3%). The only age group that continued to show a slight decline from 0.07 births per 1,000 teens in 2005 to 0.06 in 2006 was among teen girls ages 14 and younger (Kaiser Family Foundation 2007). The head of the Reproductive Statistics Branch at the CDC, Stephanie Ventura, argued that it was too early to tell if these figures were the beginning of a new trend; however she stated, "This

Figure 3.3
Birth Rates among Teens Aged 15–19 Years

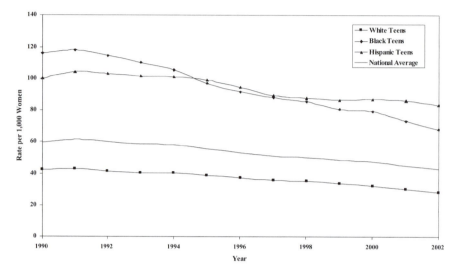

Source: Data come from the National Survey of Family Growth, 1982, 1988, 1995, and 2002. http://www.cdc.gov/nchs/nsfg.htm.

early warning should put people on alert to look at the programs that are being used to see what works" (Kaiser Family Foundation 2007, 1).

Neither the dramatic increase in teen pregnancy from 1987 to 1990, nor the sharp decline during the 1990s has been completely explained (see Figure 3.1). Overall, the majority of teen pregnancies, almost 8 in 10, are unintended (Boonstra 2002).[4] Consequently, the actual desire to have children has played a very minor role in accounting for teen pregnancy over time. In addition, the sharp increases and decreases do not necessarily correlate with abortion rates.

During the 1990s, the national abortion rate declined fairly quickly. By 1997, the teen abortion rate was 33 percent lower than the rate a decade earlier, and from 1994 to 2000, the abortion rate for 15 to 17 year olds fell by 39 percent (Boonstra 2002). Figure 3.4 contains the abortion rates throughout the 1990s and again the trends demonstrate the dramatic variation across racial and ethnic groups. African American teens experienced the steepest decline; however, their abortion rate remains markedly higher compared to Latinas and white teens.

The sharp decline in teen abortion rates and teen pregnancy rates in the 1990s suggests unintended pregnancy rates have declined as well. The reduction in unintended pregnancies may reflect an increased use of birth control, largely stemming from HIV awareness campaigns. In a 2001 survey, 90 percent of teens reported discussing AIDS at school, and 81 percent reported talking about

Figure 3.4
Abortion Rates among Teens Aged 15–19 Years

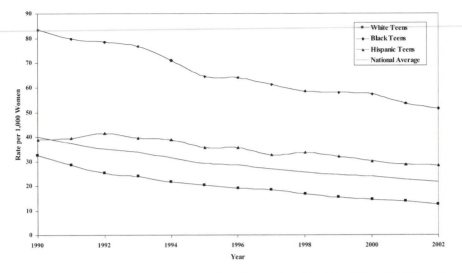

Source: Data come from the National Survey of Family Growth, 1982, 1988, 1995, and 2002. http://www.cdc.gov/nchs/nsfg.htm.

sexually transmitted infections (Lyons 2004b). These discussions likely have contributed to destigmatizing the use of condoms, which rose from 48 percent in 1988 to 63 percent by 2002 (Darroch and Singh 1998; Kaiser Family Foundation 2005b).

By 2002, more teenage women (75%) having sex for the first time were using contraception compared to 65 percent in 1988 (Darroch and Singh 1998; Kaiser Family Foundation 2005b). Sexually active teens also have access to effective, long-term birth control methods, such as implants and injectables. More than one in eight teens uses a long-acting method of contraception (Boonstra 2002). Sexual health experts attribute three-fourths of the decrease in the teenage pregnancy rate from 1988 to 1995 to increased contraceptive use among sexually active teenagers, and the remaining one-fourth to an increase in abstinence on the part of teens (Boonstra 2002; Darroch and Singh 1998).

TEENAGE SEXUAL BEHAVIOR AND PRACTICES

Adolescents are receiving the abstinence message. The majority of teens (77%) report hearing the abstinence-only-until-marriage message, and a sizable percentage (56%) of them believe young people should abstain from sex until marriage (Lyons 2004b). Young women are more inclined to verbally support abstinence until marriage compared to young men (64% and 48%, respectively).

Since 1991, sexual activity has, however, declined more sharply among teen males: 57 percent reported being sexually active in 1991, and by 2003, this declined to 48 percent. During this time period, sexual activity for teenage females dropped from 51 to 45 percent (Lyons 2004b).

Most poll questions, like the Gallup Youth Survey discussed previously, ask teens questions about "sex" without defining whether it means sexual intercourse exclusively, or includes oral sex or other sexual activity.[5] Thus, it is not clear from this particular poll whether teens are supporting the idea of abstaining and actually abstaining from sexual intercourse only, or if they are abstaining from all forms of sexual activity. The abstinence-only instruction supported by the Christian Right calls for teens to abstain from all forms of sexual activity, with the exception of kissing. Yet, research shows that a number of teens view oral sex as an alternative to intercourse, one that allows them to maintain the status of *virgin* while still engaging in sexual activity. More than half of all teenagers aged 15–19 reported engaging in oral sex in 2002 (Dailard 2006). Oral sex is more common among older teens and those who have participated in vaginal intercourse, but it is still a fairly popular practice among those who have not had vaginal intercourse (12% of males and 10% of females; Guttmacher Institute 2006).

To further complicate the picture of teen sexual activity, despite the increase in abstinence, overall, teens' behavior does not necessarily reconcile with their stated, and often conflicting, beliefs. Abstinence until marriage is supported by teens. At the same time, the majority (62%) of youth also believe teens are responsible enough to have sex at 18 years of age or younger, which is much earlier than the average age of marriage for men (26 years old) and women (25 years old; Carlson 2005).

Teens also are aware of the risks associated with unsafe sex and unwanted pregnancy even though their sexual practices do not always reflect their concerns. Most teens, two-thirds, cite the risk of pregnancy and disease transmission as "somewhat serious" and "very serious" problems among their friends (Marullo 2004). According to the figures reported by the Centers for Disease Control and Prevention, teens' evaluation of the seriousness of these problems is accurate. Although pregnancy rates decreased in the teen population, the risk of pregnancy and pregnancy scares remain high. Four in ten sexually active teenagers have taken—or had their partner take—a pregnancy test (Kaiser Family Foundation 2003), and 34 percent of sexually active young women become pregnant before the age of 20 (Centers for Disease Control and Prevention 2006b).

On a subtler but important level, youthful passions and sentiments of love have always played a role in shaping adolescents' decision making, even though their feelings often are discounted by adults. Their decisions to be sexually active largely hinge on emotions: 89 percent of teens say their decisions to engage in sexual activity are influenced by the level of trust they have in their partners (Kaiser Family Foundation 2002b). Trust also influences teens' sexual practices: Teens that trust their partners are more likely to participate in discussions about their sexual health, including issues such as sexual histories, intimacy, STDs, contraception, and their feelings (Kaiser Family Foundation 2002a, 2003). Emotions contribute to both male and female adolescents' sexual decision making.

Teens also remain vulnerable to disease transmission. A significant portion of the sexually active teen population (37%) did not practice safe sex (using a condom) during their most recent sexual encounters (Centers for Disease Control and Prevention 2006b). One in five teens do not think disease transmission can occur through oral sex, and it is considered a safer sexual activity by two in five teens (Kaiser Family Foundation 2003). In 2002, 48 percent of sexually transmitted infections were accounted for by 15 to 24 year olds (Centers for Disease Control and Prevention 2006b). Teenage girls and minorities are particularly vulnerable to HIV/AIDS. In 2002, African Americans accounted for 65 percent of AIDS cases reported among 13–19 year olds, Latino teens represented 20 percent, and overall, teen girls accounted for 51 percent of the cases reported among 13–19 year olds (Kaiser Family Foundation 2005b).

In addition to sexual practices, teens hold erroneous beliefs about contraceptives and safer sex. In one study, a surprising number of teens, one-fifth, mistakenly believed that condoms are "not effective" in preventing HIV/AIDS and STI transmission, and one in five erroneously believed birth control pills provide protection against sexually transmitted diseases (Kaiser Family Foundation 2003). In a nationally representative survey of teens, half of the adolescent women surveyed erroneously reported that condoms are ineffective in preventing the transmission of HIV/AIDS and other STDs (Kaiser Family Foundation 2002c). Adolescents' sexual beliefs, activities, and practices reflect a mix of their complicated and often contradictory emotions as well as the varying levels of information, resources, and support made available to them.

Despite the layers structuring teen's sexual decision making, they are still primarily constructed and in turn studied (and discussed) in dichotomous terms. Behavior is described in either–or terms: Teens either have had sex or not, and sexual activity was either "wanted" or "unwanted." This construction of adolescent sexual behavior undermines prevention (of risk-taking behavior) efforts by prescribing a "one size fits all" approach to sexual education (Muehlenhard and Peterson 2005; Whitaker, Miller, and Clark 2000). Teens do not simply absorb the lessons taught in *any* sex education curriculum; rather, adolescent sexual behavior is a product of hundreds of "risk and protective" factors that occur at the individual, familial, communal, and societal level (Kirby 2001). Sex education is one added factor in their decision-making process.

Adolescence is a precarious time for many teens. They are in the process of individuating themselves and seeking greater personal autonomy; yet, they still need guidance from the adults in their lives. Most adolescents become sexually active in their later teen years. Only 13 percent of teens have sexual intercourse by age 15; this number jumps to 7 in 10 by the time teens reach 19 years of age (Guttmacher Institute 2006). Emotions and communication strategies play a big role in determining when, under what conditions, and with whom teens become sexually active (Kaiser Family Foundation 2002a, 2003).

SECRECY AND SUPPRESSION

Policy debates over how to define abstinence and which specific sexual practices should be considered "off limits" are somewhat at odds with the way that public discourse about sexuality has been shrouded in secrecy, particularly with regard to young women's actual sexual practices.[6] If teen women are defined as innocent and in need of protection, then frank and accurate discussions of sex may be perceived as contaminating young minds. The lack of real discussion about sexuality means that a trivialized view of adolescent sexuality prevails, one that neither describes nor aids in understanding the myriad issues involved with sexuality (Lorber 1994; Rose 2005; Thompson 1995). Religious conservatives who champion abstinence-only sex education support "official silence" about sexuality in the public schools, arguing that "by not teaching about sexuality, adolescent sexual behavior will not occur" (Fine 1992, 33).

Particularly for teens, the paucity of accurate information and open discussion about sex and sexuality affects their access to basic knowledge and the ability to use that knowledge to make informed decisions about whether, how, when, and with whom to become sexually active. Teens report feeling a significant amount of peer pressure to engage in sex, and the majority (four in five) report that sexual double standards for young men and women are ascribed to by their parents and peers, with young women citing the existence of sexual double standards twice as frequently as young men (Kaiser Family Foundation 2002c). In the face of such pressures and sexual double standards, accurate information about sexual health and support for teens as they navigate decision-making takes on even more importance.

Many of the young women we interviewed criticized the lack of factual sexual information teens receive and the rareness of candid discussions about both the emotional and physical aspects of sex (see also Rose 2005). If young women expected to learn such lessons from their parents, some were disappointed: "Half the students seriously don't even know [about sex]. I mean there's some students out there who don't get told about sex. Their parents keep it hidden from them like a secret" (Interview with Tracy, age 17).

Communication between teens and their parents, health care providers, and educators, goes a long way in equipping teens with decision-making and communication skills to in turn use in their intimate relationships. Parents provide guidance to their adolescent children and can help them make healthy choices. However, surprisingly little communication takes place in the home. According to a national survey of teens aged 15–17, the majority rarely talk to their parents about their intentions to become sexually active: Only 1 in 10 discusses his or her intent with parents (Kaiser Family Foundation 2002a). Once sexually active, a quarter of teens reported telling their parents, and another one fifth report that their parents discovered their sexual activity "some other way." The remaining teens are silent, which accounts for nearly 40 percent of them (Kaiser Family Foundation 2002a). Communication is not any better with health care providers: One in five sexually active teens have discussed their sexual health with a doctor. This pattern of silence also extends to the classroom. More than half of the teens surveyed said sex education did little to prepare them to communicate on these "hard-to-talk-about topics" (Kaiser Family Foundation 2002a).

The silence surrounding sex is an impediment to teens' sexual health because experts cite parent–child communication as an extremely effective means of delaying the age of sexual initiation for teens as well as making healthier choices (such as using contraception) once sexually active. Despite the benefits of communication, very little takes place. Nearly half of the surveyed teens have never discussed sexual decision making with their parents, and among sexually active teens, 56 percent have never had these conversations (Kaiser Family Foundation 2002a). According to sexually active and inactive teens, five of the major barriers to parent–child communication are: concern over their parents' reactions, concern that their parents will automatically assume they are sexually active, embarrassment, feeling ill-equipped to bring up the topic of sex, and fearing their parents will not understand (Kaiser Family Foundation 2002a).

Just as adolescents often do not talk to their parents about sex, so is there sometimes silence between sexually active teens themselves. The four most significant reasons teens do not talk to their partners about sexual health include: They are concerned what their partner might think (stigma), they lack the ability to broach the subject, they are embarrassed, and they simply do not know enough (Kaiser Family Foundation 2002a). This absence of communication can color teens' sexual decisions and experiences. Lacking the communication skills to discuss sexual health issues with their partners—and receiving inadequate help from parents, doctors, and educators—many teens turn to media sources. Most teens (three in four) believe seeing characters on television shows model conversations about sexual decision-making would help them overcome some of the current barriers to communication (Kaiser Family Foundation 2002a).

Stronger connectivity to family, school, and church organizations helps to explain differences between teens who are not sexually active and those who are (Kirby 2001; Whitaker et al. 2000). It also helps account for the behavioral differences among teens that are sexually active (e.g., why some teens engage in riskier sexual behavior).

Once sexually active, connectivity continues to play a role in determining future decisions about sexual behavior and under what conditions sexual behavior occurs. Out of the teens that are already sexually active, those who are poorly connected to social institutions reported engaging in riskier behavior including higher frequencies of drug and alcohol use (Whitaker et al. 2000). Family connectivity again plays a significant role among teens that are at a heightened risk (often due to socioeconomic disadvantage) for unsafe sexual behavior (Kalmuss et al. 2003; Markham et al. 2003).

SEXUAL ASSAULT

An early initiation into sexual activity is associated with riskier future sexual behavior. Teens report feeling significant pressure to have sex and believe that prolonging sexual initiation may be a "nice idea, but nobody really does it" (Kaiser Family Foundation 2003). There are several factors associated with early entry into sexual activity. Social norms and the influence of peer groups influence teens' sexual decision making; socializing with sexually active teens increases the chance that a teen will experience an earlier initiation into sexual activity and decreases the likelihood that safe sex will be practiced (Kaiser Family Foundation 2003; Kalmuss et al. 2003). The premature onset of puberty also increases the likelihood of engaging in sex at a younger age (Kalmuss et al. 2003), while depression in middle and high school students increases the probability of participating in sexually risky behavior (Lehrer et al. 2006).

For some youth, early entry into sexual activity was not a choice. Childhood victimization is linked to an increased risk of being victimized in adulthood and a contributing factor to engaging in future high-risk sexual behavior (Howard and Wang 2003; Valois, Oeltmann, and Hussey 1999). Rape myths about victims, perpetrators, and sexual assault itself continue to shape the definition of sexual assault, the treatment given victims, and the prosecution of assailants. These myths are linked to social constructions informing society about gender, sexuality, and violence. The belief that a victim's clothing and behavior (particularly involving drinking) means that she "asked for it" plays on the historical construction of male sexuality as uncontrollable, based in urges, and unstoppable once triggered by tantalizing clothing and "inviting" behavior (Buddie and Miller 2001; SmarterSex.org 2002; Vachss 2003). The biological construction of male sexuality is reinforced by other myths, such as the idea that men rape when they have been sexually deprived, and by extension, those that have ample opportunities for sex do not rape.

The dichotomous and conflicting construction of female sexuality is also reflected in commonly held rape myths. The narrow virgin/whore construction creeps up in several pernicious ways. Women who are sexually active prior to an assault may be understood as "unworthy" and lacking credibility (Buddie and Miller 2001; SmarterSex.org 2002; Vachss 2003). More than any other crime, society is much more prone to believe that women "cry rape" and make false accusations when in reality, only 2 percent of reported assaults are false, which is no higher than false reports for other crimes.

Yet, in the face of these longstanding myths, statistics indicate that young women are very much at risk for sexual assault, and often, that means assault by men that they know. In fact, young women aged 16 to 19 and low-income women are in the highest risk groups for sexual assault (U.S. Department of Justice 1994). Results from the National Violence against Women Survey reported that of women who had been raped in their lifetimes, 54 percent were under the age of 18 at the time of the rape (Tjaden and Thoennes 2000).

Sexual assault is the most frequently committed violent crime in society, and women between the ages of 15 to 24 are particularly vulnerable: The risk of rape is four times higher among this age group (Danenet.org 2006). For women who became sexually active before the age of 20, 10 percent reported that their first sexual experience was involuntary (Guttmacher Institute 2006). The younger a woman was at sexual initiation, the more likely she is to have been assaulted. On the National Women's Survey of 714 adult women, 32.2 percent reported experiencing forcible rape in their adolescent years (Danenet.org 2006). Other studies suggest that teens may be subject to significant verbal coercion and often know their rapists (Jones et al. 2003). Seventy-four percent of teen victims knew their attackers (Kilpatrick, Saunders, and Smith 2003), and 43 percent of victims aged 18 and younger were assaulted in their homes (Danenet.org 2006).

Studies show that these realities of teen experience play out differently depending upon the ethnicity and class of the women involved. A study by Lefley et al. argues that in general, Latinos have more traditional views of gender than whites and blacks, and that these views intersect with and shape Latinas' acceptance of rape myths. In comparing white, black, and Latina attitudes toward rape, Latinas were said to have the "highest level of perceived victim-blaming and victim distress" (Asencio 2002, 142), based on respondents' reported beliefs about whether men can "control their sexual urges and beliefs about women having control of rape situations" (Asencio 2002, 142; Lefley et al. 1993). Another study reported that 60 percent of white and black male high school students deemed it "acceptable for a boy to force sex on a female in one or more situations" (quoted in Asencio 2002).

The prevalence of involuntary, coerced, and forced sexual initiation is difficult to track because most people do not report their victimization to law enforcement. Victimization surveys, however, indicate the proportion of perpetrated sexual crimes is substantially higher compared to what is reported in crime statistics. Despite the variation in figures, all experts agree that the estimates of sexual violence are grossly low. For example, only 39 percent of assaults were reported to law enforcement in 2002 (U.S. Department of Justice 2003). Roughly 9 percent of high school students report having forced sex. This number varies across racial groups: 12.3 percent of African American students, 10.4 percent of Latino students, and 7.3 percent of white students (Centers for Disease Control and Prevention 2004). Gender plays a significant role in sexual violence: 11.9 percent of female high school students compared to 6.1 percent of male students report being sexually assaulted. Most rape victims are women (78%), and the majority of sexual violence occurs early in a young woman's life. Fifty-four percent of female victims were assaulted before the age of 18, and out of those women, 22 percent were assaulted before the age of 12 (Tjaden and Thoennes 2000).

Risk factors including individual and social factors can increase the probability of being a victim or perpetrator of sexual violence. The likelihood of being a target of sexual violence increases with a prior history of sexual assault for women and for youth (Tjaden and Thoennes 2000). Alcohol and drug consumption (particularly binge drinking and drug use), high-risk sexual behavior (which is also a consequence of being victimized at an early age), ethnicity (American Indian and Alaskan Native women are more likely to report being assaulted), and poverty (which creates a more dangerous community environment) are also "vulnerability" factors that increase the probability of being a target of sexual violence (Champion et al. 2004; Howard and Wang 2003; Valois et al. 1999). Although less is known about preventative measures to combat sexual violence, research suggests that connectivity not only plays a role in teens' sexual choices, it is linked to prevention of sexual violence (Borowsky, Hogan, and Ireland 1997).

Somewhere between sexual agency and coercion is another layer of adolescent sexuality—the role of ambivalence. Sexual desire and pleasure drive sexual choices, but these motivating factors for engaging in sexual activity are mired in contradictory emotions. Sexuality becomes expressed in a discourse of ambivalence for many teens and adults, but it is more acute for young women (Lamb 2001; Tolman and Szalacha 1999). "The adolescent woman herself assumes a dual consciousness—at once taken with the excitement of actual/anticipated sexuality and consumed with anxiety and worry" (Fine 1988, 35).

Within the limited and contradictory construction of sexuality, ambivalence can play out as "token resistance" to sex: expressing a lack of desire for sex when in reality sexual activity is desired by the individual. Under these conditions, when sexual activity occurs, researchers have noted a paradoxical situation. Females report more negative feelings compared to when sex does not take place, even though they initially wanted to engage in sex, suggesting that a more nuanced model of sexuality is necessary for understanding the complexities involved in sexuality (Muehlenhard and Peterson 2005). Other researchers have qualitatively documented similar competing and contradictory expressions of sexual desire—experiencing pleasure while feeling vulnerable—particularly among females (Tolman and Szalacha 1999).[7]

CHAPTER SUMMARY

Popular conceptualizations of adolescence tend to reflect simplistic, dichotomous, and contradictory understandings of teens as dependent/independent, vulnerable/dangerous, immature/culpable, and virginal/promiscuous. These overly simplified and often competing social constructions of sexuality have been used as the basis for forming policies. In practice, fewer teens are having sex, and teen pregnancy rates have been trending downward along with abortion rates. But teens continue to face several complex issues regardless of their sexual activity status, such as whether to become sexually active, stay sexually active, engage in safe sexual practices (physically and emotionally), and under what conditions sexual negotiation should occur.

Teens often do not voice their concerns about sexual health because a culture of silence continues to characterize communication patterns between many teens and their parents, partners, doctors, and educators. When sexuality is shrouded in secrecy, teens are left to themselves to decipher and negotiate the intersections between sexual experimentation and the social construction of female sexuality. Furthermore, many teens are victims of sexual violence, which shapes future sexual behavior. From this perspective, the extent of sexuality education that teens need is much more complex than what many are offered, particularly in terms of curricula limited to an abstinence-only approach.

Abstinence until marriage is being prescribed as a means of reining in what is perceived as rampant sexual permissiveness in society. Against this backdrop, abstinence-only education surfaced as a policy solution to social problems in the 1990s. In the next chapter, four leading abstinence-only curricula are closely analyzed to examine the lessons they present—and do not present—teens about sex and sexuality.

NOTES

1. Post traumatic stress disorder (PTSD) is a psychiatric condition that follows a traumatic, life-threatening experience. Although PTSD has been noted in documents dating back to ancient times (often following wars), it started to gain attention following the Vietnam War, when a significant number of veterans were suffering from psychological disorders resulting from their combat experiences. This disorder often surfaces in survivors

of military combat, sexual assault, domestic violence, terrorist attacks, natural disasters, or serious accidents. It causes biological and psychological changes in a person, often marked by flashbacks, nightmares, insomnia, feelings of detachment, and estrangement, which can impair the daily functioning of a person and interfere with their ability to perform a job, maintain a relationship, parent, or interact socially. This disorder can be treated with therapy, and many survivors return to normal functioning once treated for PTSD (National Center for PTSD 2006).

2. Historians point to the Victorian Era as a key point during which women, particularly middle- to upper-class white women, were increasingly constructed as virtuous, able to resist vice, capable of self-restraint, and devoid of passion. The Victorian "angel" was acquiescent, passive, asexual, and uninterested in sex. She engaged in sexual activity for two express purposes: procreation and fulfillment of her wifely duties. Within this context, the angel was aligned with purity, leaving little room for the role of pleasure and desire in female sexuality (Degler 1974; Peterson 1984).

Sexual repression and control most obviously symbolized affluence, and by extension, the absence of those qualities became tied to beliefs about lower-class values. The implication was that the lower class subscribed to a different set of sexual values (Rosenberg 1973). These differences were reflected in and helped to further construct the dominant Victorian ideology regarding "proper" women's sexuality, that middle-class women were pure and asexual. The link between uncontrolled sexual desire and lower-class values became solidified, and this association persists into current times.

As the public began to embrace adolescence as a distinctive developmental stage, they also increasingly came to understand it as a time of great vulnerability for children, particularly for young women (Moran 2000; Odem 1995). The Victorian personification of white, upper-class women as "angels" was transferred to adolescent white, upper-class women, who were constructed as "angels in training" (Peterson 1984). The angel's qualities, such as virtue, innocence, and purity, became more pronounced as they related to young women and came to construct and inform society's understandings of young girls. Female youth, innocence, and dependence—for white, elite young women—became inexorably linked in the public psyche. Much like the "angel-wife," unmarried adolescent women were portrayed and idealized as devoid of sexual knowledge, curiosity, or desire.

3. The outrage over teen childbearing has dominated the political conversation during the past two decades even though teen pregnancy rates declined throughout the 1990s and reached a record low in 2002 (Ventura, Abma, Mosher, and Henshaw 2006; see also Boonstra 2002; Luker 1996; Luttrell 2003).

4. The rate of unintended pregnancy has remained relatively unchanged for the past 10 years, however, the rate has increased among poor women (29%) while decreasing (20%) among economically advantaged women (Wind 2006).

5. The Gallup poll question: "Do you think young people should abstain from sex until marriage, or do you think it doesn't matter one way or the other?" (Lyons 2004b).

6. Historians have noted similar tensions between knowledge and silence about teen sexuality in the Victorian Era. In the early 1900s, educators were uncomfortable discussing adolescent sexuality. Educating young women about sexuality was viewed as a corrupting

agent that would simply contaminate the innocence and purity of young women (Odem 1995). Not all members of society were satisfied with this version of Victorian morality and worked on ushering in a more progressive view of sexuality toward the end of the 1900s. Social reformers criticized the construction of young women as innocent and pure "angels," noting that it contributed to a "conspiracy of silence" surrounding sexuality, reinforcing the social taboo against open and accurate discussions of sex-related issues. But rather than ushering in a sexual revolution aimed at deconstructing popular images and faulty "biological" beliefs about female and male sexuality, reformers focused on the physical consequences of sexually transmitted infections from a "scientific" perspective (Burnham 1973; Moran 2000; Odem 1995). Social hygienists attempted to educate the public about the dangers of disease and prostitution by publishing pamphlets and giving public lectures on these topics.

7. Muehlenhard and Peterson (2005) have documented ambivalence in young men and women, leading them to move beyond dichotomous conceptualizations of sexuality. They reconfigure sexuality in a multidimensional conceptualization that recognizes the difference between wanting sexual activity but not the consequences, or conversely, not wanting sex but wanting the outcomes. Gender factors into ambivalence (females are more likely to possess ambivalent feelings) because many of the negative outcomes of sexual activity are uniquely salient to women: unwanted pregnancy, a higher rate of contracting certain sexually transmitted infections, and sexual double standards.

Sexual ambivalence also is expressed by participating in unwanted sexual activity because the outcomes of the activity are desired by the individual. Lucia O'Sullivan and Elizabeth Rice Allgeier (1998) conducted a study examining sexual activity among young men and women in committed dating relationships. Participants were required to keep a journal for two weeks detailing their sexual activity. Over the course of the study, 50 percent of females and 26 percent of males reported engaging in unwanted sexual activity. The majority of respondents cited "desired outcomes" (such as relationship maintenance, intimacy, fulfilling their partners' needs, or decreasing relationship stress) as the motivation for participating in unwanted sex. O'Sullivan and Allgeier point to several factors contributing to young women's greater rate of consenting to unwanted sexual activity. Many of these reasons tie into gender role expectations and social constructions of female sexuality and sexual desire such that male pleasure (and the belief that men "need" sex more frequently and cannot "control" their desire) is often the focal point of sexuality.

The gender difference in consenting to unwanted sexual activity has been found in other studies (Impett and Peplau 2003). Consensual unwanted sex is a murky area of sexuality. In O'Sullivan and Allgeier's research, they found that both young men and women largely reported having positive outcomes for consenting to unwanted sex. This finding has been replicated in other studies, suggesting that consenting to unwanted sexual activity falls along a continuum ranging from unwanted consensual sex to unwanted coercive sex. The consequences of participation depend on the reasons for consenting to the activity. When individuals consent to unwanted sex because they want to foster intimacy, the outcomes are generally positive. Consenting to unwanted sex out of fear, however—which commonly occurs among battered women—has negative consequences (Jacobson and Gottman 1998). Adolescent women are vulnerable to dating violence and therefore at a higher risk of "consenting" out of fear. Studies have indicated that 1 in 10 teen couples experience relationship violence (Danenet.org 2006).

BIBLIOGRAPHY

Asencio, Maysol. 2002. *Sex and Sexuality Among New York's Puerto Rican Youth.* Boulder, CO: Lynne Rienner Publishers.

Boonstra, Heather. 2002. "Teen Pregnancy: Trends and Lessons Learned." *The Guttmacher Report on Public Policy* 5 (February 1): 7–10.

Borowsky, I. W., M. Hogan, and M. Ireland. 1997. "Adolescent Sexual Aggression: Risk and Protective Factors." *Pediatrics* 100 (6): E7.

Brodie, Janet Farrell. 1994. *Contraception and Abortion in 19th Century America.* Ithaca, NY: Cornell University Press.

Buddie, Amy M., and Arthur G. Miller. 2001. "Beyond Rape Myths: A More Complex View of Perceptions of Rape Victims." *Sex Roles: A Journal of Research* 45 (3–4, August): 139–60.

Burnham, John C. 1973. "The Progressive Era Revolution in American Attitudes Toward Sex." *The Journal of American History* 59 (4): 885–908.

Butler, Judith. 1990. *Gender Trouble: Feminism and the Subversion of Identity.* New York: Routledge.

Carlson, Darren K. 2005. "Teen Survey: What's the Responsible Age for Smoking, Drinking, Sex?" *The Gallup Poll* (August 2). Available at: http://www.poll.gallup.com. Subscription required.

Centers for Disease Control and Prevention. 2004. "Youth Risk Behavior Surveillance—United States, 2003." *MMWR* 53(SS-02)1–96.

Centers for Disease Control and Prevention. 2006a. "Youth Risk Behavior Surveillance—United States, 2005." *MMWR* 55 (SS-5) 1–112.

Centers for Disease Control and Prevention. 2006b. "Healthy Youth! Sexual Behaviors." Available at: http://www.cdc.gov/HealthyYouth/sexualbehaviors.

Champion, H. L., K. L. Foley, R. H. DuRant, R. Hensberry, D. Altman, and M. Wolfson. 2004. "Adolescent Sexual Victimization, Use of Alcohol and Other Substances, and Other Health Risk Behaviors." *Journal of Adolescent Health* 35 (4): 321–28.

Crenshaw, Kimberle. 1992. "Whose Story is it Anyway? Feminists and AntiRacist Appropriations of Anita Hill." In *Race-ing Justice, En-gendering Power,* ed. Toni Morrison, 402–40. New York: Pantheon.

Dailard, Cynthia. 2001. "Recent Findings from The 'Add Health' Survey: Teens and Sexual Activity." *The Guttmacher Report on Public Policy* 4 (4, August): 1–3. Available at: http://www.guttmacher.org/pubs/tgr/04/4/gr040401.html.

Dailard, Cynthia. 2006. "Legislating against Arousal: The Growing Divide between Federal Policy and Teenage Sexual Behavior." *Guttmacher Policy Review* 9 (3, Summer): 1–4. Available at: http://www.guttmacher.org/pubs/gpr/09/3/gpr090312.html.

Danenet.org. 2006. "Teen Sexual Assault and Abuse Information Sheet." Available at: http://www.danenet.wicip.org/dcccrsa/saissnes/teen2.html.

Darroch, Jacqueline E., and Susheela Singh. 1998. "Why Is Teenage Pregnancy Declining? The Roles of Abstinence, Sexual Activity and Contraceptive Use." *Occasional Report*

(January). Available at: http://www.alanguttmacherinstitute.org/pubs/or_teen_preg_decline.html.

Degler, Carl N. 1974. "What Ought To Be and What Was: Women's Sexuality in the Nineteenth Century." *The American Historical Review* 79 (5, December): 1467–90.

Department of Justice. 2003. "Criminal Victimization 2002." Available at: http://www.ojp.usdoj.gov/bjs/pub/pdf/cv02.pdf.

Doan, Alesha E. 2007. *Opposition and Intimidation: The Abortion Wars and Strategies of Political Harassment*. Ann Arbor: University of Michigan Press.

Driscoll, Catherine. 2002. *Girls: Feminine Adolescence in Popular Culture and Cultural Theory*. New York: Columbia University Press.

Fausto-Sterling, Anne. 1992. *Myths of Gender: Biological Theories About Women and Men*. New York: Basic Books.

Fine, M. 1988. "Sexuality, Schooling, and Adolescent Females: The Missing Discourse of Desire." *Harvard Educational Review* 58 (1): 29–53.

Fine, Michelle. 1992. *Disruptive Voices: The Possibilities of Feminist Research*. Ann Arbor: The University of Michigan Press.

Freedman, Estelle B. 1982. "Sexuality in Nineteenth-Century America: Behavior, Ideology, and Politics." *Reviews in American History* (December): 196–215.

Gordon, Linda. 2002. *The Moral Property of Women: A History of Birth Control Politics in America*. Urbana: University of Illinois Press.

Guttmacher Institute. 1999. "Teen Sex and Pregnancy." *AGI Facts in Brief*. Available at: http://www.guttmacher.org/pubs/fb_teen_sex.pdf.

Guttmacher Institute. 2004. "Teenagers Sexual and Reproductive Health: Developed Countries." *Facts in Brief*. Available at: http://www.alanguttmacherinstitute.org/pubs/fb_teens.html.

Guttmacher Institute. 2006. "Facts on American Teens' Sexual and Reproductive Health." *Facts in Brief*. Available at: http://www.guttmacher.org/pubs/fb_ATSRH.html.

Haffner, Debra W. 1995. "Facing Facts: Sexual Health for America's Adolescents: The Report of the National Commission on Adolescent Sexual Health." *SEICUS Report* 23 (6, August/September): 2–8.

Hamilton, Brady E., Joyce A. Martin, Stephanie J. Ventura, Paul D. Sutton, and Fay Menacker. 2005. "Births: Preliminary Data for 2004." *National Vital Statistics Reports* 54 (8): (December 29): 1–20.

Harris, Anita. 2004. *Future Girl: Young Women in the Twenty-First Century*. New York: Routledge.

Howard, D. E., and M. Q. Wang. 2003. "Risk Profiles of Adolescent Girls Who Were Victims of Dating Violence." *Adolescence* 38: 1–14.

Impett, E. A., and L. A. Peplau. 2003. "Sexual Compliance: Gender, Motivational, and Relationship Perspectives." *Journal of Sex Research* 40 (1): 87–100.

Jacobson, N., and J. Gottman. 1998. *When Men Batter Women: New Insights into Ending Abusive Relationships*. New York: Simon and Schuster.

Jones, J. S., L. Rossman, B. N. Wynn, C. Dunnuck, and N. Schwartz. 2003. "Comparative Analysis of Adult versus Adolescent Sexual Assault: Epidemiology and Patterns of Anogenital Injury." *Academic Emergency Medicine* 10 (8): 872–77.

Kaiser Family Foundation Publication. 2002a. "Communication." SexSmarts: A Public Information Partnership #3240 (July). Available at: http://www.kff.org/entpartner ships/upload/Teens-and-sexual-health-communication-summary-of-Findings.pdf.

Kaiser Family Foundation Publication. 2002b. "Relationships: A Series of National Surveys of Teens about Sex." SexSmarts: A Public Information Partnership #3257 (October). Available at: http://www.kff.org/entpertnerships/upload/Relationships-Summary-of-Findings.pdf.

Kaiser Family Foundation Publication. 2002c. "Gender Roles: A Series of National Surveys of Teens about Sex." SexSmarts: A Public Information Partnership #3309 (December). Available at: http://www.kff.org/entpartnerships/upload/Gender-Roles-Summary.pdf.

Kaiser Family Foundation. 2003. "National Survey of Adolescents and Young Adults: Sexual Health Knowledge, Attitudes and Experiences." Available at: http://www.kff.org/youthhivstds/3218-index.ctm.

Kaiser Family Foundation. 2005a. "Sex on TV." News Release (November). Available at: http://www.kff.org/entmedia.

Kaiser Family Foundation. 2005b. "U.S. Teen Sexual Activity" (January). Available at: http://www.kff.org/youthhivstds/3040-02.cfm.

Kaiser Family Foundation. 2007. "U.S. Teen Birth Rate Increases by 3% in 2006; First Increase Since 1991, According to CDC." Daily Reports (December 7). Available at: http://www.kaisernetwork.org/daily_reports.

Kalmuss, Debra, Andrew Davidson, Alwyn Cohall, Danielle Laraque, and Carol Cassell. 2003. "Preventing Sexual Risk Behaviors and Pregnancy among Teenagers: Linking Research and Programs." *Perspectives on Sexual and Reproductive Health* 35 (2): 87–93.

Kaplan, Elaine Bell. 1997. *Not Our Kind of Girl: Unraveling the Myths of Black Teenage Motherhood.* Berkeley: University of California Press.

Kilpatrick, D. G., B. E. Saunders, and D. W. Smith. 2003. *Youth Victimization: Prevalence and Implications.* Washington, D.C.: National Institute of Justice, Office of Justice Programs, U.S. Department of Justice.

Kirby, Douglas. 2001. "Understanding What Works and What Doesn't in Reducing Adolescent Sexual Risk-Taking." *Family Planning Perspectives* 33 (6, November/December): 276–81.

Lamb, S. 2001. *The Secret Lives of Girls: What Good Girls Really Do—Sex, Play, Aggression, and their Guilt.* New York: Free Press.

Lefley, Harriet P., Clarissa S. Scott, Maria Llabre, and Dorothy Hicks. 1993. "Cultural Beliefs About Rape and Victims' Response in Three Ethnic Groups." *American Journal of Orthopsychiatry* 63 (4): 623–32.

Lehr, Valerie. 2006. "Sexual Agency in Risk Society." Conference paper presented at the 2006 Annual Meeting of the Midwest Political Science Association, Chicago, April.

Lehrer, Jocelyn A., Lydia A. Shrier, Steven Gortmaker, and Stephen Buka. 2006. "Depressive Symptoms as a Longitudinal Predictor of Sexual Risk Behaviors among US Middle and High School Students." *Pediatrics* 118 (1): 189–200.

Lesko, Nancy. 2001. *Act Your Age!: A Cultural Construction of Adolescence.* New York: Routledge.

Levine, Judith. 2002. *Harmful to Minors.* Minneapolis: University of Minnesota Press.

Lorber, Judith. 1994. *Paradoxes of Gender*. New Haven, CT: Yale University Press.

Luker, Kristin. 1996. *Dubious Conceptions: The Politics of Teenage Pregnancy*. Cambridge, MA: Harvard University Press.

Luker, Kristin. 2006. *When Sex Goes to School: Warring Views on Sex—and Sex Education—Since the Sixties*. New York: W.W. Norton & Company.

Luttrell, Wendy. 2003. *Pregnant Bodies, Fertile Minds: Gender, Race, and the Schooling of Pregnant Teens*. New York: Routledge.

Lyons, Linda. 2003. "Teens' Marriage Views Reflect Changing Norms." *The Gallup Poll* (November 18). Available at: http://www.poll.gallup.com.

Lyons, Linda. 2004a. "How Many Teens are Cool with Cohabitation?" *The Gallup Poll* (April 13). Available at: http://www.poll.gallup.com. Subscription required.

Lyons, Linda. 2004b. "Teens: Sex Can Wait." *The Gallup Poll* (December 14). Available at: http://www.poll.gallup.com. Subscription required.

Markham, Christine M., Susan R. Tortolero, S. Liliana Escobar-Chaves, Guy S. Parcel, Ronald Harrist, and Robert C. Addy. 2003. "Family Connectedness and Sexual Risk-Taking Among Urban Youth Attending Alternative High Schools." *Perspectives on Sexual and Reproductive Health* 35 (4): 174–79.

Marullo, Shannon. 2004. "Teens: Pregnancy, STDs Problems Among Peers." *The Gallup Poll* (April 27). Available at: http://www.poll.gallup.com. Subscription required.

Mast, Coleen Kelly. 2001. *Sex Respect: The Option of True Sexual Freedom*. Student Workbook. Sex Respect. Bradley, IL: Respect Incorporated.

McGlen, Nancy E., and Karen O'Connor. 1998. *Women, Politics, and American Society*. Upper Saddle River, NJ: Prentice Hall.

Moran, Jeffrey P. 2000. *Teaching Sex: The Shaping of Adolescence in the 20th Century*. Cambridge, MA: Harvard University Press.

Morone, James A. 2003. *Hellfire Nation: The Politics of Sin in American History*. New Haven, CT: Yale University Press.

Muehlenhard, Charlene, and Zoe D. Peterson. 2005. "Wanting and Not Wanting Sex: The Missing Discourse of Ambivalence." *Feminism and Psychology* 15 (1): 15–20.

National Center for PTSD. 2006. "What is Post Traumatic Stress Disorder?" Available at: http://www.ncptsd.va.gov/facts/general.

Odem, Mary E. 1995. *Delinquent Daughters: Protecting and Policing Adolescent Female Sexuality in the United States, 1885–1920*. Chapel Hill: University of North Carolina Press.

O'Sullivan, Lucia F., and Elizabeth Rice Allgeier. 1998. "Feigning Sexual Desire: Consenting to Unwanted Sexual Activity in Heterosexual Dating Relationships." *Journal of sex Research* 35 (3): 234–43.

Peterson, Jeanne M. 1984. "No Angels in the House: The Victorian Myth and the Paget Women." *The American Historical Review* 89 (3): 677–708.

Roberts, Dorothy. 1999. *Killing the Black Body: Race, Reproduction, and the Meaning of Liberty*. New York: Vintage Books.

Rose, Susan. 2005. "Going Too Far? Sex, Sin and Social Policy." *Social Forces* 84 (2): 1207–32.

Rosenberg, Charles E. 1973. "Sexuality, Class and Role in Nineteenth-Century America." *American Quarterly* 35 (May): 131–53.

Rubin, Gayle. 1984. "Thinking Sex: Notes for a Radical Theory of the Politics of Sexuality." In *Pleasure and Danger*, ed. Carole Vance, 267–319. New York: Routledge.

SmarterSex.org. 2002. "Facts and Myths about Date Rape." Available at: http://www.smartersex.org/date_rape/facts_myths.asp.

Solinger Rickie. 2000. *Wake Up Little Susie: Single Pregnancy and Race before Roe v. Wade*. New York: Routledge.

Teen Aid. 1998. *Sexuality, Commitment and Family*. Spokane, WA: Teen Aid, Inc.

Thompson, Sharon. 1995. *Going All The Way: Teenage Girls' Tales of Sex, Romance, and Pregnancy*. New York: Hill and Wang.

Tjaden P., and N. Thoennes. 2000. *Full Report of the Prevalence, Incidence, and Consequences of Violence Against Women: Findings From the National Violence Against Women Survey*. Washington, D.C.: National Institute of Justice. Report NCJ 183781.

Tolman, D. L., and L. A. Szalacha. 1999. "Dimensions of Desire: Bridging Qualitative and Quantitative Methods in a Study of Female Adolescent Sexuality." *Psychology of Women Quarterly* 23 (1): 7–39.

U.S. Census Bureau. 2001a. "U.S. Adults Postponing Marriage, Census Bureau Reports." *U.S. Census Bureau News* (June 29). Available at: http://www.census.gov/Press-Release/www/2001/cb01-113.html.

U.S. Census Bureau. 2001b. "Households and Families: 2000." *Census 2000 Brief* (September). Available at: http://www.census.gov/prod/2001pubs/c2kbr01-8.pdf.

U.S. Department of Justice. 1994. *Violence Against Women*. Washington, D.C.: Bureau of Justice Statistics.

Vachss, Alice. 2003. "The Charge of Rape, the Force of Myth." *The Washington Post* (November 2) Op-Ed.

Valois, R. F., J. E. Oeltmann, and J. R. Hussey. 1999. "Relationship between Number of Sexual Intercourse Partners and Selected Health Risk Behaviors among Public High School Adolescents." *Journal of Adolescent Health* 25 (5): 328–35.

Vance, Carole Susan. 1991. "Anthropology Rediscovers Sexuality: A Theoretical Comment." *Social Science and Medicine* 33 (8): 875–84.

Ventura, S. J., J. C. Abma, W. D. Mosher, and S. K. Henshaw. 2006. "Recent Trends in Teenage Pregnancy in the United States, 1990–2002." *Health E-stats*. Hyattsville, MD: National Center for Health Statistics. Released December 13, 2006.

Walters, Ronald G. 1976. "Sexual Matters as Historical Problems: A Framework of Analysis." *Societas* 6 (Summer): 157–75.

Whitaker, Daniel J., Kim S. Miller, and Leslie F. Clark. 2000. "Reconceptualizing Adolescent Sexual Behavior: Beyond Did They or Didn't They?" *Family Planning Perspectives* 32 (3): 111–17.

Wind, Rebecca. 2006. "A Tale of Two Americas for Women." *Media Center, News Release, Alan Guttmacher Institute* (May 4).

CASES CITED

Eisenstadt v. Baird, 405 U.S. 438 (1972)

Griswold v. Connecticut, 381 U.S. 479 (1965)

Roe v. Wade, 410 U.S. 113 (1973)

4

Resurrecting the Chastity Belt: Lessons from Abstinence-Only Curricula

For the past several decades, abstinence has been taught to almost all teens in various forms through sexuality education. An abstinence-only curriculum is not the first to teach abstinence to teens; however, it takes a very distinct approach to the importance of abstinence. Abstinence-only curricula insist all individuals, teens and adults, remain abstinent until marriage. Using content analysis, paired with a deconstruction of the dominant narratives contained in the curricula, we closely examine what lessons are taught to teens through abstinence-only education.

Abstinence-only curricula vary to some degree in their genesis, orientation, and focus. Nevertheless, as the following analysis of the curricula bears out, some important commonalities exist. First, the four curricula analyzed in this study generally follow the Title V, Section 510 guidelines found in the Personal Responsibility and Work Opportunity Reconciliation Act (PRWORA). Second, each curriculum addresses a battery of topics that generally can be organized around three larger themes: expected standards of behavior, consequences of premarital sex, and sexuality education. Under the rubric of each major theme, we examine and analyze abstinence-only education's approach to multiple salient issues and deconstruct the implicit lessons targeted to adolescents by the curricula.

HEATHER'S STORY

Heather, a 15-year-old virgin, describes herself as a Christian for whom the Bible provides clear directives regarding how she should live her life. A recipient of abstinence-only education in school, her church youth group, and through a church-sponsored conference run by *True Love Waits,* Heather fully embraces the abstinence-only message. For Heather, *True Love Waits* in particular—which weaves its religious teachings with an abstinence-only directive—presents an effective and appealing way to live her life:

> *True Love Waits* is one of several approaches to challenging teenagers and college students to make a commitment to sexual abstinence until marriage. Created by LifeWay Christian Resources, *True Love Waits* is designed to encourage moral purity by adhering to biblical principles. This youth-based international campaign utilizes positive peer pressure by encouraging those who make a commitment to refrain from pre-marital sex to challenge their peers to do the same. (LifeWay Student Ministry 2001)

As Heather talks about teen sexuality and her own choices, she relies heavily on the ideas of "purity," "adhering to biblical principles," and using "positive peer pressure" to maintain her own and her friends' virginity until marriage. And for Heather, abstinence means significantly more than simply not having sexual intercourse: "Where do I draw the line? I think pretty much after kissing—I'm not saying pecking but as far as making out or something. I have no problem with people showing affection for each other and showing that they like them or love them or whatever, but I think anything as far as them touching you or doing anything, I just think your body [is off limits]."

Heather and her friends utilize both biblical teachings and one another's support to remain true to their convictions. Surrounded by a culture that they perceive works against their attempts to remain "pure," Heather explains how she adheres to her beliefs and goals:

> Everything on earth right now is so temporary, it's just like nothing on earth is worth risking [eternal life]. So I always think about that when I'm either wanting to do something or whatever, I just think to line up—the Bible's what I live by and so it says in the Bible do not have any sexual immorality. It's kind of like I don't know how you prevent it, because the world always promotes that, but it's hard but you just keep striving to become more pure, and not completely because the world brings out so much stuff, but you can try.

Heather has like-minded friends from her church who provide a support system for one another, helping each other not to weaken in the face of cultural pressure to be sexual.

These particular aspects of the abstinence message, however, are much more explicitly addressed in the church-related activities in which Heather participates, as compared to their more indirect treatment in her school curriculum. In school, Heather was taught to abstain from sexual activity until marriage as a means to avoid pregnancy, HIV/AIDS, and other STIs. As Heather describes it, her school's abstinence-only curriculum also tried to provide strategies to help teens remain abstinent, by including

> a unit on positive relationships. . . . The first step is spending time with them, maybe not at night time or any time alone, just trying to get to know them, just develop friendship. I think we had a whole unit just on how family comes into it and how you should get them involved. And for me, if you have sex before you're married, on your marriage night what is there to look forward to?

For the advocates, authors and teachers of abstinence-only curricula, the fact that Heather so firmly and clearly articulates the beliefs and choices at the heart of abstinence-only instruction is a triumph. Heather's unconditional acceptance of the abstinence message, and her considerable knowledge of and ability to reiterate reasons to remain abstinent until marriage, however, are somewhat unique among the teens we interviewed. Heather's interview better shows the ideal end goal of abstinence-only education than the current reality facing the majority of teens. As we discussed in chapter three, teens are more likely to verbally support abstinence than to remain abstinent in practice, particularly in the later teen years.

The curricula we analyze are written for use in the public schools, and so their abstinence-only messages do not overtly teach many of the points that Heather discusses. However, a close look at the specifics of the curricular messages indicates that many of the religious lessons articulated by Heather underlie abstinence-only instruction, suggesting abstinence-only education has moved sex education in a new direction.

THE DATA

This study analyzes four abstinence-only curricula written for the high school level: *Sex Respect, Sexuality, Commitment, and Family (SCF); Sex Can Wait;* and *Choosing the Best Life*. These curricula were chosen for a variety of reasons, the most important being their widespread use in schools and community programs and the nationwide attention they have garnered, as indicated in reports and evaluations of abstinence-only education.[1] We also assessed these curricula because three of them were cited by SIECUS, an organization that attempts to closely track the use of abstinence-only curricula and programs, as among the nine leading abstinence-only curricula that use "fear-based" tactics to encourage abstinence until marriage (Kempner 2001). Additionally, several key national studies of abstinence-only education focus on these curricula among the programs they analyze. The U.S. House of Representative's Committee on Government Reform's report (commonly known as the Waxman Report) cites *Sex Can Wait*; *Me, My World, My Future*; Teen Aid's junior high school curriculum; and *Choosing the Best Life* among "the most popular abstinence-only curricula used by grantees of the largest federal abstinence initiative, SPRANS (Special Programs of Regional and National Significance Community-Based Abstinence Education)" (U.S. House of Representatives 2004, i). Mathematica Policy Research's 2002 report, one of the first systematic evaluations of abstinence-only education, examines the use of *Sex Can Wait* in one program in Mississippi and *Choosing the Best Life* in a Virginia program.

In addition to their inclusion in national studies of abstinence-only education, *Sex Respect* and *Sexuality, Commitment and Family* are used in the areas in California where we conducted our teen interviews. In the late 1990s, *Sex Respect* was cited as the most frequently used abstinence-only program in California (Burlingame 1997, 5), and *Sexuality, Commitment, and Family* is taught in two of the five high schools attended by some of the teens we interviewed.

Sex Respect and *Sexuality, Commitment, and Family*, both written for high school age students, have the clearest ties to the Christian right. *Sex Respect* is a program "developed and funded by the Committee on the Status of Women," a well-known conservative Christian organization founded by Phyllis Schlafly (Burlingame 1997, 6). The author of *Sex Respect*, Coleen Kelly Mast, has extensive ties with the Catholic Church. She runs a weekly radio program titled "Catholic Answers," has worked for the U.S. Catholic Conference, National Council of Catholic Bishops, and also has written a religiously based curriculum titled *Love and Life: A Christian Sexual Morality Guide for Teens*.[2]

Similarly, Teen Aid, publisher of *Sexuality, Commitment, and Family*, has a Web site that contains numerous links to leading Christian right organizations, including Focus on the Family, Passion 4 Purity, and the Family Research Council. Its Board of Directors offers such "inspirational statements" as "Make prayer your first resource-not your last resort," and "The Purity of the next generation depends on the integrity of this generation" (Teen Aid, Inc. n.d.).

Choosing the Best Life is a high school curriculum targeted to grades 8 through 10 and written by Bruce Cook (2003). He has also authored *Choosing the Best*

Path for grades 7 and 8 and *Choosing the Best Way* for grades 6 and 7, among other abstinence-only curricula. Though he formerly authored other educational and training materials, *Choosing the Best* appears to be Cook's first foray into developing a sex education curriculum. Cook has dubbed *Choosing the Best* an "abstinence-focused sex education curricula," but it differs little in comparison to SCF and *Sex Respect*. It also better meets the accepted definition of abstinence-only education as compared to abstinence-based education (Landry, Kaeser, and Richards 1999).

We also evaluated *Sex Can Wait*, written by Pennie Core-Gebhart, Susan J. Hart, and Michael Young (1994) under the auspices of the Arkansas Family Life Education Project (AFLEP), a project of the Program in Health Sciences at the University of Arkansas. The AFLEP, established in 1982, works with schools to develop and update sexuality education; the staff specializes in sexuality education and has expertise in the area through the sexuality research they have conducted. *Sex Can Wait* is published and distributed by ETR Associates, a nonprofit organization that publishes health-related materials for use in public schools and community organizations.

The authors of *Sex Can Wait* claim that their curriculum is medically appropriate and accurate, free of the kind of bias studies have pointed to in other abstinence curricula. While most comprehensive sexuality education programs are authored by public health experts, the abstinence-only curricula we consider (with the exception of *Sex Can Wait*) are not written by experts in the field of sexuality education. This is the only curriculum of the four that were studied that was authored by experts in the field of sexuality education. Their Web site notes that *Sex Can Wait* "is one of only two curricula listed in the Waxman Report on Abstinence Education that did not 'Contain major errors and distortions of public health information'" (University of Arkansas n.d.). *Sex Can Wait* does strike a significantly more neutral tone with regard to teen sexuality and relationships, particularly as compared to *Sex Respect* and SCF; *Sex Can Wait* also lacks an obvious conservative religious tone or message. Like *Choosing the Best*, the authors of *Sex Can Wait* identify it as an "abstinence-based" rather than abstinence-only curriculum. But again, it better fits the accepted definition of abstinence-only education in that it contains almost no references to contraception nor broadly based discussions of sex and sexuality.

METHODOLOGY

Although there is a growing pool of literature analyzing abstinence-only education, a gap remains in terms of thoroughly examining the *actual* content of abstinence-only across a range of curricula. This analysis attempts to fill the gap through an examination of the content and approach of four abstinence-only curricula. We conduct two types of analyses to provide both a systematic overview and a nuanced study of the curricula: content analysis and narrative deconstruction.

A content analysis was conducted in two stages. The first stage entailed coding the manifest content—the visible and straightforward text of the curricula (Babbie 2005). We were interested in documenting the breadth and frequency of the major issues addressed daily and weekly in the texts. Coding was done paragraph by paragraph and included the main point of the paragraph—such as a discussion of relationships and dating, sexual activity, gender roles, virginity, and the like—and the tone of the material.[3] Thirty-eight different issues were identified in the curricula, and 35 of them clustered around three general themes: expected standards of behavior, consequences of premarital sexual activity, and sexuality education.[4]

The second stage of the content analysis focused on coding the latent content of the texts to assess the underlying meaning, or tone, in which the themes were addressed (Babbie 2005). Tone was coded into three categories: positive, negative, and neutral. In the curricula, gender norms are frequently discussed; however, simply noting the frequency of the topic does not address the context in which gender norms are presented. By coding the discussion as positive, negative, or neutral, we were able to gauge how the themes are taught to students. If traditional gender norms were ascribed to in the paragraph, it was coded as negative tone. Conversely, if gender was talked about in an egalitarian manner, it was coded as positive tone. Finally, if gender was discussed neutrally, it received a neutral tone code.[5]

Tone assessment is central to deconstructing the dominant narratives found in the curricula. We focus on narratives because they play an important discursive role in teaching lessons about sexuality, gender, and adolescence. Individuals learn about themselves and their links to the larger community through narratives. Narratives interact with individuals and help them "understand their progress through time in terms of stories, plots which have beginnings, middles, and ends, heroes and antiheroes, epiphanies and denouements, dramatic, comic, and tragic forms" (Alexander and Smith 1993, 156). Mason (2002) refers to this dynamic between a narrative and the reader of the narrative as a process of interpellation and defines this as "the process in which a reader of a narrative—or social situation—comes not only to sympathize but also to identify with what he is taking in and reacts to it in a way that gives him a new social role or even identity. Although he might think he has chosen or freely accepted this new idea of himself, the process is actually structured and bound by the narrative, not him" (Mason 2002, 7).

Symbolic codes and narratives play a key role in explaining social change, social process, and social meanings (Jacobs 1996). Examining the story abstinence-only curriculum tells adolescents about themselves and the larger society they belong to is instructive in assessing how the text builds on, reinforces, and creates new socially constructed understandings and identities of youth. Narratives also play a role in shaping behavior and structuring choices based on the worldview being espoused through a particular narrative. As noted by many scholars, narratives do not *cause* behavior; rather they play a role in the process of social change, learning, and identity formation. By examining the narratives presented in abstinence-only curricula, we attempt to contextualize the systematic content analysis and demonstrate how the narratives compliment and reinforce a particular understanding of teens, gender, and sexuality.

LIMITATIONS

Because we analyze the definition and funding of abstinence-only curricula as it appears in welfare reform, we have sought to centrally address the ways that race and racism shape abstinence and sex education as political issues. Welfare policy has been racialized since its inception, which impacts sexuality education as it dovetails with welfare reform. In particular, low-income black and Latina women have been defined as overly sexual and unable to delay gratification. In order to address these issues, when seeking teens to interview, we purposely set out to overrepresent young women of color.

In selecting which abstinence-only curricula to analyze, we had the same concerns and interests in mind. We found, however, that the curricula did not overtly address race and ethnicity, racial stereotypes, or the extent to which race, ethnicity, class, and sexual orientation shape social constructions of sexuality and lived experience for teens. Rather, the curricula are "colorblind," approaching discussions of sexuality as if racial and ethnic categories, stereotypes, and differences do not exist.

A primary assumption underlying a colorblind text is that of neutrality. That is, by "ignoring race," the curricula is supposed to be sufficiently neutral and qualified to speak to a broad audience. Yet, many scholars have argued that a supposedly colorblind text is racialized; it is raced white, where whiteness is perceived as the norm, normal, and without need for explanation or deconstruction (Frankenberg 1993; Morrison 1993). The *colorblind* curricula, then, are far from impartial and unbiased. All four curricula are racialized by their attempts to be colorblind. Ethnocentrism erases the racial, ethnic, and class differences among students, and in turn is used to judge those differences as strange or wrong. These ethnocentric judgments often are internalized and reproduced in the stories of the young women interviewed in this study.[6]

The curricula approach colorblindness primarily by erasing race as a discussion topic or explicit reference. Two of the curricula give a brief nod to the existence of racial differences through names and pictures, but do not examine or even mention race as a category of analysis. Specifically, both *Sex Respect* and *Choosing the Best Life* attempt to represent some diversity in their curricula through photographs or drawings of teens. White teens appear in most of these pictures, but there are some exceptions. Smatterings of photos contain racial and ethnic minorities. These attempts to be inclusive are punctuated in the narratives of these curricula with references to names such as "LaWanda" in *Sex Respect* or "Antonio" and "Raoul" in *Choosing the Best Life*. *Sexuality, Commitment, and Family* uses illustrations in its text, and almost all of them depict white teens. In *Sex Can Wait*, there are very few illustrations of any kind throughout the text.

The curricula's colorblind approach limits our analysis. Because we focus on and deconstruct the explicit language used by the curricula, without overt discussion of race and ethnicity, the narrative deconstruction lacks inclusiveness and is not as rich as it could have been were the curricula to address race and ethnicity. Yet, social constructions of race clearly underlie the abstinence message, and race shapes sexual beliefs and experiences. Race is both everywhere and nowhere in the curricula.

FINDINGS: CONTENT ANALYSIS

The content analysis provides a quantitative overview of the primary themes in each curriculum. At first blush, many individual issues appear to be an insignificant portion of a total curriculum; however, by grouping together similar topics pertaining to a common theme, we provide a more accurate reflection of the interaction between topics and lessons, as well as their prominence in the texts. We organize and compile the topics into three primary, or overarching, themes: expected standards of behavior, consequences of premarital sex, and sexuality education. (All of the issues used in the analyses appearing in Tables 1–3 are contained in the Appendix). The texts vary in terms of their overall length (ranging from a total of 478 paragraphs in *Sex Can Wait* to 2,071 in *SCF*) as well as the extent of the treatment given to a particular issue.[7] Each issue is therefore displayed as a percent of the total curriculum to more precisely reflect its prominence in each curriculum.

The curricula exhibit the most parity in terms of the portion of each text discussing expected standards of behavior. *Choosing the Best Life* spends the least amount of text (17%) compared to *Sex Respect*'s treatment (29%). *Sex Can Wait* and *SCF* fall in the middle at 19 percent and 21 percent, respectively. While the overall total does not vary tremendously, the individual issues addressed show more fluctuation, particularly in terms of how much text is reserved for teachings on gender roles, marriage and family, and commitment and values. *Sex Respect* and *Choosing the Best Life* designate more time for discussions about gender roles (4.9% and 5.3%, respectively).

Table 4.1
Percent of Curriculum Discussing Expected Standards of Behavior

	Sex Respect[a]	Sexuality, Commitment & Family (SCF)[b]	Choosing the Best Life[c]	Sex Can Wait[d]
Curriculum Themes:				
Gender Roles	4.9%	1.2%	5.3%	1.7%
Marriage & Family	8.9%	8.9%	0.85%	3.1%
Relationships	7.6%	4.3%	6.3%	7.5%
Commitment & Values	3.2%	4.1%	2.6%	6.7%
Divorce	0.21%	0.24%	0%	0%
Virginity	3.9%	1.7%	2.4%	0%
Homosexuality	0.14%	0.14%	0%	0%
Total[e]	29%	21%	17%	19%

[a] *Sex Respect* page count includes student workbook and teacher manual.

[b] *Sexuality, Commitment & Family (Teen Aid)* page count includes curriculum text.

[c] *Choosing the Best Life* page count includes leader guide, student manual, and video transcripts.

[d] *Sex Can Wait* page count includes curriculum text.

[e] Total percent is rounded.

Aside from these differences, the data presented in Table 4.1 indicate commonalities across curricula, particularly in the emphasis on certain issues and silence on others. Instructions about behavioral expectations predominately hinge on traditional notions of a nuclear, heterosexual family (gender roles, commitment, and values). These issues are addressed to the exclusion of topics, namely divorce and homosexuality, which stand in conflict with traditional understandings of the family.

Even though approximately one in five adults have experienced divorce, indicating a significant number of the students exposed to these curricula have been affected by divorce within their households (U.S. Census Bureau 2005), it is a little discussed topic in the curricula. Aside from divorce, many adolescents reside in homes characterized by nontraditional living arrangements where their parents may be single, cohabiting, remarried, or widowed, to name a few (Acs and Nelson 2003). For example, approximately 50 percent of African American children are born to unmarried parents. Single parent households, impoverished households, and communal childrearing, where extended family and support networks contribute to parenting, also are more common among African Americans than other racial groups (Cain and Combs-Orme 2005). In this study, however, colorblind texts mask these important cultural and resource differences across racial and ethnic groups. The curricula uniformly provide little information about growing up in a nontraditional (or nonwhite) family even though household environment is a significant factor in shaping adolescents' outlook and decision making toward sexuality (Kirby 2001; Whitaker, Miller, and Clark, 2000).

While the curricula pay little attention to alternative family structures, they simply erase alternatives to heterosexuality. Homosexuality is referenced in both *Sex Respect* and *SCF*, but only to note that gay men are considered a high-risk population for contracting HIV. Beyond these brief mentions, homosexuality is absent across the curricula.

In contrast to Table 4.1, Table 4.2 shows a larger disparity among the curricula in terms of time designated to teach students about the consequences of premarital sex. *Sex Can Wait* spends the least amount of time (16%) on consequences while *Choosing the Best Life* reserves almost half (48%) of its curriculum for these lessons. Considerable variation also exists across the curricula in discussing three consequences of premarital sex: unmarried pregnancy, abortion, and adoption. *Sex Can Wait* is the only curriculum that excludes abortion and adoption from its texts. The remaining three curricula cover all three topics, although the coverage is not evenly divided. *Choosing the Best Life* spends more time on unmarried pregnancy, while *Sex Respect* is nearly equivalent in its coverage of pregnancy, abortion, and adoption. *SCF* stands out because relative to pregnancy and adoption, it concentrates more time on abortion.

Despite the variation in curriculum totals, an interesting pattern surfaces from the results in Table 4.2. All four texts emphasize two main consequences to premarital sexual activity: psychological and physical damage. Compared to the other issues falling under consequences, *Sex Respect*, *SCF*, *Choosing the Best Life*, and *Sex Can Wait* allot a considerable portion of their curricula to the psychological and emotional effects associated with engaging in sex outside of marriage (12.8%, 5.0%, 9.6%, and 5.9%, respectively). These effects include physical, emotional, and social consequences resulting from premarital sex.

Only the fear of contracting a sexually transmitted infection rivals the amount of text spent on psychological consequences. The omission of racial, ethnic, and class differences is particularly prominent in relation to these topics because of the disparity in transmission and infection rates across subpopulations (Kaiser Family Foundation 2005, 2007).[8] While all of the curricula gloss over these differences, they vary in terms of how much emphasis is placed on sexually transmitted infections compared to HIV/AIDS. Even though contracting an STI is more common, *Sex Respect* opts to spend 4.3 percent of the text on STIs while overemphasizing HIV/AIDS (12.5%). *Sex Can Wait* chooses a different tack, underemphasizing HIV/AIDS (0.63%) and concentrating its efforts on the con-

Table 4.2
Percent of Curriculum Discussing Consequences of Premarital Sexual Activity

	Sex Respect[a]	Sexuality, Commitment & Family (SCF)[b]	Choosing the Best Life[c]	Sex Can Wait[d]
Curriculum Themes:				
Psychological & Emotional Effects	12.8%	5.0%	9.6%	5.9%
Sexual Coercion	0.48%	0.68%	1.4%	0.63%
Drugs & Alcohol	2.5%	2.6%	8.7%	0%
Sexually Transmitted Infections	4.3%	4.5%	10.8%	7.1%
HIV/AIDS	12.5%	4.3%	11.5%	0.63%
Out-of-Wedlock Pregnancy	1.2%	1.8%	5.6%	1.5%
Abortion	1.2%	2.5%	0.34%	0%
Adoption	1.4%	1.0%	0.20%	0%
Total[e]	36%	22%	48%	16%

[a] *Sex Respect* page count includes student workbook and teacher manual.
[b] *Sexuality, Commitment & Family (Teen Aid)* page count includes curriculum text.
[c] *Choosing the Best Life* page count includes leader guide, student manual, and video transcripts.
[d] *Sex Can Wait* page count includes curriculum text.
[e] Total percent is rounded.

sequences of sexually transmitted infections (7.1%). The two other curricula split their text more evenly between the two. *SCF* spends 4.5 percent of the text teaching about STIs and 4.3 percent on HIV/AIDS, and *Choosing the Best Life* allocates 10.8 percent and 11.5 percent, respectively, to these topics.

Much like the findings represented in Table 4.1, the curricula highlight certain issues with respect to the consequences of premarital sex, but spend relatively little time on drugs, alcohol, and sexual coercion. These issues merit special attention because adolescence is often a time when teens are initially exposed to drugs and alcohol, as well as being most vulnerable to sexual coercion and violence (Tjaden and Thoennes 2000). With the exception of *Choosing the Best Life*, the curricula devote a trivial amount of time to instructing teens about drugs and alcohol or on issues related to sexual coercion and assault. There is an established link between alcohol and sexual assault, as well as racial, ethnic, and class differences in victimization rates (Centers for Disease Control and Prevention 2004). Rather than candidly addressing these risk factors, the "colorblind" curricula ignore these variations. The silence on these issues is more salient in light of studies indicating that a substantial portion of unintended pregnancy is a product of childhood sexual and psychological abuse and power differentials in adolescents' relationships (Landry and Forrest 1995; Olenick 2000).

Table 4.3 pulls together issues associated with teaching sexuality education. One significant finding illustrated in Table 4.3 is the curricula's collective emphasis on decision making—how to make the *right* decision when faced with alternative choices. If gay or lesbian relationships, drug and alcohol use, and sexual coercion are understood as the result of poor decision making, from this viewpoint the logical solution is strengthening students' decision-making skills rather than drawing students' attention to *wrong* choices. Decision making is supplemented and reinforced in all of the texts with teaching students refusal skills—or to "just say no." Improving decision-making and refusal skills is part of equipping students, among other things, to achieve the final goal—remaining abstinent until heterosexual marriage. Although abstinence is the goal, explicit teachings on it comprise similar, and relatively small, portions of the text across curricula, ranging from 4.8 percent to 6.7 percent.

The remaining issues are given different treatment across the curricula. Biology, which includes content on reproductive parts or anatomy, is a significant portion of the SCF and *Sex Can Wait* curricula, but not in the other two. *Sex Can Wait* further stands out with respect to the attention it gives to parenting and self-esteem. The time dedicated to birth control also fluctuates across the curricula from hardly a mention in both *Choosing the Best Life* and *Sex Can Wait* to over 4 percent in *Sex Respect* and SCF.

Overall, the content analysis systematically reveals the degree of variation and, alternatively, the consistency in scope and emphasis of certain issues across the curricula. This investigation portrays the explicit content and lessons contained in abstinence-only curricula as well as highlights the problems inherent in employing a colorblind approach to many of these lessons. The content analysis, however, does not reveal the implicit messages that underlie the lessons. Scrutinizing abstinence-only curricula through a deconstruction of the dominant narratives provides a closer examination of the subtext of the curricula, which helps to inform and shape socially constructed understandings of gender and sexuality.

FINDINGS: NARRATIVE DECONSTRUCTION

We explore several dominant themes in our deconstruction of the curricula's narratives, focusing on the construction of gender and sexuality, sexual assault, premarital sex, marriage and relationships, abortion, and birth control. Though

Table 4.3
Percent of Curriculum Discussing Sexuality Education

	Sex Respect[a]	Sexuality, Commitment & Family (SCF)[b]	Choosing the Best Life[c]	Sex Can Wait[d]
Curriculum Themes:				
Biology	2.8%	10.9%	1.5%	11.1%
Birth Control	4.9%	4.2%	0.85%	0.21%
Parenting	3.9%	4.7%	2.1%	7.1%
Self-Esteem	1.4%	5.3%	1.9%	12.8%
Decision Making	8.8%	18%	12.6%	24.1%
Refusal Skills	3.9%	5.6%	4.6%	0.42%
"Just Say No"/ Abstinence	5.9%	4.8%	6.7%	4.8%
Total[e]	32%	54%	30%	61%

[a] *Sex Respect* page count includes student workbook and teacher manual.

[b] *Sexuality, Commitment & Family (Teen Aid)* page count includes curriculum text.

[c] *Choosing the Best Life* page count includes leader guide, student manual, and video transcripts.

[d] *Sex Can Wait* page count includes curriculum text.

[e] Total percent is rounded.

we analyze gender and sexuality in a separate section, they provide an important context for all the subtopics addressed by the curricula.

Trudell (1993), Morgan (1996), and others have suggested that most sexuality education—regardless of how it teaches abstinence—underscores rather than questions traditional norms. The curricula in this study generally support such conclusions, though to varying degrees and in different ways. As a whole, the curricula range from the overt and aggressive assertion of traditional gender norms in *Sex Respect,* to the mild questioning—without fully specifying alternative gender norms—in *Sex Can Wait.* We define traditional norms of gender to include the notions that men's and women's biological differences translate to significant differences in temperament, capacity for emotion, views and experiences related to sexuality, and life choices and abilities, including in school, career, and family. At times the curricula also offer a view of gender based in biblical teachings, and we define this too as traditional while recognizing that it differs from more secularized traditional views of gender.

Though traditional views of gender predominate, the curricula are not always clear about the appropriate roles for young men and women, or consistent in their constructions of male and female gender and sexuality. The curricula generally portray girls as lacking sexual desire and defined by their sexual and emotional innocence, while boys are cautioned not to take advantage of girls' innocence or need for love by pressuring them for sex (see also Fine 1992). At times, however, the curricula seem less concerned about young women's "purity," and construct young women as temptresses, likely to flaunt their sexuality with inappropriate clothing while young men are trying to maintain a platonic relationship. But in the face of such temptation, the curricula suggest, young men can be carried away by their physiological reactions, implying that young women are responsible for sexual aggression through the messages they send to young men.

Both the religious and secular traditional views of gender stand in contrast to egalitarian views of gender. Egalitarian definitions of gender rarely appear in abstinence-only curricula; in this study, *Sex Can Wait* is the only curriculum that discusses gender norms in a relatively egalitarian manner. Egalitarian views of gender tend to perceive fewer differences between women and men and to argue that biological differences, when they exist, do not necessarily extend to other perceived social and cultural differences between women and men. These views of gender tend to emphasize that gender is a socially constructed phenomenon— and thus is cultural and political—rather than a biological phenomenon.

GENDER AND SEXUALITY CONSTRUCTION

The curricula generally conceptualize gender and sexuality in ways that reflect and help to sustain existing dominant cultural constructions of femininity and masculinity. Moreover, gender and sexuality repeatedly are constructed in terms of one another; gender is perceived as a biological category that shapes sexual attraction and choices. In the first pages of *Sex Respect's* student workbook, students learn that gender differences are biological and extend to men's and women's physical attraction to the "opposite sex":

> Before your heart starts beating, the gift of your gender has been assigned. As soon as we are born, or even beforehand looking at the ultrasound screen, people eagerly ask, "Is it a boy or a girl?" Our physical identity in the world is already being formed. Indeed, our sexuality, or the way we express ourselves as a male or female person, is part of us from the very beginning of life. . . . Although men and women equally deserve respect, they were not made exactly the same emotionally, physically and psychologically. This notion of comparing the genders on the same scale set up marriage and relationships for many surprises. Individuals found that they couldn't understand and communicate with the opposite sex. (Mast 2001b, 6)

Male and female gender and sexuality are defined in opposition to one another. Just as gender is biologically assigned and so is fixed and immutable, according to *Sex Respect*, so (hetero)sexuality is inherent and assumed to extend to all teens.[9]

The emphasis on traditional gender norms corresponds to a narrow and traditional approach to sexuality. *Sex Respect* assumes that teens define themselves as heterosexual, evidenced by the constant emphasis on heterosexual marriage. In the curricula, heterosexuality and traditional gender norms structure one another, as in the previous passage and similarly in the *Sex Respect* parent guide, where there is a chapter titled, "What is Freedom?" The answer to that question appears in the subtitle, "Knights in Shining Armor and Honorable Ladies of the Court!" (Mast 2001c, 29). The curriculum then goes on to state:

> Throughout the history of humanity, man has come with a desire to conquer. Whether it was the need to slay dragons or capture enemy lands, the desire both to conquer and to be a hero have emerged at all ages. . . . During the sexual conquests of the past few decades, many men have chosen to conquer the honor and virtue of women. Furthermore, the women, thinking they have become modern and liberated, have often willingly become victims of this emotional violence, blind to the future consequences. In these battles, neither is free. . . . How can the men and women of the 21st Century become heroes and helpmates? (Mast 2001c, 29)

The passage suggests that there is something *natural* or innate about "man's" (i.e., *men's*) "need to conquer and to be a hero," because they have been driven by such desires throughout history, while women have no such innate leanings. If individuals step outside the bounds of their appropriate identities, as women do when they think themselves "modern and liberated," they are apt to either victimize (as do men) or become victims (as do women).

The ties between gender and sexuality, and the gender and sexuality differences between males and females, are underscored and reified by emphasizing biological arguments and claims: "Testosterone, a male hormone, leads men to interest in the desire for sexual release and pleasure. The estrogen in females tends to focus them primarily on nurturing, warmth, closeness and security" (Mast 2001a, 20). The student workbook goes on to say,

> because they generally become physically aroused less easily, girls are still in a good position to slow down the young man and help him learn balance in a relationship . . . the girl may be showing her interest in the guy, but he thinks she is interested in sex. If their communication isn't clear, the boy may sometimes misread this behavior and get carried away by his physical reactions to that behavior. (Mast 2001b, 12–13)

Choosing the Best Life echoes these ideas—that biological differences between men and women mean that they have differing levels of sexual desire and different physiological reactions and needs. In the anatomy portion of the curriculum, *Choosing the Best Life* asserts: "If we combine brain activity with sex hormones, how does this help explain how guys and girls view sex differently? (Guys can focus more easily on the *physical side of sex* without necessarily being in a relationship. Girls tend to have a broader view of sex that emphasizes the *total relationship* rather than the physical aspect alone)" (Cook 2003a, 7, emphasis in original). The accompanying video lesson underscores this idea when the teacher in the video segment contends: "Boys and girls are different and boys have very different physical needs than girls have and they see sex very differently than girls do. For boys I think, first is a biological urge. And for girls I think there is a biological urge but it's also incorporated in through their emotional needs . . . they see sex more as an intimacy rather than just biological" (Cook 2003b).

The *Choosing the Best Life* curriculum offers multiple, complex, and sometimes contradictory lessons about sexuality. First, by suggesting that innate differences lead to distinct biological urges with regard to sex, teens learn that "normal" young women will not want to participate in sexual activity except in relationships, and that "normal" young men will be satisfied with—even seek—sex without emotional commitment. Boys do not have the same emotional range and depth as girls and do not link sex with emotion. Second, the curriculum focuses on male pleasure and ignores or downplays female desire (Fine 1992). A girl's role is to understand and monitor male desire, rather than identify with her own. Girls lack the strong "biological urges" that boys have, or at least girls are not ruled by such urges as are boys. Finally, if young women can control their sexual desires, then they carry the burden of preventing premarital sex; she becomes responsible both for his and her own behavior. This responsibility has significant implications when taught within the framework of abstinence-only instruction, because the primary message is that serious, lifelong, negative effects result from premarital sex.

In *Choosing the Best Life* and *Sex Respect*, sexual differences are presented as biological fact with no supporting evidence. The curricula's assertion that hormones drive men and women's sexual responses both physiologically and emotionally is incorrect. Although found in different levels, hormones that are classified as female (estrogens) and male (androgens) are present in both sexes (Discovery Health 2002). Such notions of biological difference related to sexual desire have not been proven. "Sex drive is much more likely to be affected by external stimuli (sights, sound, touch) than by variations in sex hormones, except in extreme cases" (Discovery Health 2002, 1). If some men and women view and react to sex differently, it is because they are taught that those are the proper gendered responses to sex. In fact, by asserting that such differences exist and are natural, the curricula themselves push a particular view of women as without innate sexual desire and men as driven by uncontrollable desire. John Stoltenberg contends,

> Male sexual identity is the conviction or belief, held by most people born with penises, that they are male and not female, that they belong to the male sex. In a society predicated on the notion that there are two "opposite" and "complementary" sexes, this idea not only makes sense, it *becomes* sense; the very idea of a male sexual identity produces sensation, produces the meaning of sensation, becomes the meaning of how one's body feels . . . sexuality does not *have* a gender; it *creates* a gender. It creates for those who adapt to it in narrow and specified ways the confirmation for the individual of belonging to the idea of one sex or the other. (Stoltenberg 2003, 257–8)

BIBLICAL UNDERTONES

In addition to constructing gender and sexuality in traditional and biological terms, the curricula may reference biblical notions of these categories as well. The authors and publishers of *Sex Respect* and *SCF* have the clearest connections to the religious right, and not surprisingly, these curricula sometimes make implicit references to biblical ideas. For example, when the *Sex Respect* text asks, "How can the men and women of the 21st Century become heroes and help-mates? (Mast 2001c, 29), the reference is to a passage in Genesis. To recommend that young men should strive to be heroes while young women support them as helpmates rests on an active subject position for males and a subservient, object position for females. The biblical notion of woman as *helper*, taken from the introduction of Adam and Eve in Genesis, underlies the lesson. We read in Genesis 2:18 through 2:23:

> [18]And the LORD God said, It is not good that the man should be alone; I will make him a helper as his partner.
>
> [19]So out of the ground the LORD God formed every animal of the field, and every bird of the air; and brought them to the man to see what he would call them; and whatever the man called every living creature, that was its name.
>
> [20]The man gave names to all cattle, and to the birds of the air, and to every animal of the field; but for the man there was not found a helper as his partner.
>
> [21]So the LORD God caused a deep sleep to fall upon the man, and he slept; then he took one of his ribs, and closed up its place with flesh.
>
> [22]And the rib that the LORD God had taken from man he made into a woman and brought her to the man.

[23] Then the man said, "This at last is bone of my bones and flesh of my flesh; this one shall be called Woman, for out of Man this one was taken."

According to *Sex Respect*, if women and men follow the gendered paths set out for them in the Bible, they can find the freedom that they seek. When the curricula base gender norms on biblical notions of male and female, they contain no critical analysis of their arguments, nor make explicit references to the Bible. Rather, biblical references are implicit and serve to underscore the idea that men and women achieve their natural roles by joining together their complementary, though biologically opposite, emotional and physical selves.

GENDER EQUALITY

In contrast to *Sex Respect* and *Choosing the Best Life*, *Sex Can Wait* addresses gender roles from a more egalitarian perspective. *Sex Can Wait* offers two chapters that focus on gender roles, the first a general chapter and the second a more specific consideration of masculinity. The authors openly question traditional views of gender, arguing that as gender roles change, so do our "concepts of sex and sexuality" (Core-Gebhart et al. 1994, 107). They sum up the chapter on masculinity by emphasizing that traditional gender roles are "limiting" and that teens must respond to changing notions of gender:

> Our focus today has been on the role of young men in responsible sexual decision making. The video and our discussion provided a starting point for young men to begin to talk about society's and peers' expectations of them and to create strategies for coping with pressures to conform to stereotypes. Young men are also affected by the legal and emotional consequences of early sexual involvement. We must learn how to break old, limiting stereotypes for both males and females and to create more positive and balanced gender roles. (Core-Gebhart et al. 1994, 127–28)

Sex Can Wait, then, achieves more gender neutrality than the other curricula; even focusing more on men's sexuality than women's based on the idea that as a culture, we usually hold men less responsible for sexual activity than women.

Sex Can Wait, however, fails to offer the teacher or students much factual information to ground the discussion of gender roles and stereotypes. There are numerous questions designed to get the students to talk about their own beliefs, but little information for the teacher to use to guide the discussion or refute stereotypes. A student would come away from most lessons with the sense that gendered notions of masculinity and femininity—whether more or less traditional—are based largely on individual beliefs and preferences.

In particular, the curriculum does not provide a way to analyze the power differentials between teen women and men and how constructions of gender relate to access to personal, social, economic, and physical power. One exercise has students moving between signs marked with "Agree" and "Disagree" in response to statements such as "It is OK for women to be truck drivers, corporate presidents, and surgeons"; "Male/female relationships were easier before the women's liberation movement started"; and "It is up to the man to initiate sexual activities, but it is up to the woman to say yes or no" (Core-Gebhart et al. 1994, 114). Students then return to their seats and are asked whether males and females in the class had different opinions and why that might be the case. Neither the teacher nor the students have access to reading material or other information addressing the questions they have been asked. Nothing tangible is provided, detailing, for example, how many women currently hold positions of truck drivers or surgeons, and whether that has changed throughout history and why. Nor has there been any definition for or discussion of the "women's liberation movement," so students are left to define that term for themselves.

SEXUAL ASSAULT

Culturally, from sources like the media and their peers, teens receive mixed messages about sexual assault and whether girls carry responsibility for boys' violence. Abstinence-only curricula sometimes play on—and even provide authoritative support for—the idea that boys are not completely to blame for coercive sexual behavior if they have been "tempted" or "teased" by a girl. Reinforcing commonly held rape myths, the curricula suggest that girls' clothing send a message to boys about their sexual availability, that boys are physiologically unable to stop themselves once they have become sexually excited, and overall, that girls are responsible for sexual assault.

In *Sex Respect's* discussion of dating, the curriculum exhorts young women: "Knowing that what we wear can advertise our attitudes, we can be aware of clothes that are too tight, too low-cut or too short. Deep down, you know that your friend's plunging necklines and short skirts are getting the guys to talk about her. Is that what you want? To see girls who drive guys' hormones when a guy is trying to see her as a friend?" (Mast 2001b, 94). This instruction on appropriate clothing warns girls that their clothes send a message to boys, and that skimpy, tight clothes engender a physiological reaction in boys. A boy cannot control his physiological reactions; thus it is the girl's fault for tempting and provoking him by dressing provocatively when a "guy is trying to see her as a friend." The implications of this lesson resonate with the idea that girls are responsible for sexual assault by "asking for it," by advertising their availability by dressing provocatively, going "too far" sexually, or the like. Young men and women both learn that a biological justification exists for boys who rape, reinforcing existing myths about the causes of sexual assault.

Sex Can Wait contains some of the same notions about sexuality and sexual assault, but it also attempts to undermine rape myths to some degree. It is, however, hampered by a lack of real information to counter stereotypes and rape myths, just as with its discussion of gender norms. This results in mixed messages about sexuality and sexual assault. *Sex Can Wait* primarily concentrates on date rape in its chapter on abstinence. The teacher is directed to ask the students to consider and comment on cultural stereotypes, asking the students: "What is date rape? Is it really rape? Is it true that once a male gets 'turned on' he's got to go 'all the way'? If a female dresses provocatively, is she responsible for date rape?" (Core-Gebhart et al. 1994, 307). The teacher receives no curricular materials about rape or information to counter such rape myths. It is difficult to precisely ascertain what the authors of the curriculum are trying to teach students about rape, because the lesson seems to begin and end with these questions.

The section closes with the following authoritative guidance for students on the subject of rape:

> Taking responsibility for yourself means recognizing that others may not be willing to take responsibility for their own actions. Taking responsibility means taking extra measures to ensure that you are protecting yourself against your own vulnerability to whatever extent possible. Should rape or exploitation occur, it is important to recognize that it is not your fault. Ask for adult help when you need it. (Core-Gebhart et al. 1994, 308)

First, the passage is directed at girls, exhorting them to protect themselves. And not only are girls responsible for stopping "rape or exploitation," the passage seems to blame girls themselves, instructing them to protect "yourself against your own vulnerability," rather than to protect themselves against men, presumably. Men are not the actors here, the ones who rape; rather, it is women's vulnerability that acts to put women in danger. Precisely how to "take extra measures to ensure that you are protecting yourself" is not clear, and so even if a young woman also is told that rape "is not your fault," lingering doubts exist for students of both sexes. Did she take enough precautions? Was she being responsible, and isn't the rape evidence of her irresponsibility, or at least failure at being fully responsible?

The next page in the *Sex Can Wait* curriculum (and final page of the section) further adds to the mixed messages. Titled "Avoiding Sexual Exploitation in Dating Relationships," the handout contains nine statements relating to dating and date rape:

Know your sexual limits. Believe in your right to set those limits. If you are not sure, stop.

Communicate. Talking is the basis of any good relationship. Tell your girlfriend or boyfriend what you want. Find out what she or he thinks and feels.

Be assertive. Passivity may be interpreted as permission. Be direct and firm with someone who is pressuring you sexually. Say no when you mean no. Move away. Leave if possible or necessary.

Be aware of the messages you may be sending. People may assume that "sexy" clothing and/or flirtation indicate you want to have sex.

Accept a "No" at face value. "No" always means no, no matter how quietly or shyly it is said. Don't continue after a "stop" or "please don't," or a "no."

Place the greatest importance on verbal messages. Don't assume that because a person dresses in a sexy manner and/or flirts that he or she wants to have sex.

Previous permission does not apply to the present. A yes yesterday can still be a no today. A person has the right to change his or her mind.

Trust your intuition. When you first get the feeling that things aren't OK, say something or do something to try to get out of the situation.

Avoid alcohol and drugs. Clear thinking and effective communication are difficult when "under the influence." Responsibility for actions remains. (Core-Gebhart et al. 1994, 309)

Some of these admonitions are directed at young men while others are aimed at young women, calling on both males and females to be aware of and active in preventing sexual assault. Yet, at the same time, these statements run the gamut from blaming young women for sexual assault based on the "message" their clothes send to men and their assumed passivity, to instructing young men to listen to and respect women's wishes with regard to sexual activity, to suggesting that sexual assault is caused by bad communication rather than power differentials and coercion. Such conflicting lessons no doubt leave teens confused as to how to define sexual assault and who holds responsibility for assault. This is made worse by the fact that overall, *Sex Can Wait* offers little concrete instruction in an area fraught with misconceptions and cultural stereotypes. Because such misconceptions may be held by the instructor as well as the students, it seems imperative that *Sex Can Wait* provide much clearer and more detailed instructional material if the authors wish to undermine traditional norms regarding rape.

The point is not that abstinence-only curricula are producing myths about rape; rather, the lessons about sexual assault that teens learn from the curricula intervene in a struggle to define rape that already exists in numerous forms and forums in society—a struggle that is based in a contest for social and cultural power. The debate, at its most simple, is one over how to define sexual assault and who is responsible for sexual assault. One set of arguments, dominated by feminist articulations of rape, maintains that rape is a violent crime, committed to underscore male power: "Gender based violence, theoretically, is derived from a system of beliefs that legitimates a male's use of violence to control a female's behavior" (Asencio 2002, 142). Feminists argue that rape can and does happen to women (and to a much lesser extent men) of all ages, races, and classes, and that men rape both because they have more power than women and in order to claim and reify that power.

In defining rape as an act of violence, feminists are combating and responding to various rape myths that exist to normalize, explain, excuse, and justify male sexual assault. These myths blame women for assault rather than men. A central myth asserts that women provoke rape or "ask for it" by wearing suggestive clothing, being in a "private" location with a man, such as a bedroom or hotel room, or by drinking alcohol or taking drugs (SARP Center n.d.). When a woman does any of these things, she indicates that she is available for sex, so therefore she cannot be raped. Another rape myth declares that regardless of her verbal "no," a woman says "yes" to sex by engaging in other (noncoital) sexual activity with a man, and that a man reaches a point when he physiologically cannot stop himself from having sex. In this case, she is still "asking for it" because she assented to a certain degree of sexual activity. An accompanying myth states that most rapes happen in a dark alley at night by a stranger, not a person the victim knows and not in someone's home. Finally, Stephen Schulhofer argues that in both acquaintance and stranger rape situations, if a woman cannot show that she has fought back vigorously, and if the rapist has not used physical force to restrain her, then in law and practice, she is considered to have had consensual sex, even when she was raped (Schulhofer 1998).

Michael Kimmel demonstrates the extent to which rape myths are related to and supported by arguments that gender and sexuality are biologically based. The same process that constructs gender and sexuality as fixed, immutable, and biologically based constructs sexual assault as the natural outcome of differential gender identities. It is "natural" for boys to "need" sex, and their needs are so strong as to excuse them for using pressure or force against young women. For girls to be considered "natural," they must have little sexual desire but obvious interest in the "opposite" sex. Young women hold the responsibility for monitoring and controlling sexual interactions. To the extent that these social constructions of gender and sexuality support and justify rape myths, they also further gender inequality:

> Gender inequality is reinforced by the ways we have come to assume that men are more sexual than women, that men will always try to escalate sexual encounters to prove their manhood, and that women—or, rather,

"ladies"—either do not have strong sexual feelings, or that those they do must be constantly controlled lest they fall into disrepute. . . . when sexual pleasure happens, it's often seen as his victory over her resistance. (Kimmel 2000, 222–23)

It is no wonder that sexuality has been called "the linchpin of gender inequality," as these notions of natural and "proper" femininity are used by schools, churches, families, and even the state to police women's actions (Kimmel 2000, 223). When abstinence-only curricula advance these ideas, they do so in a context where such a construction of female sexuality—teen and adult—already exists. This helps to further develop and reify such notions (and particular constructions of gender and sexuality) while teaching students about sexual assault.

MARRIAGE AND RELATIONSHIPS

The portions of abstinence-only curricula that focus on gender norms and roles, on sexuality, and on sexual assault are related to one another in the context of the curricula's principal lessons about remaining abstinent until marriage. Portraying the institution of marriage as the only moral and safe place to have sex reflects the influence of conservative religious advocates on abstinence-only education. As the introduction to SCF declares, "*Sexuality, Commitment and Family* is based upon a tradition of moral and value principles. It strongly supports the family and teaches that the deepest meaning of the sexual act derives from the marriage commitment" (Teen Aid 1998, 8). These "moral and value principles" are not necessarily precisely the same in all of the curricula, but with the exception of *Sex Can Wait*, all the curricula in this analysis seem to be influenced by conservative Christian religious views.

Both SCF and *Sex Respect* emphasize the importance and centrality of heterosexual marriage. *Sex Respect* instructs students about the depth of their sexual choices by emphasizing marriage: "You ARE worth waiting for, so you can learn about real love. For the price of keeping your clothes on and keeping cool now, you could have a priceless treasure—years of reaping the benefits of premarital virginity in your marriage" (Mast 2001b, 74). This passage emphasizes the particular way that sexuality and relationships are defined in abstinence-only education: Virginity until marriage is framed as a "priceless treasure" that will make a marriage stronger. The implied message for teens is that not remaining abstinent until marriage will have the opposite result, inflicting harm on a marriage.

SCF and *Sex Respect* characterize marriage as the natural and expected result of dating, and they imply that marriage is somewhat imminent for dating teens. SCF lists the "purposes of dating"; the first on the list is "to choose a marriage partner and prepare for a lasting relationship" (Teen Aid 1998, 57). A "dating partner" is referred to as one's "prospective spouse" (Teen Aid 1998, 66). Similarly, *Sex Respect* refers to dating as a "method of choosing a mate" for marriage (Mast 2001b, 81). And when *Sex Respect* offers a list of character traits that teens should aspire to, it lists, among others, temperance, frugality, sincerity, and chastity. Chastity is defined as "purity of the body and mind . . . sexual self-control at the service of married love" (Mast 2001c, 28).

Sex Can Wait and *Choosing the Best Life* contain far fewer references to marriage and family, and *Sex Can Wait* also offers a more neutral orientation toward these topics. While it supports abstinence until marriage and disapproves of teenage sexual activity, it leaves open the possibility that adults may have sex outside of marriage without the depth of negative repercussions suggested in other abstinence-only curricula. In fact, "Waiting to have sex until you are married *or involved in a mutually monogamous relationship with an uninfected partner*" is listed as a "Safe Behavior" (Core-Gebhart et al. 1994, 213, emphasis added), reinforcing the idea that "Sex belongs in committed, adult relationships" (Core-Gebhart et al. 1994, 44). This more progressive tone may be attributable to the reduced influence of the Christian Right on this curriculum.

SEX AND DEVIANCE

The few passages in *Sex Can Wait* suggesting that premarital sex may be acceptable are the exception within the abstinence-only curricula assessed in this study. SCF refers to sexually active teens as "displaying destructive behavior" and warns teachers to deal carefully with such students: "In sex education policy it is best that we not place the spotlight (and the glamor?) [*sic*] on those teens who are having illicit sex and putting themselves, their future children, and society at risk" (Teen Aid 1998, insert, 13).

Abstinence-only education often represents sexually active girls as negative examples; ironically, sexually experienced teens make up the majority of the audience for sex education. Studies show that approximately 80 percent of teens are sexually active by the age of 18 (Rabasca 1999). SCF tries to include these teens in the abstinence discourse by providing teachers with a directive:

> Remediation should be available for those who, for whatever reason, deviate from the best choice, but it is absolutely essential that this be done in private individual counseling and not in the classroom. It is unwise and unfair to allow the sexually dysfunctional faction of students to set the standard for developing district-wide programs. Classroom discussions for these students may degenerate into sensational exhibitions creating negative peer pressure. (Teen Aid 1998, insert, 15)

Deriving from this segment, sexually active students threaten to contaminate the rest of the classroom with their dysfunctional ideas and choices. Notwithstanding other curricular references to young women as temptresses, here we see the norm—and the majority of teens—portrayed as appropriately innocent and devoid of sexual knowledge and desire. From this vantage point, including those who are sexually active in classroom discussions becomes problematic.

A suggestion is also made in the *SCF* passage that those who engage in sexual activity outside marriage need counseling to overcome their mistakes. Simply by virtue of the fact that they are sexually active, teens are defined as dysfunctional. *Choosing the Best Life* echoes this idea and takes it further by emphasizing the mental health complications brought about by teen sexual activity through the following teacher guided questions and answers for the students:

> Why might sexually active teens experience depression? (Investment in another results in pain when breakup occurs; feels like a failure; feels deeper pain because already sees events in emotional way.) What consequences can this depression have? (May lead to attempted, or successful, suicide. One study showed that girls who had been sexually active were six times more likely to attempt suicide than those who were virgins).[10] (Cook 2003a, 9)

Here sexual activity is linked to mental instability in the form of depression and even suicide. While both *SCF* and *Choosing the Best Life* focus on psychological damage, *Choosing the Best* emphasizes the negative effects of sexual activity as it is turned inward, while the *SCF* curriculum focuses on the damage sexually active teens can cause other students. The sources that they cite, however, are misused and misquoted. *Choosing the Best Life* cites a study to support its claims that suicide is linked with sexual activity. In fact, the authors of the study itself do not support the curriculum's implication that teen sexual activity may lead to suicide (U.S. House of Representatives 2004, 21).[11]

FEAR AS DETERRENCE

Given the deeply negative associations with teenage sex promoted by abstinence-only education, sexually active teens have little opportunity to find guidance from the curricula.[12] Framing all teen sexual activity as destructive leads to the notion that sexually active teens are by definition "at risk," and that sexual activity is a "risky behavior." Many of the lessons are built around the potential consequences stemming from premarital sex. These discussions are designed to instill an almost visceral fear of premarital sex in students. *Sex Respect* teaches:

> If premarital sex came in a bottle, it would probably have to carry a Surgeon General's warning, something like the one on a package of cigarettes.

There's No Way To Have Premarital Sex without Hurting Someone. . . . Some people still think premarital sex is okay as long as they and their partner aren't hurting anyone. After all, sex is a personal, private decision, and it's nobody else's business what they do with their bodies—right? Wrong! Because of the special and mysterious nature of human sexuality, premarital sex ends up hurting someone. (Mast 2001b, 47–48)

Likewise, the first directive to teachers in the "consequences of adolescent sexual activity" section of *SCF*, reads:

Emphasis should be placed on the serious risks and responsibilities *inherent in teenage sexual activity.* As a general principle, the students should be encouraged to consider the *long-range* effects of a decision made impulsively and without adequate factual information. (Teen Aid 1998, 235, emphasis in original text)

The section goes on to describe the social and psychological consequences of premarital sex:

loss of reputation, limitations in dating/marriage choices, negative effects on sexual adjustment—Premarital sex, especially with more than one person, has been linked to the development of difficulty in sexual adjustment. (Guilt has been found to be a pervasive problem in this regard.) . . . development of emotional illness, loss of self esteem . . . [and] confusion regarding personal value (e.g. "Am I loved because . . . I am a sex object?"). (Teen Aid 1998, 236–37)

Though carefully worded to appear mostly gender neutral, the message (and risk) is clearly directed to girls; culturally, men generally do not fear these consequences.

In addition to the psychological and social effects of teen sexual activity, abstinence-only lessons portray STIs as a likely result of sex. Abstinence-only curricula generally contain detailed discussions about the symptoms and outcomes associated with gonorrhea, chlamydia, HPV, and others (Cook 2003a; Mast 2001a; Teen Aid 1998). Information is technical and impersonal and divorced from relationships (Trudell 1993; Wolf 1997).

The risk of STIs represents an important basis for shaming adolescents by linking sex with hazard and peril. These topics easily relate to abstinence-only curricula's messages about the loss of reputation and marriageability for sexually active girls. Specifically, contracting an STI provides proof that sexually active teens are "dirty" and "unpure"; their reputations are sullied as their bodies are sullied. *Sex Can Wait* is an exception and is less likely than the other curricula to use the possibility of contracting an STI to instill fear and shame in teens.

Choosing the Best Life introduces STIs with a long and detailed study of infection rates, physical manifestations of the various infections, and difficulties in detection. A video accompanying the *Choosing the Best Life* STI chapter contains graphic, close-up slides of infected genitalia. Teachers are directed to warn their students that, "Today there are more than 25 STDs, some of which are incurable and can lead to serious health consequences such as infertility, cancer, or even death" (Cook 2003a, 18). HIV/AIDS, addressed in a later chapter, provides further basis for instilling fear of infection and death in students should they engage in premarital sex.

The *Choosing the Best Life* curriculum introduces condoms in the context of its discussion of STIs and safer sex, stressing repeatedly that condoms can "break," "slip off," and "weaken and deteriorate" due to their sensitivity to heat and cold. It cites research that indicates only 5 percent to 21 percent of couples use condoms consistently and correctly, and more importantly, even with correct usage, condoms do little to protect against diseases. Though the author notes that studies differ, such as with chlamydia, where "some studies indicate limited risk reduction, yet other studies show no risk reduction at all" (Cook 2003a), the emphasis is clearly on the fact that condoms do little to nothing to protect against STIs. Downplaying the efficacy of condoms runs contrary to vast scientific research indicating the opposite: Consistent condom use is an effective method for reducing the risk of infection contraction and transmission (U.S. House of Representatives 2004).[13]

Throughout these lessons, fear and shame are used to deter teens from engaging in sexual activity prior to marriage. In reality, these tactics do little to achieve this goal. Fear and shame simply serve to reinforce fatalistic behavior among the sexually active (i.e., condoms offer little protection therefore do not use them). Studies indicate that around 20 percent of teens do not think condoms are effective in preventing HIV/AIDS and STI transmission, and one in five teens erroneously believe birth control pills provide protection against sexually transmitted diseases (Kaiser Family Foundation 2003).

Fear and shame tactics may encourage a secondary effect as well. They inadvertently encourage teens to experiment with other sexual practices perceived to be safer. Oral sex has become fairly popular among teens: Over half of teens aged 15–19 reported participating in oral sex in 2002 (Dailard 2006). Many teens think oral sex is safer than vaginal sex, and approximately 20 percent of adolescents do not think disease transmission is possible through oral sex (Kaiser Family Foundation 2003).

ABORTION

In general, abstinence-only education presents abortion as another hazard (to be feared) facing sexually active young women. References to abortion in the curricula unambiguously demonstrate the influence of religious conservatives in shaping specific lessons in abstinence-only curricula. The curricula's analysis of abortion is almost entirely negative in tone. *SCF* states:

> The *legal definition* of "abortion" is the emergence of the fetus from the uterus before 20–24 weeks, menstrual age (depending on state law). After this time, separation of the fetus from the mother is called a "delivery." The popular definition of the term "abortion," however, automatically implies an *intent to kill the unborn*, and is used for procedures performed at any stage of pregnancy. The live-born fetus (baby) is considered a "complication" of second trimester abortions, posing "difficult medical, legal, and ethical problems." (Teen Aid 1998, 250 emphasis in the original text)

In the first two sentences, the passage teaches that delivery of a baby and abortion of a fetus are comparable, describing abortion as the "emergence of the fetus." The curriculum highlights the arbitrary division (20–24 weeks) used to delineate between a legal abortion compared to a birth of a baby. In other words, *SCF* indicates the issue is one of legalese and semantics, but the end result is the same. It makes this point more forcefully in the next sentence by defining abortion as the "intent to kill the unborn." This argument is central to religious conservative groups' claim that life begins at conception, and thus, abortion involves the taking of an innocent and defenseless life. Finally, the passage erroneously represents abortion as delivery of a "live-born fetus," presumably that could live outside the woman's body, and further implies that second-trimester abortions are the norm, rather than a small percentage of abortions performed.

SCF goes on to teach students that significant "psychological aftereffects" plague most women after they have abortions. The curriculum states: "most, if not all, parties of the abortion" suffer "a chronic grief reaction" after abortion (Teen Aid 1998, 255). *SCF* cites a study where, after having an abortion, as many as 62 percent of women became suicidal, "with 20% actually making suicide attempts, 30% began drinking heavily, and 40% experienced nightmares" (Teen Aid 1998, 255).

The book cited to support these claims, *Aborted Women: Silent No More*, is a polemic against legal abortion, not a scientific study with a controlled sample such as would normally be constructed to test social beliefs or experiences. The author, David Reardon, has no credentials as a scholar or academic, but rather, a personal interest in pressing his particular beliefs about abortion. His lack of credentials is reflected in the unscientific "study" that Reardon devised. He bases his assertions about the psychological and emotional effects of abortion on interviews that he completed with women from a group called Women Exploited By

Abortion (WEBA). This group provides a "place of refuge, a place where women could share their abortion experiences, share their pain, share their strengths, and rebuild their lives" after being devastated by having an abortion (Reardon 1987, xxii). WEBA was founded by and for women who felt so emotionally scarred by abortion that they sought a group to join to heal themselves; these women are not representative of the general population of women who have had abortions, so basing a study on their perspectives does not yield unbiased information that can be used to make general claims about women who have had abortions. Yet, this is precisely what Reardon does and precisely what SCF does when it uses Reardon's arguments in the curriculum.

The issues with bias and the specificity of the women's experiences in Reardon's study are far more problematic when they show up in SCF for several reasons. Students, teachers, and parents do not have access to *Aborted Women* in order to see from where the information comes, so they have no idea that these claims are based on just a few women's experiences. Nor do they know that these women are self-selected to prove the negative ramifications of abortion; in other words, that Reardon sought out women who would speak about the pain of abortion in order to prove the pain of abortion. Without that information, students cannot assess the extent to which SCF is offering a religiously and politically based polemic in public school curricula. Reardon cannot even find interviews to support some of his claims, claims that SCF echoes in the curriculum. For example, there are no interviews cited in *Aborted Women* to support Reardon's assertion that abortion and child abuse are linked. Here, Reardon's most compelling evidence—since *Roe v. Wade* the rate of legal abortions has increased and so has reported incidences of child abuse—is anecdotal at best.

Aborted Women is published by Crossway Books, a division of Good News Publishers. As their Web site indicates, books published by Good News/Crossway explicitly press an evangelical agenda:

> Good News Publishers is a not-for-profit Christian ministry and exists solely for the purpose of proclaiming the gospel through publishing and all other means in order, by God's grace;
>
> 1. to bring men, women and children to Christ as their Lord and Savior;
> 2. to help individual Christians and the church grow in knowledge and understanding of the Christian life;
> 3. to bear witness to God's Truth, Beauty and Holiness, and to the Lordship of Christ in every area of life; and
> 4. to glorify our Lord and Savior Jesus Christ in every way. (Good News & Crossway n.d.)

Aborted Women is not an unbiased discussion or scholarly study; rather, it specifically intends to present the case against abortion using a very specific religious argument. The fact that this book is presented as scholarly support for the teachings in a public school curriculum points to the influence of a fundamentalist religious agenda on the lessons learned by all public school teens.

Contrary to the evidence presented in *Aborted Women*, the scientific evidence points to just the opposite reaction to abortion. A study based on data from the National Longitudinal Survey of Youth found that abortion had no effect on a woman's self-esteem or general psychological well-being (Edwards 1997). The American Psychiatric Association concurs, as an expert panel indicated that, "for the vast majority of women, an abortion will be followed by a mixture of emotions, with a predominance of positive feelings" (cited in U.S. House of Representatives 2004, 14).

Similarly, no scientific evidence underlies the even more outlandish claims that SCF makes linking abortion and child abuse. According to SCF, an equally important "psychological aftereffect" of abortion is the tendency toward child abuse of subsequent children: "after one has aborted a child, an individual loses instinctual control over rage," and women who have had abortions experience "the loss of the social taboo against aggressing the defenseless" (Teen Aid 1998, 255). The curriculum goes on to state that women who have abortions are likely to subsequently devalue children, and their "guilt and self-hatred may be displaced onto the child" (Teen Aid 1998, 255).

BIRTH CONTROL

Though a concern about the "immorality" or "hazards" of abortion might lead to a focus on the use of birth control, abstinence-only education avoids any clear explanation or comparison of birth control methods. Because abstinence-only education teaches about birth control failure rates exclusively, birth control does not appear in the curricula as a method to avoid either pregnancy or abortion for sexually active teens. While *Choosing the Best Life* skims over birth control methods rather quickly, SCF and *Sex Respect* spend considerably more time on birth control. All three focus on the failure rates for stopping pregnancy. *Sex Can Wait* has virtually no discussion of birth control; its one paragraph contains a negative tone toward its use.

In discussing birth control, abstinence-only curricula self-consciously avoid providing any information about how to access or use various contraceptive methods, their individual advantages and drawbacks, or medical risk factors, among other issues. A student exposed to the contraceptive sections of the curricula, then, will come away with little more information about contraceptives than their names and their failure rates. SCF directs teachers to focus on contraceptive failure rates without giving out more information: "As the awareness of freedom gained by abstinence dawns, teens may ask about contraceptives which were previously held up as the ticket to freedom. Questions should be answered considering contraceptive failure rates, and comparing those to the 'failure' rates for refraining adolescents" (Teen Aid 1998, insert, 13).

Sex Respect's Student Workbook asks: "So does birth control help teens become free? The facts show the opposite. Even when teenagers were using contraceptives and using them more consistently than ever before, the number and rate of premarital pregnancies continued to rise" (Mast 2001b, 42). And *Sex Respect* does more than suggest that birth control does not help to prevent pregnancy. The workbook goes on to connect numerous dire consequences to the use of birth control:

> The adults who thought that they were helping, found out that birth control was only an illusion of help. They discovered that the chemical forms of birth control damage the inside of a young girl's body in ways that can affect her fertility later on, too. They found that birth control shots, pills and implants affected a girl's moods and often made her gain weight. They found that many teens that used birth control had a 10 to 20% chance of getting pregnant anyway. They found that many more sexually transmitted diseases were being spread among teens. The abortion rates were much higher among people who used birth control that failed. The emotional and psychological effects of teen sex only got worse. (Mast 2001b, 42)

Capitalizing on fears that are particularly salient to young women—fertility, pregnancy, abortion, disease infection—this passage is furthering myths about the uselessness of birth control that are not supported by scientific evidence. In fact, existing evidence points to the opposite of many of the claims made here (U.S. House of Representatives 2004). The preponderance of negative associations with birth control, however, is likely to dissuade young people from using birth control when they do become sexually active, as some of the literature suggests. The birth control lessons, like many of the lessons contained in abstinence-only curricula, are woven together with a common thread of fear and shame.

CHAPTER SUMMARY

Maintaining virginity until marriage is the primary focus of the abstinence-only curricula. To this end, the curricula address a range of issues related to teenage sexuality. A content analysis and narrative deconstruction were performed on four abstinence-only curricula. The findings indicate that many discussions about teen sexuality are generally shaped by a conservative religious view of gender and sexuality. These views ultimately shape a narrow perspective about sexuality, as well as structure the consequences involved with sex outside of marriage.

The analyses also suggest that abstinence-only sex education virtually ignores the gendered aspects of sexuality that teen women seem most affected by, specifically, gendered norms regarding sexuality that lead to a power imbalance in intimate relationships. When the curricula does address themes with which teen women say they grapple—particularly the impact of the social construction of gendered sexuality and sexual assault—the curricula tend to underscore traditional interpretations of gender and sexuality and to buttress rape myths.

The implicit discourse underlying the explicit lessons in the curricula also promote an ethnocentrism that champions white, middle-class, social and religious conservatism as the cultural standard and ideal. The inclusion of abstinence within a welfare reform law may be read as an attempt to instill "middle-class" values of delayed childbearing in young girls caught in the culture of poverty, which assumes that young, poor (and likely minority) women are promiscuous. This is woven throughout the different texts and apparent in the colorblind writing of the curricula. Little to no attention is given to racial, ethnic, or class differences among adolescents.

These ethnocentric judgments often are internalized and reproduced in the stories of the young women interviewed in this study. Many of the teenage women's experiences were shaped by their intersecting location in poverty and as a member of a racial or ethnic minority. For these teenage girls, becoming sexually active often was not a question of whether or not to have sex, but how to navigate and make sense out of their sexual relationships. Moreover, teens lament the lack of informative discussion about relationships that might assist them in making choices about sex and help them make sense of the constant stream of conflicting messages about sexuality that they receive in their daily lives.

APPENDIX

Issues Coded for Analyses, Tables 4.1–4.3

Table 4.1

Gender Roles
Gender: Any discussion about traditional gender roles, expectations, or behavior.

Marriage & Family
Marriage: Any discussion about marriage or family.
Postmarital: Any discussion about sex after marriage.[a]

Relationships
Relationship: Any discussion about relationships or dating.

Commitment & Values
Values: Any discussion about values, morals, or ethics.
Commit: Any discussion about commitment (i.e., to yourself, friend, partner, parents).[b]

Table 4.1(Continued)

Divorce
Divorce: Any discussion about divorce.

Virginity
Female Virginity: Any discussion specifically about female virginity.
Male Virginity: Any discussion specifically about male virginity.
Virginity: Any general discussion about virginity; not gender specific.
Second: Any discussion about secondary virginity.[c]

Homosexuality
Homosexuality: Any discussion about homosexuality.

---

[a] Marriage and postmarriage are combined into one variable in Table 4.1, "Marriage & Family."

[b] Commitment and Values are combined into one variable in Table 4.1, "Commitment & Values."

[c] Female virginity, male virginity, virginity, and second are combined into one variable in Table 4.1, "Virginity."

Table 4.2

Psychological & Emotional Effects
Physical: Any discussion on the physical effects of sex/sexuality.
Emotional: Any discussion on the emotional effects of sex/sexuality.
Social: Any discussion on the social effects of sex/sexuality.
General: Any general discussion about sex/sexuality.
Premarital: Any discussion about premarital sex.[a]

Sexual Coercion
Rape: Any general discussion about rape or pressuring people into sex.
Victim: Any discussion about rape or pressuring person into sex, where victim is blamed for activity.[b]

Drugs & Alcohol
Drugs: Any discussion on drugs or alcohol.

Sexually Transmitted Infections
STIs: Any discussion about sexually transmitted infections/disease.

HIV/AIDS
HIV/AIDS: Any discussion about HIV or AIDS.

Out-of-Wedlock Pregnancy
Out-of-Wedlock Pregnancy: Any discussion about pregnancy outside of the context of marriage; premarital pregnancy.

Abortion
Abortion: Any discussion about abortion.

Adoption
Adoption: Any discussion on adoption.

---

[a] Physical, emotional, social, general, and premarital are combined into one variable in Table 4.2, "Psychological & Emotional Effects."

[b] Rape and victim are combined into one variable in Table 4.2, "Sexual Coercion."

Table 4.3

Biology
Biology: Any discussion on reproductive parts or anatomy.

Birth Control
Birth Control: Any discussion about birth control.

Parenting
Pregnancy: Any discussion of pregnancy after couple is married.
Parent: Any discussion about parenting or raising children.[a]

Self Esteem
Self Esteem: Any discussion about self-esteem, self-worth, or self-respect.

Decision Making
Decision Making: Any discussion about decision making or goal setting.
Media: Any discussion on media's influence on decision making.
Pressure: Any discussion about peer pressure or pressures teens face making decisions.[b]

Refusal Skills "Just Say No"
Refusal: Any discussion about refusal skills or ways to say "no" to sex.

Abstinence
Abstinence: Any discussion about abstinence.

---

[a] Pregnancy and parenting are combined in Table 4.3, "Parenting."

[b] Decision making, media, and pressure are combined in Table 4.3, "Decision Making."

NOTES

1. While SIECUS, among others, cites the curricula that we analyze among those that are most popular, they caution that attempts to quantify which curricula are most widely used have significant limitations. According to SIECUS, "It is difficult to know exactly how many schools and community-based programs across the country are using these curricula. Local school districts and communities are responsible for choosing what curricula they will use with their students and, even when programs are federally funded, there is little government oversight" (SIECUS n.d.). Although SIECUS has tracked many of the most popular abstinence-only curricula, they caution that their statistics relating to which curricula are used in which states are not completely accurate. For example, SIECUS was able to track the use of *Choosing the Best* in 17 states as of July 2006, but warned that "while we have found many of the locales that are using these curricula in no way have we found all of them" (SIECUS 2006). Thus, SIECUS states on its Web site: "It is likely, however, that these programs are used in federally, state, and privately funded programs in many other states and communities. Respect Inc.'s website, for example, boasts that their curriculum has been used in all 50 states and 23 foreign countries. Choosing the Best, Inc. suggests that since 1993, more than 700,000 students have participated in Choosing the Best programs in 2,500 school districts in 50 states" (SIECUS n.d.).

2. We also evaluated *Love and Life: A Christian Sexual Morality Guide for Teens* in order to compare this overtly Christian curriculum, not written for use in public schools, to *Sex*

Respect, which Mast authored specifically for public schools. We did not include this text in the analysis because Mast wrote *Love and Life* for church groups and parochial schools, and so employs explicitly religious language and lessons throughout the curriculum. *Love and Life*, then, differs from *Sex Respect* in the overt way it makes use of biblical teachings to promote abstinence; however, *Sex Respect* has some of the same kinds of lessons, secularized for a public school audience. Similar to *Sex Respect*, *Love and Life* describes gender and sexuality using a traditional notion of women and men as binary opposites, depicting a heterosexual and complementary construction of female and male. In comparing *Love and Life* to *Sex Respect* we found that they echo one another in their references to gender as a biological rather than socially constructed, or cultural, phenomenon. And (hetero)sexuality and gender are intimately connected, as men and women accomplish their natural places by joining together their complementary, though biologically opposite, emotional and physical selves.

3. We had three coders who initially coded a trial section of one curriculum. After norming the content of each category, the three coders were asked to code the same curriculum. We compared the results of each coder and the inter-coder reliability was very high.

4. Out of 35 issues, several were combined with similar variables in the analysis. For example, under the issue of *virginity*, four separate topics were included: female virginity, male virginity, non–gender specific virginity, and secondary virginity. Even though these were initially coded separately, they were aggregated into one issue for the analyses reflected in the tables.

5. All of the variables were entered into Statistical Package for the Social Sciences (SPSS). We conducted cross tabulations on the data to obtain the frequency of specific themes, broken down by the tone of the message. The quantitative results provide a general and systematic overview of the curricula. They also provide a more accurate account of how much attention is given to each issue and theme in the curricula.

6. These links are more clearly reflected in chapter 5, where we examine the interviews with teens.

7. Most of the content (95% to 97% of the total text for each curriculum) was accounted for through the content analysis.

8. African Americans and Latinos have a much higher rate of infection. For example, the Massachusetts Department of Public Health released a report in 2007 pointing out the "grossly disproportionate" cases of HIV/AIDS among African Americans and Latinos in 2005. These two subpopulations comprise over half of all people living with HIV/AIDS even though they only make up 6 percent of the state's population, respectively (12% total). The disparity is even starker when looking at gender: 83 percent of women infected with HIV/AIDS in the state are African American or Latina (Kaiser Family Foundation 2007).

9. Medical experts have long noted the existence of intersexual bodies, where individuals' physiology includes a mixture of male and female characteristics (Fausto-Sterling 2000). Beyond physiology, the concept of a fixed sex has also been challenged by the transgendered community. Transgender "more aptly refers to the transgressing of gender norms, or being freely gendered, or transcending gender altogether in order to become

more fully human" (Boswell 2000, 121). From both a biological and social perspective, ascribing sex in binary categories is limiting and not reflective of the range of sexual identities in society.

10. The Waxman Report cites this *Choosing the Best* passage as an example of an unscientific claim that mental health problems are "simple problems that can be fixed by abstaining from sexual activity" (U.S. House of Representatives 2004, 20).

11. The study specifically states that "We are not suggesting that premature sexual experience is a cause or leads to the other negative behaviors" (cited in U.S. House of Representatives 2004, 21).

12. Abstinence-only education may mention the advantages of "secondary virginity," sometimes offering a "personal commitment card" or "contract" where teens promise to stop having sex and become a "secondary virgin." But this entails their willingness to recognize that their past behavior has been "risky" and even "dysfunctional" and to promise to change their "lifestyles." Secondary virginity is not easily attained.

13. *The Waxman Report* criticizes the efforts of abstinence-only curricula to argue that condoms do not protect against STIs. As the report asserts,

> The curricula fail to note that rates of important sexually transmitted diseases, such as syphilis and gonorrhea, have been dropping over the past decade. Contrary to the assertions in the curricula, the most recent data show that consistent condom use is associated with: Reduced acquisition of syphilis by women and men; Reduced acquisition of gonorrhea by women; Reduced acquisition of urethral infection by men; Faster regression of HPV-related lesions on the cervix and penis, and faster clearance of genital HPV infection in women. (U.S. House of Representatives 2004, 11)

The *Waxman Report* goes on to fault abstinence-only curricula for "distort[ing] information about the risks of sexual activity" (U.S. House of Representatives 2004, 18), including the claims that STIs are a likely result of sex, and condoms provide little protection against common STIs.

BIBLIOGRAPHY

Acs, Gregory, and Sandi Nelson. 2003. "Changes in Family Structure and Child Well-Being: Evidence from the 2002 National Survey on America's Families." Urban Institute. Available at: http://www.urban.org/url.cfm?ID=311025.

Alexander, Jeffrey C., and Philip Smith. 1993. "The Discourse of American Civil Society: A New Proposal for Cultural Studies." *Theory and Society* 22: 151–207.

Asencio, Maysol. 2002. *Sex and Sexuality Among New York's Puerto Rican Youth.* Boulder: Lynne Rienner Publishers.

Babbie, Earl. 2005. *The Basics of Social Research,* 3rd ed. Belmont, CA: Wadsworth.

Boswell, Holly. 2000. "The Transgender Paradigm Shift Toward Free Expression." In *The Social Construction of Difference and Inequality: Race, Class, Gender, and Sexuality,* ed. Tracy E. Ore, 120–24. Mountain View, CA: Mayfield.

Burlingame, Phyllida. 1997. "Sex, Lies, and Politics: Abstinence-Only Curricula in California Public Schools." Oakland, CA: Applied Research Center.

Cain, Daphne S., and Terri Combs-Orme. 2005 "Family Structure Effects on Parenting Stress and Practices in the African American Family." *Journal of Sociology and Social Welfare* 32 (June 2): 19–40.

Centers for Disease Control and Prevention. 2004. "Youth Risk Behavior Surveillance—United States, 2003." *MMWR* 53(SS-02)1–96. Available at: http://www.cdc.gov/mmwr/PDF/SS/SS5302.pdf.

Cook, Bruce. 2003a. *Choosing the Best Life: An Abstinence Focused Curriculum, Leader Guide,* 2nd ed. Atlanta: Choosing the Best.

Cook, Bruce. 2003b. *Choosing the Best Life: An Abstinence Focused Curriculum,* Video, 2nd ed. Atlanta: Choosing The Best.

Core-Gebhart, Pennie, Susan J. Hart, and Michael Young. 1994. *Sex Can Wait: An Abstinence-Based Sexuality Curriculum for High School.* Santa Cruz, CA: ETR Associates.

Dailard, Cynthia. 2006. "Legislating Against Arousal: The Growing Divide Between Federal Policy and Teenage Sexual Behavior." *Guttmacher Policy Review* 9 (3 Summer): 1–4.

Discovery Health. 2002. "Estrogen and Testosterone Hormones." *Sinclair Intimacy Institute.* Available at: http://www.health.discovery.com/centers/sex/sexpedia/hormone_print.html.

Donovan, Patricia. 1998. "School-Based Sexuality Education: The Issues and Challenges." *Family Planning Perspectives* 30 (4): 188–93.

Edwards, S. 1997. "Abortion Study Finds No Long-Term Ill Effects on Emotional Well-Being." *Family Planning Perspectives* 29 (4): 193–94.

Fausto-Sterling, Anne. 2000. "The Five Sexes: Why Male and Female are Not Enough." In *The Social Construction of Difference and Inequality: Race, Class, Gender, and Sexuality,* 2nd ed., ed. Tracy E. Ore, 115–19. Boston: McGraw-Hill.

Fine, Michelle. 1992. *Disruptive Voices: The Possibilities of Feminist Research.* Ann Arbor: The University of Michigan Press.

Frankenberg, Ruth. 1993. *White Women: Race Matters: The Social Construction of Whiteness.* Minneapolis: University of Minnesota Press.

Good News and Crossway. n.d. "About Us." Available at: http://www.gnpcb.org/home/about.

Jacobs, Ronald N. 1996. "Civil Society and Crisis: Culture, Discourse, and the Rodney King Beating." *The American Journal of Sociology* 101 (5): 1238–72.

Kaiser Family Foundation. 2003. "National Survey of Adolescents and Young Adults: Sexual Health Knowledge, Attitudes and Experiences." Available at: http://www.kff.org/youthhivstds/3218-index.cfm.

Kaiser Family Foundation. 2005. "U.S. Teen Sexual Activity" (January). Available at: http://www.kff.org/youthhivstds/3040-02.cfm.

Kaiser Family Foundation. 2007. "Minorities Make up Large Proportion of HIV/AIDS Cases in Massachusetts, Report Says." Daily Reports (December 7). Available at: http://www.kaisernetwork.org/daily_reports.

Kempner, Martha E. 2001. *Toward a Sexually Healthy America: Abstinence-Only-Until-Marriage Programs that Try to Keep Our Youth "Scared Chaste."* New York: Sexuality Information and Education Council of the United States.

Kimmel, Michael. 2000. *The Gendered Society*. New York: Oxford University Press.

Kirby, Douglas. 2001. "Understanding What Works and What Doesn't in Reducing Adolescent Sexual Risk-Taking." *Family Planning Perspectives*. 33 (6): 276–81.

Landry, David, Lisa Kaeser, and Cory L. Richards. 1999. "Abstinence Promotion and the Provision of Information about Contraception in Public School District Sexuality Education Policies." *Family Planning Perspectives* 31 (6): 280–86.

Landry, David J., and Jacqueline Darroch Forrest. 1995. "How Old Are U.S. Fathers?" *Family Planning Perspectives* 27: 159–61, 165.

LifeWay Student Ministry. 2001. "True Love Waits." Available at: http://www.lifeway.com/tlw.

Mason, Carol. 2002. *Killing for Life: The Apocalyptic Narrative of Pro-Life Politics*. Ithaca: Cornell University Press.

Mast, Coleen Kelly. 2001a. *Sex Respect: The Option of True Sexual Freedom*, Teacher's Manual. Sex Respect. Bradley, IL: Respect Incorporated.

Mast, Coleen Kelly. 2001b. *Sex Respect: The Option of True Sexual Freedom*, Student Workbook. Sex Respect. Bradley, IL: Respect Incorporated.

Mast, Coleen Kelly. 2001c. *Sex Respect: The Option of True Sexual Freedom*, Parent Guide. Sex Respect. Bradley, IL: Respect Incorporated.

Morgan, Kathryn Pauly. 1996. "The Moral Politics of Sex Education." In *The Gender Question in Education: Theory, Pedagogy, and Politics*, ed. Ann Diller and Barbara Houston, 170–78. Boulder: Westview Press.

Morrison, Toni. 1993. *Playing in the Dark: Whiteness and the Literary Imagination*. New York: Vintage Books.

Olenick, I. 2000. "Women Exposed to Childhood Abuse Have Elevated Odds of Unintended First Pregnancy as Adults." *Family Planning Perspectives* 32 (1).

Rabasca, Lisa. 1999. "Not Enough Evidence to Support 'Abstinence-Only.'" *APA Monitor Online* 30 (11).

Reardon, David C. 1987. *Aborted Women: Silent No More*. Westchester, IL: Crossway Books.

SARP Center. n.d. "Myths and Facts about Sexual Assault." San Luis Obispo, CA: Sexual Assault Recovery and Prevention Center.

Schulhofer, Stephen. 1998. *Unwanted Sex: The Culture of Intimidation and the Failure of Law*. Cambridge, MA: Harvard University Press.

SIECUS. n.d. "SIECUS Reviews Fear-Based, Abstinence-Only-Until-Marriage Curricula." Available at: http://www.siecus.org/reviews.html.

SIECUS. 2006. "SIECUS State Profiles: A Portrait of Sexuality Education and Abstinence-Only-Until-Marriage Programs in the States." Available at http://www.siecus.org/policy/states.

Stoltenberg, John. 2003. "How Men Have (A) Sex." In *Reconstructing Gender: A Multicultural Anthology*, 3rd ed., ed. Estelle Disch, 253–62. Boston: McGraw-Hill.

Teen Aid. 1998. *Sexuality, Commitment & Family*. Spokane, WA: Teen Aid, Inc.

Teen-Aid Inc. n.d. "Board of Directors." Available at: http://www.teen-aid.org/About_Teen-Aid/Board_of_Directors.htm.

Tjaden, Patricia, and Nancy Thoemmes. 2000. "Full Report of the Prevalence, Incidence, and Consequences of Violence Against Women." *Findings from the National Vio-*

lence Against Women Survey. Washington, D.C.: National Institute of Justice. Report NCJ183781.

Trudell, Bonnie Nelson. 1993. *Doing Sex Education: Gender Politics and Schooling*. New York: Routledge Press.

University of Arkansas. n.d. "Sex Can Wait." Available at: http://www.uark.edu/depts/hepoinfo.

U.S. Census Bureau. 2005. "Number, Timing, and Duration of Marriages and Divorces: 2001." *Household Economic Studies* (February). Available at: http://www.census.gov/prod/2005pubs/p70-97.pdf.

U.S. House of Representatives. 2004. "The Content of Federally Funded Abstinence-Only Education Programs." Committee on Government Reform-Minority Staff. Prepared for Rep. Henry A. Waxman.

Whitaker, Daniel J., Kim S. Miller, and Leslie F. Clark. 2000. "Reconceptualizing Adolescent Sexual Behavior: Beyond Did They or Didn't They?" *Family Planning Perspectives*. 32 (3): 111–17.

Wolf, Naomi. 1997. *Promiscuities: The Secret Struggle for Womanhood*. New York: Random House.

CASES CITED

Personal Responsibility and Work Opportunity Reconciliation Act (PRWORA) of 1996, Pub. L. no. 104-193, 110 Stat. 2105 (1996).

5

In Their Own Words: Sexuality, Knowledge, and Power

Through interviews with 32 young women, we explore how abstinence-only lessons fit into teens' sexual experiences, perceptions, and understandings of their sexualities. Four primary topics surfaced throughout the interviews—exposure to sex education from school and other sources, the gendered experience of sexual relationships, the cultural focus on female virginity, and the lack of intentionality in terms of teens' decisions to become parents. All of these general topics are interrelated and, more importantly, help explain why crafting policy around teen sexuality is so difficult and so contentious.

Teen sexuality, as described by young women themselves, is a convoluted and multilayered issue; the idea that teens should remain abstinent until marriage does not begin to connect with many of these young women's lived experiences. Rather than focusing on abstinence, most teens discussed their struggles to define themselves in a culture fraught with images of women as sexual objects, commented on gender differences in the experience and interpretation of teen sexuality, and bemoaned the lack of detailed and meaningful information about sex and sexuality available to assist them in understanding themselves and their relationships.

TERESA'S STORY

Teresa, an eleventh grader, responds to interview questions with mostly one- or two-line answers, until a question about why teens have sex unleashes a torrent of reasons that Teresa perceives as specific to young women:

> Just to try to get away from things, or there are some teens that think that it's better to be out with your boyfriend and do things with them if you have no attention from your family. And they think, "oh my God, he's the only one that really knows what's going on in my life, and if I make him feel good, then I will be able to have someone" . . . There's some people that do give up and just say "yeah, okay, we'll do it." Just like in my case, that was my case. Some people that I know they just do it because maybe they have nothing else or they just want to try it. And there are people that don't do it because they think it's disrespectful for their family.

At 17, Teresa has had one sexual partner. A year ago, she ended an eight-month relationship that started primarily as a sexual relationship, though the young man later became Teresa's boyfriend. She describes how the relationship began:

> We mostly would talk on the phone and he would tell me, "oh come on," just because he had already done it and I was still a virgin. So you know it was kind of pressure on me now that we were talking, and he just wanted me to do it. I was just like, "no, I'm gonna wait, I'm gonna wait," and then that's what I always said because my friends always said we're all going to wait. . . . So then he started pressuring me and he would call me every day and he told me, "come on, come on," and that was the main subject.

Eventually, Teresa succumbed to the pressure and had sex with her boyfriend, though she felt that she had been pushed unwillingly into the relationship by him.

During the six months that they engaged in sex, Teresa and her boyfriend never used birth control. Teresa states that she planned to begin taking the pill, but before she could start, she broke up with her boyfriend. She now asserts that she does not plan to have another sexual relationship for the foreseeable future, partly because she fears pregnancy: "People always think, 'oh it can't be me, it can't be me'—that they'll get pregnant. People just don't think it can be you . . . the way I think now it could happen to me."

When she is older, Teresa maintains, she will be ready to have sex again: "If something were to happen, then I could be stable enough to recognize my mistake, and too if I were to have a baby, then I'd rather be positively sure that

I could take care of it, because if I can't, I still have to take care of it no matter what. It's my responsibility and I should be able to take care of it." If she did become pregnant unintentionally, Teresa does not see abortion as an option, which she defines as "killing this innocent little baby that is just coming to have his own life." Either giving up the baby for adoption or getting married and raising the baby would be preferable to Teresa, though she acknowledges that either of those choices would be difficult.

Teresa's perspectives and experiences reflect her individual circumstances, but at the same time mirror the experiences of many teen women in this study. Teresa's first sexual encounter happened because of verbal pressure from her boyfriend, which was an oft-heard occurrence in the interviews. In addition to her sense that she was not in control of her decision whether or not to have sex, Teresa never used birth control while sexually active. When she became sexually active at age 15, Teresa's parents had not taught her anything about sex, and she could not recall what, if anything, she had been taught in school regarding sex education. In the face of her lack of knowledge and control over her sexuality, Teresa, like many teens, embraces the language of personal responsibility with regard to pregnancy and parenting. Finally, her anti-abortion beliefs were also echoed by most of the young women we interviewed and are tied up with her rhetoric of personal responsibility regarding teen sexuality.

METHODOLOGY

From April 2001 to February 2002, we conducted open-ended interviews with 32 teenage women to assess their experiences with and interpretations of abstinence education, in the context of their perceptions and analyses of their own sexual experiences and sexualities. Interview questions asked about a teen's family background; her past and present sexual activity, including access to birth control; exposure to sex education, and specifically to an abstinence message; and perceptions about gender, sexual activity, and virginity. The teen women we interviewed included those who were sexually active, never sexually active, pregnant, and parenting.

Interviews were conducted with female teens from central, northern, and southern California. The young women interviewed came from several agencies in California that work with low-income or "at-risk" teens, including an alternative high school, AmeriCorp, and the Economic Opportunity Commission's Teenage Academic Parenting Program in San Luis Obispo county. Other teens came from a church youth group and from a group home for teens in foster care. These agencies provided us with access to teenagers but did not mandate that teens participate in the interviews. Instead, we spoke to groups of teens about our project, speaking for a few minutes to an hour, depending on the group, and asking for volunteers to be interviewed.[1] Teens who voluntarily agreed to participate in our interviews were guaranteed both confidentiality and anonymity.[2]

Table 5.1 contains several general descriptive statistics for the respondents. The 32 teen participants were all between the ages of 14 and 19 with an average age of 17 years old. Seventeen of our respondents were white, eight Latina, and seven biracial, defined by each teen as some combination of African American, Native American, Latina, and white. Two young women's parents were middle class; the majority came from low-income families, which is reflected in the number of families who received welfare assistance. At the time of the interview, 12 of the teens' families received some type of assistance, for example cash aid, food stamps, WIC, and Medicaid. An additional 8 teens indicated that their families had received assistance in the past.

We focus on female adolescents, rather than both males and females, because so many of abstinence-only curricula's lessons target young women, even when the lessons are cloaked in gender neutral language. Partly, abstinence-only's orientation toward young women can be traced to concerns over a so-called crisis of teen pregnancy that the curricula attempt to address. The definition of and response to this crisis have long converged on theories about the actions and decisions of young women much more than men.[3] Likewise, concerns over teen sexualization and teen promiscuity also concentrate on young women. We were interested, then, in interviewing young women who spanned the spectrum of sexual experience. Among the teenagers we interviewed, six teens were virgins, nine teens had had one sexual partner, six teens had two partners, and six teens had between three and five partners. Five teens had more than 10 partners; of this group, four had been sexually assaulted early in their adolescence or childhood. The majority of teens involved in a relationship at the time of the interview were in monogamous relationships.

Our interviews with young women first attempted to get teens' assessments of their sex education classes and the extent to which abstinence-only instruction predominated, but teens could not provide detailed, specific information about the lessons they had learned in school. Abstinence-only curricula—indeed sex education classes more generally—were but one source among many that presented to teens various attitudes, beliefs, and theories about sexuality. For teens to isolate the lessons they learned about abstinence from their high schools' curricula was nearly impossible, as sex education instruction interacted with and built upon lessons learned about sexuality from their families and peers and from U.S. culture, including such sources as television, movies, books, advertising, and religion. In fact, the young women we interviewed provided only brief descriptions of what they had learned in sex education classes; were not likely to know whether they had abstinence-only, abstinence-based, or comprehensive sexuality education; and had difficulty defining abstinence.

Table 5.1
General Information about Respondents

Variables	Number of Respondents	Percent
All Teens (N = 32)		
Race		
White	17	53%
Latina	8	25%
Bi-racial	7	22%
Welfare Use		
Current	12	38%
Past	8	25%
Never	12	38%
Sexual Status		
Virgin	6	19%
1 Partner	9	28%
2 Partners	6	19%
3–5 Partners	6	19%
10+ Partners	5	16%
Sources of Sex Education		
Grade and Middle School	25	78%
High School	15	47%
Parents	5	16%
Clinics	6	19%
*Other Sources	24	75%
Sexually Active Teens (N = 26)		
Access to Contraception		
Difficulty Obtaining	15	56%
Cost Prohibitive	9	35%
Experience with Sexual Aggression		
Pressured into Sex	8	31%
Sexual Assault	12	46%
Sexual Initiation by		
Force or Pressure	16	62%
Parenting and Pregnant Teens (N = 15)		
Pregnancy Intentions		
Unintentional	12	80%
Did Not Care	3	20%
Intentional	0	0
Support from Father of Child		
Emotional and Financial	6	40%
Financial Only	1	7%
Emotional Only	2	13%

Table 5.1 (*Continued*)

Variables	Number of Respondents	Percent
Sporadic Support	4	27%
No Support	2	13%
Abortion Beliefs		
Don't Believe in Abortion	10	67%
Considered It an Option	4	26%
Considered Adoption	5	33%

* Other Sources primarily references' friends, but may also include sibling, partner, or media.
Percents may not total to 100 due to rounding.

Because teens were so vague about their sex education, we do not argue for direct connections between what young women learn in sex education classes and how they think about and experience their sexuality. Rather, the picture is far more complex, with teen women learning about sexuality through multiple sources including sex education classes, parents, peers, and the media. Instruction from these numerous sources interacts with social constructions and cultural norms regarding gender, sexuality, and adolescence.

LIMITATIONS

In comparison to the U.S. teen population, the stories of the young women we interviewed both show unique patterns and experiences and demonstrate general truths about teen girls' sexuality. The teens in this study became sexually active earlier, are more likely to be teen parents, disproportionately experienced sexual abuse, and are more likely to be women of color as compared to the overall population of teen women. Specifically, while the median age at first premarital sex in the United States is closer to 17 (Finer 2007), all but two of the sexually active teens we interviewed were sexually active by the age of 15. While the teen pregnancy and birth rates have been dropping since the early 1990s—to a birthrate of 41.6 per 1,000 teens aged 15–19 in 2003 (Guttmacher Institute 2006b)—we purposely sought teen parents to interview, eventually including 14 teen parents in our sample. And though most studies report between 10 and 30 percent of high school–age teens have been raped, 12 of 26 sexually active teen girls we interviewed (46%) had experienced nonconsensual sex at some point in their lives.[4] Finally, 17 (53%) of the teens we interviewed were white, though whites make up 69 percent of the U.S. population.

These differences, as compared to the general population, serve a number of purposes. First, the teens we interviewed reflect the population whose behavior welfare reform advocates seek to influence. Thus, in choosing sites to find teens to interview, our concern was not to locate a random sample of teen women; rather, we wished to focus attention on young, poor, women of color, those most clearly considered to be the key recipients of an abstinence policy that is nested within welfare policy. These young women are likely to have their sexualities socially constructed as deviant and in need of outside control, and they also are more likely to have poor access to birth control and other reproductive health needs as compared to middle- and higher-income teens (Fields 2005; Kaplan 1997; Roberts 1999).[5] Additionally, low-income teens who are black and Latina are perceived to be at the heart of the "crisis" of teen pregnancy and unmarried pregnancy more generally (Fields 2005; Kaplan 1997; Roberts 1999).

While the construction of their sexualities as deviant—impure or "at risk"—may be particularly potent for the teens we interviewed, we argue that their stories portray the obstacles that many teen girls face in adolescence. And while the teens we interviewed may experience rather intense surveillance of their sexualities, the interviews highlight the ways that many young women face scrutiny with regard to their sexualities. Though we overrepresent teens that are sexually active early, are parents, and have been raped, their numbers in the sample serve to crystallize some of the issues addressed in abstinence-only curricula. In this way, the stories of teens in this study serve to bring specific concerns into focus while exploring teen experience more generally.

Though we set out to overrepresent some aspects of teen experience and some portions of the population, we did not do so purposefully with regard to sexual orientation. Specifically, none of the teens we interviewed defined themselves as other than heterosexual. In fact, although we asked open-ended questions intended to include discussion of heterosexual, lesbian, and bisexual sexual activity, the teens revealed only heterosexual activity in their interviews. On one hand, this is not a surprising finding given the heterosexism and homophobia in U.S. culture. Abstinence-only curricula all but ignore gay, lesbian, and bisexual youth and constantly emphasize the importance of heterosexual marriage. The curricula provide a particularly egregious example of heterosexism because organizations may receive public funding to support writing and publicizing the curricula, and the lessons are taught to youth in a publicly funded setting (see Tolman 2002). Because of the state's role in defining and funding abstinence-only curricula, the lessons in abstinence-only programs underscore the state's role in pressing on teens the notion that heterosexuality is the expected standard and should structure sexual behavior and sexual object choice. Given the wide-ranging cultural and "official" silence about lesbian experience, then, we were not surprised by teens' reticence in discussing their own nonheterosexual experiences.

On the other hand, the interviews are characterized by wide-ranging and extremely personal discussions of teen sexualities and sexual experiences. Most of the young women in this study were quite candid and unguarded in describing their experiences and did not appear to edit or regulate their opinions on parenting, sex, abortion, and the like. As Ken Plummer notes in *Telling Sexual Stories*, such candid retellings of sexual experiences have become central to U.S. culture: "Sex, then, has become the Big Story. . . . a grand message keeps being shouted: *tell about your sex*" (1995, 4). Given the cultural context, then, and in light of teens' frankness about other aspects of their sexual lives, we would have expected more teens to relate lesbian or bisexual experiences.[6] Finally, it is possible, given the relatively small number of teens we interviewed, that they all were heterosexual.

In the interviews, young women shared their beliefs and experiences about sexual experimentation; virginity; sexual assault, including rape and incest; abortion; birth control; pregnancy; and parenting. We analyze these rich and multi-layered interview responses, showing how teen women's attitudes and choices about sexual activity relate to—and at times collide with—lessons about sexuality from various sources.

SEX EDUCATION: INSIDE AND OUTSIDE OF THE CLASSROOM

School sex education courses have been the leading source of sexual information for teens. Twenty-five teens (78%) received sex education in either grade school or junior high.[7] In terms of what teens remembered learning from the grade school and junior high school classes, their responses were very similar. Most teens described learning a very clinical explanation of physiology that focused on the function and location of their reproductive organs. For example, when asked what she had learned, Barbara responded "I remember a little bit from fifth grade and eighth grade. All I know was it wasn't enough. At the time I felt like it should have been more cause they only like showed you the body. . . . They never really showed why sex happens or anything like that." Similarly, Tracy describes her sex education class:

> I remember in fourth grade . . . it was just like telling you about your body and how it works and your period . . . and they had the guys separated from the girls so we didn't learn about the guys. We just learned about the girls. . . . And then when I got into junior high that's when they started talking more about sexual intercourse. But they didn't really talk about sexual intercourse itself, like being with another person . . . there was really

no, um, not descriptive maybe is the word I'm looking for. It wasn't as detailed into the thing, it was just more of a lecture.

Both Barbara and Tracy, 18 and 17 years old at the time of the interviews, lament the shallowness of the information taught in their sex education classes. Importantly, the teens refer to junior high courses as lacking context that would help them discern and consider "why sex happens" and to think "about sexual intercourse itself" rather than physiology and the mechanics of sex. In talking about what they mean by "why sex happens," the teens referred to the intersections between sexual experimentation and the social construction of female sexuality, including pressure to have or not have sex, the emotional connections associated with sex, and the cultural (and particularly peer) responses to young women's sexual activity. Their peers tended to react to young women's sexual activity primarily by addressing whether or not they had come to be perceived as "sluts," though some young women described guarded approbation from their close friends.

Unfortunately, for many of the teens, focusing on reproductive body parts to the exclusion of other kinds of information in junior high school is problematic given that 17 (65%) of the 26 sexually active young women interviewed had sexual intercourse before entering high school. Some teens stated that they would have liked to receive more direct and detailed information on birth control methods, while others, like Barbara and Tracy, would have appreciated assistance in navigating the emotions, pressures, and complexities of adolescent sexuality.

Once in high school, a smaller portion of teens were exposed to any form of sex education. Although the majority of the women interviewed received some type of education in elementary and junior high school, only 15 (47%) of them received sex education in high school. Mirroring their grade school experiences, teens who received sex education recount learning clinical explanations of sexually transmitted infections (STIs) and for some, relatively brief discussions of contraception. For many, a primary focus of their sex education was the discussion of STIs, including STI names and symptoms, infection rates, and the threat they posed to nonmarried, sexually active teens and adults.

As a result of sex education classes, teens were fairly sophisticated about STIs; most could recount detailed lists and descriptions of various infections. In fact, teens were unable to explain any other topic from their high school sex education curricula in any detail at all, with the exception of STIs. Recalling the general topics covered in her high school sex education course, Janice asserted, "Oh like how you can get STDs and diseases . . . you can get crabs . . . I remember the STDs like gonorrhea, herpes and just knowing that I didn't want to get any of those especially if you hear that someone got something like that at school, I mean you never hear the end of it." Along with getting pregnant, Janice indicated that the threat of getting an STI—and the shame involved with other students knowing about it—was the "number two" reason she had chosen to remain a virgin.

Outside of school, 24 teenagers (75%) were receiving sex education information from other sources—primarily from parents, friends, siblings, churches, and clinics. The accuracy of the information being passed along varied greatly, particularly from friends. Amanda describes how she has learned about sex:

> It's just something that you see in your everyday life with movies and stuff like that and then. . . . and like maybe you talk with your friends about it. . . . you mess around, you say things and you hear new things. And you're like, "what's that?" Like you ask your friends, "You know what that is" or something. I remember that in junior high. People would say something and I'd like laugh with them on a joke but I didn't really know what it was.

Though information from friends was not always clearly explained or accurate, teens indicated that this was the most uninhibited form of information exchange about sex.

Although they comprised a small number of the respondents (16%), the five teens that learned or discussed sex with their parents fared better in terms of the accuracy and validity of the information they received, which is a similar finding to other studies (Blake et al. 2001). Claudia explained the value of her interactions with her mother: "I was well educated about sex and birth control by my mom before I went into it [junior high school]." However, information from parents was much more limited than information from peers in terms of its availability and the level of reticence that accompanied parents' attempts to educate their children about sexual activity (see Rose 2005). Likewise, only six teens (19%) were exposed to information from a clinic. When teens received information from clinics, just as with parental information, their knowledge was more medically accurate.

For teens like Nancy, who were relying on their schools for sexuality education, the class felt gendered. Although not overtly designed to be a class for girls only, the content and the way the teacher explained the information made it clear to Nancy that it was girls' sexuality that was on display, suspect, and in need of explanation:

> Mostly the girls are the ones that are paying attention 'cause the girls pretty much have . . . questions to ask but you're afraid to ask them 'cause you're embarrassed. . . . Interviewer: And what did they teach the boys? Nancy: They didn't really teach them [the boys] anything. They were just telling girls if you don't want to do it—and if like you feel that you want to do it, they tell them about birth control—but if you didn't want to do it and you were just afraid of the guy or anything to just say no. If he got angry, just say

no stronger and to walk away and stuff like that. And the guys were in the room, but they didn't really teach the guys anything.

Gendered assumptions and the social constructions of femininity and masculinity underlie much of what Nancy's sex education class taught her and the other students, but the social construction of gender was not analyzed within the class. The messages Nancy learned coincide with many aspects of abstinence-only sex education that were addressed in the previous chapter. First is the idea that sex education is for girls, not boys, because it is girls who are responsible for birth control, both getting and using it. Relatedly, girls make the decision about whether or not to have sex. The fact that boys might not want to have sex, and might similarly be making such decisions, never surfaced because of the social construction of male sexuality that interprets men as always ready for and interested in sex. Finally, the course taught both young women and men that girls are responsible for negotiating and stopping sexual assault. The lesson that could have been focused on young men and their responsibility to not pressure or force young women to have sex was simply absent from Nancy's curriculum.

In addition to complaining about the lack of valid, well-explained information, many teens expressed difficulty in obtaining contraception. Of the 18 sexually active teens who answered the question, slightly more than half (56%) claimed that they had a difficult time gaining access to birth control, while 6 (35%) stated that the cost of birth control was problematic. Concurring with other studies (Frost and Oslak 1999; McFarlane and Meier 2001), teens in this study often expressed knowledge of where to receive birth control, but they experienced barriers to access, from lack of parental support in obtaining contraceptives to difficulty persuading boyfriends to wear condoms. Cara, for example, stole condoms from the store because she was sexually active, but her parents would not help her get birth control. For Kim, a confluence of parental resistance and living in a semirural area (where attaining birth control is challenging without transportation) kept her from protecting herself:

I was trying to tell my Mom, "I'm having sex with this guy, and I want to be on birth control" and she kept on telling me "You don't need to be sexually active. You don't need to be on birth control. You don't need to have sex." And you know, I told her and she didn't want to believe it. But I kept on telling her, "Mom, I'm not a virgin. I have not been a virgin ever since I was fourteen years old." And my mom didn't like, comprehend, or you know, or she just like blew it off and said whatever you know, "I don't want to hear it cause I know it's not true." And then when I moved here . . . I told my grandma I'd been, you know, I'm with this guy, I've been with him for three months, you know. I slept with him and I need to be on birth control. Well my grandma kept on saying "Okay, I'll take you to the doctor's. I'll get you birth control, blah, blah, blah."

Kim's grandmother never followed through, and because Kim lives "in the country," some distance from the nearest clinic, she was unable to transport herself. Before she finally found someone in her family to assist her to get contraceptives, Kim became pregnant. Though she did not want to have a baby, having begged her parents to assist her in obtaining contraceptives, Kim resolved to carry her pregnancy to term because she did not "believe in" abortion or adoption. However, early in her pregnancy, Kim miscarried.

Diane describes a combination of parental refusal to teach her about sex or assist her in acquiring birth control, and inconsistent use of birth control, that led to her pregnancy at age 15:

I was a teenage mother and I wasn't planning on getting pregnant. At that age I was just—hormones were high and I was sexually active. . . . You can teach them about it [birth control and teen pregnancy], but they're still going to have sex. And there's that still that one percent, or that three percent, that they can get pregnant . . . but half the girls here aren't using birth control at all. . . . When I was fifteen, no one really taught me anything [about sex]. And it was hard to get condoms and things like that. Now that I'm eighteen years old, and I have a child, everyone's like "Oh, a kid." And I'm like "I wish you would have done that when I was fifteen." But a lot of parents don't—my Mom was like that—don't want their child to know anything about it, don't teach them.

According to Diane, there are multiple complex issues at play as sex education intersects with various aspects of teen sexuality. She refers to problems with access to birth control, birth control failure, inconsistent use of contraceptives, and lack of sexual knowledge and education. Further explaining Diane's contention that teens do not use contraceptives reliably even when they have access to them, Claudia states: "Girls are afraid to say 'Hey, you need to put a condom on before we have sex.' I think they're just too shy or whatever." If girls are afraid to assert themselves, then lack of female power in a relationship can affect contraceptive use. And if girls are too shy to assert themselves, then we see the social construction of femininity used by abstinence-only education at play, which defines *normal* girls as lacking sexual desire or experience. This makes it unlikely that a girl would want to risk appearing too sexually knowledgeable by demanding condom use.

In the context of Kim's, Diane's, and other teens' experiences, sex education seems deficient in several areas. First, earlier education—in grade school and junior high—primarily focused on physiology. Once in high school, classes portrayed sexuality in simplistic terms of the risks of sexually transmitted diseases and contained limited discussions of effective contraception use. When education about birth control was taught in abstinence-based or comprehensive sexuality education, it often occurred after teens had become sexually active. And abstinence-only education precluded discussion of birth control outright. Other than school, the majority of teens used their peers as an informational source. Additionally, teens experienced numerous barriers to obtaining and using contraception reliably.

TEENS' CONFUSION ABOUT ABSTINENCE

In probing young women about their sex education courses, we also asked them to talk about abstinence. Unlike their level of recall about STIs, teens did not use one clear definition to explain the meaning of abstinence. Some described abstinence as "not having sex," meaning sexual intercourse, but indicated that other sexual activity, such as oral sex, was acceptable. A few indicated that all sexual activity, even "deep kissing," was off limits. A number of young women maintained that abstinence was having sex but using birth control, while other teens could not define it at all (see Horan, Phillips, and Hagan 1998; Remez 2000).

Several young women seemed to think that they could, in a sense, define abstinence for themselves. Janice, for example, proudly showed off a ring she wears to symbolize her choice to remain abstinent, to wait, but when pressed, she revealed the ways she renegotiates the meaning of abstinence to fit her circumstances:

> It means not having sex, not doing anything, like not even taking off clothes, not even going that far to see the other person's body at all. But you know abstinence for many people is just not going . . . I mean clothes are off, you've done everything else except that last thing. . . . Truthfully I can't really say that I'm abstinent. I know it means something completely different to me and to them.

Janice is, in part, pointing to the difference between a clinical definition of abstinence that requires that one abstain from sexual intercourse, and a definition of abstinence promulgated by Christian conservatives that extends to abstinence from most kinds of sexual activity unless married. For Janice, as for many teens, a teen could be considered *abstinent* even if she had engaged in oral sex or other sexual activity. The Christian conservative definition, however, suggests that even some kissing is off limits; thus, one cannot be considered abstinent if one has engaged in practically any sexual activity at all. Due to the Christian Right's influence on abstinence-only education, most abstinence-only curricula use the extensive definition of abstinence.

Teens' participation in the debate over how to define abstinence suggests that the young women we interviewed usually did not remember the most transparent or specific lessons from sex education, and rarely did they memorize terms and definitions, with the exception of STIs. They did, however, absorb the underlying lessons about sex and sexuality that reflect traditional cultural norms. In particular, teens in our study repeatedly emphasized that sex and virginity are differently experienced and mean something different for boys and girls. Abstinence-only sex education teaches them that sexually active girls are suspect, in particular that they have bad reputations and no one wants a serious relationship with them. For the group of young women in this study, most of whom were sexually active, these "lessons" placed them in an uncomfortable position: Sexually active teens are used as an example by some abstinence-only curricula to illustrate the immorality of teen sexual culture and marked as likely to "pollute" other teens.

Abstinence-only education's failure to address the complex issues of teenage sexuality is reflected in teens' perceptions of it. Many of the teen women questioned the efficacy of abstinence-only curricula because it overlooks male sexuality while focusing on female sexuality, ignores or demeans sexually active teens, and often is perceived as adults telling teens what to do with their lives. While a few teens (both sexually and nonsexually active) believed teaching abstinence was a good idea, most expressed reservations, believing abstinence education is lost on young people, especially young boys because sex tends to increase their status with their peers. "Guys losing their virginity is a good thing, a big step for them, they can tell everybody" (Interview with Janice 2002).

Among those teenagers who were no longer virgins, they disregarded abstinence education because they believed it no longer applied to them. "I don't think they pay attention to it [abstinence education] . . . High school students, they don't care, they already experienced it [sex] . . . I didn't pay attention, I didn't care. It was more like I already did it, oh well no big deal" (Interview with Samantha 2001). Similarly, Nicole believes "they're gonna do what they want to do . . . in general they don't really care about it." Consequently, abstinence education does little to change the course of already sexually active teens, and further, does not aid sexually active teens in negotiating their current or future relationships.

Abstinence education can, however, support those students who have already decided to remain abstinent. When asked about the efficacy of abstinence education, Heather responded, "I already was on that track . . . but I don't think it's really effective 'cause it's a teacher teaching it and it's them saying don't have sex. It's kind of like, well she's an adult . . . I don't know if it would be effective on me if I did not believe in that before."

GENDER DIFFERENCES IN TEENAGE SEXUALITY

Though the interviews addressed a broad range of topics, one of the most prominent topics centered on gender differences in the experience and interpretation of teen sexuality. In the initial 22 interviews, these issues were introduced by teens themselves and not prompted by an interview question. When we realized that this subject triggered some of the most interested and sustained responses from the teens, we added a question to later interviews asking if differences existed between young women's and men's views of and experiences with sex. The young women repeatedly affirmed that culturally, teen sexual activity is interpreted differently for males and females, and young women and men diverge in their experiences of sex and sexual relationships.

Throughout the interviews, most young women repeatedly explained that having sex won young men accolades from their male peers, bolstered their egos, and left them sexually gratified. "It's totally different for boys. If they have sex they see it as they scored. It's big points for them" (Interview with Janice 2002). Likewise, Erica asserts, "[Guys] like to be cool with their friends and to say they lost their virginity and their friends didn't." According to these young women, for males, having sex provided a way to gain sway with friends and to boost one's reputation.

For sexually active young women, however, a very different picture emerged. Damita, a virgin, remarks:

> Guys want to have sex, and the more girls they get, I think it's better for the guys. But sometimes if the girl has sex, they're considered a ho. . . . Like with guys, when they do it they think that's cool you know but if a girl was to be like "oh yeah, I had sex with all these guys," then it would be like "eh." But if guys talk "I had sex with all these girls," it'd be like "yeah, good job."

Similarly, Samantha states "when a guy does it he gets props for it, he gets a handshake, 'oh yeah,' whatever, and they make a list of it. When a girl does it, it makes her reputation turn around." The very experience that enhances a young man's reputation (among other teen men), can damage a young woman's reputation. It may even lead to her being defined as a "ho," a person who has sex indiscriminately and is tainted as a result (see Tolman 2002).

According to teens, young women engaged in sexual activity for different reasons than did their male partners. The majority of the teens claimed that young girls engaged in sex either to preserve existing relationships with their boyfriends or to develop new relationships (see Martin 1996). When asked, "Why did you decide to become sexually active," Nicole explained, "He was the first boy that ever said he loved me, that's why. He really wanted to express the love and I don't know, I just wanted to I guess. . . . It was good in the beginning, [but] after a while it just went down the tubes. . . . I figured out that's all he wanted like to start out with, so everything else he told me was a lie—loving me and stuff."

Nicole's subsequent sexual experiences confirmed for her that gender differences shaped her sexual relationships and experiences:

> We were friends and we'd do it; it wasn't like we were together and it felt good at the time to be able to have someone to do that with and just be friends, but at the end it makes me feel really shitty and crappy so it ends up being bad. . . . After you do that, you're not friends and then you're a slut and you both did the same thing, but the girl always ends up to be the slut and the guy's just the cool guy.

Perhaps because the social consequences of sexual activity differ for males and females, teen women like Nicole entered into sexual relationships on the premise, and sometimes the hope, that sex would lead to a more emotional or semi-permanent connection.

Nancy became sexually active in middle school hoping to secure a relationship with a young boy she cared for. Since junior high, Nancy has had intercourse with six different young men because she liked them and continued to believe that sex would lead to a relationship. Prior to intercourse, all six teenagers told Nancy that they cared about her and wanted to date her; after having intercourse, a relationship did not materialize. Many teens had stories that mirror Nancy's—they initially believed sexual intercourse was a foundation for a relationship but quickly realized that sex does not carry the same significance for young men (see Lichtenstein 2000). According to Angelina:

> It feels different for guys and it feels different for girls. Some guys think it's all cool when you have sex and some girls think it's not, it's just to make the boys feel better . . . If they [girls] don't want to lose them [boys] they'll give it to them because they don't want to lose that person . . . Boys talk about it constantly and it makes the girls feel guilty.

Abstinence-only education's focus on the ill effects of premarital sex—loss of reputation, self esteem, and guilt—do not position young women to evaluate their own sexuality and make autonomous decisions about sexual relationships. Rather, the messages simply reinforce the negative feelings young women have after engaging in disparate sexual relations—feeling foolish for being "duped" by young men who pretended to care about them (see Martin 1996). After sex, many girls described themselves as "sluts, dirty, and stupid" because the social costs for them were great, whereas for boys the costs were minimal, and in fact, their experiences were typically positive. "Guys don't care. Guys don't get reputations" (Interview with Blanca 2001).

For the young women we interviewed, sex often was seen as something for boys, not girls; it was, in a sense, the defeat of girls' virginity in favor of boys' pleasure. Girls' pleasure is almost completely absent from teens' discussions of virginity and sexuality (see Tolman 2002). Blanca describes herself as feeling dirty after she had sex: "I'm not like, I don't get into it like 'oh yeah'. I'm not into it; I'm just like go ahead do what you want to do and that's it, you know? And they're all into it and I'm like, I don't get no fun, but its okay." Deborah Tolman argues that the "missing discourse of desire" in young women's descriptions of their sexual activity is shaped by the social construction of adolescent sexuality (Fine 1988). She criticizes "our insistence on defining female adolescent sexuality only in terms of disease, victimization, and morality and our avoidance of girls' own feelings of sexual desire and pleasure" (Tolman 2002, 14). Thus, Blanca and other teens interviewed for this study do not have access to a language or discourse of female pleasure with which to interpret their own sexual experiences; the dominant cultural understanding of young women's sexuality either ignores female pleasure or defines it as abnormal.

If sex is devoid of pleasure, it also may be because of the context in which many girls learn about sex (Abma, Driscoll, and Moore 1998; Lichtenstein 2000). Blanca's first sexual contact, for example, was rape at the age of 12. She explains how her sexual experiences have confirmed for her the feeling that girls have little choice or sexual agency:

> It's like they [guys] pressure you more into doing it . . . You could keep saying no and no and no and then you know they'll keep asking you and asking you and asking you and you'll be like no, and then finally you just get to the point, alright, alright then.
>   Interviewer: You think they're really good at pressuring girls?
>   Blanca: Yeah, or if not, they rape.

Both abstinence-only curricula and teen interviews note gender differences in teen sexuality and sexual experiences. For example, the curricula suggest that girls approach sex more emotionally than do boys, a difference mentioned by Nicole. In another example, the curricula's implication that *normal* girls will not have the same desires as boys is reflected in Blanca's focus on male pleasure. Abstinence-only education's lessons about male "urges" and girls' responsibility to "slow down the young man" serve to confirm for girls that boys have physiological desires that girls do not have (Mast 2001b, 12–13). And Damita and many other young women focused on the fact that girls may develop reputations as sluts as a result of sex, while sex enhances boys' reputations. Abstinence-only curricula repeatedly make the point that sex can lead to "loss of reputation."

Surface similarities between the teen interviews and abstinence-only lessons, however, mask deeper differences. Specifically, while both the abstinence-only curricula and teen interviews point to gender differences, teens' interview responses serve to critique the approach to gender differences found in the curricula. The curricula present the basis for gender differences as biological rather than socially constructed. These teens' interview responses suggest just the opposite—apparent gender differences are formed and reified through constructions of sexuality and actual sexual experiences. These gender differences are not innate; rather, they are created through the sexual power differentials between young women and men. And as male and female sexualities are differentiated through social constructions, so sexuality helps to construct two disparate gender identities as well. Rather than mirror young women's experiences, the curricula's construction of differences in sexual experiences as biologically based seems to undermine teen women's attempts to analyze the gendered aspects of their experiences. Teen interviews point out power imbalances and the cultural emphasis on traditional gender roles as they interpret their sexual experiences; these critiques rarely surface in the curricula. The reality of teens' sexual experiences and the shortcomings in the abstinence-only curricula are even more complicated when the role of pressure and sexual assault are considered.

SEXUAL ASSAULT

Twelve out of 26 sexually active teen girls we interviewed (46%) had experienced nonconsensual sex at some point in their sexual lives. Of the young women who experienced nonconsensual sex, all of them became sexualized at the age of 15 or younger, which does not differ dramatically from the overall group—all but two of the sexually active teens were sexually active by the age of 15. All three teens that became sexually active at the age of 11 had been sexually assaulted, and 4 out of 7 who became active when they were 13 had also been assaulted. The numbers are even more striking when teens are asked about why they initially became sexually active: Eight of the teens responded that they had been sexually assaulted, and another eight mentioned pressure from their boyfriends.

Compared to the general teen population, the young women in this study experienced sexual assault in disproportionately large numbers. Increased risk factors among this group of young women provide one explanation for the discrepancy. Statistics show that low-income women, women of color, and young women aged 16 to 19 are in the highest risk groups for sexual assault; the overlap of poverty and nonwhite racial identity among the women we interviewed may help to explain their high rate of victimization.

Nancy's first sexual encounter at age 13 was rape: "I was drunk and passed out. . . . after that happened I was scared." Nancy states that "less than half" of her subsequent sexual activity has been consensual: "Sometimes I'm too out of [it] to even realize what's going on until later . . . sometimes I'm too afraid to speak up . . . either I didn't want to have sex or it was forceful or I passed out or I just did it because I was afraid the guy wouldn't like me."

Many teens said they had been pressured to have sex, either for their first time or in subsequent encounters. Commenting on why she became sexually active at the age of 13 with her 15-year-old boyfriend, Sue explained the pressure she felt: "I was with the guy for like a month and a half and was in love. I felt pressure from him. I felt like if I didn't do it then he would be unhappy." And Ana, a 16-year-old teen parent who is currently still with the father of her child, describes why she initially had sex with him: "I remember not wanting to have sex. . . . he kept asking me, and pressuring me to do it. I didn't think that he would have left me, but he probably would have been—just kept asking me and asking me and asking me." Viewed in terms of assault and peer pressure, an overwhelming 16 out of the 26 (62%) teen girls became sexually active by force or pressure.

After some of the young women experienced intercourse, they subsequently engaged in sexual activity largely stemming from their beliefs that because they were no longer virgins, there was no point in abstaining from sex. For example, one teen who was raped at the age of 13 described the experience: "I'd been raped . . . I just pretty much after awhile I figured what's the point [of abstaining from sex]. I mean I'm not a virgin anymore."

Another striking finding from the interviews was the young women's complicated responses to their experiences with sexual assault; many did not define their experiences as rape. The denial of sexual assault and the idea that girls regulate sexual activity—and consequently are to blame for sexual assault—are both reflected in the abstinence-only curricula and reinforced by young women's experiences with unwanted sexual encounters. "I'm not gonna call it rape or anything, because I could have done more to stop it, but sometimes I'm too out of it to even realize what's going on until later" (Interview with Nancy 2002). Most women were reluctant to name their sexual experience as rape and in fact would claim that they had a choice and were ultimately responsible for their experiences. Sue explains: "I had slept with two guys within five minutes apart and I was telling them no. But I had a choice to do it or not, I could have forced them off but I didn't want to struggle so I just let it go." Similarly, Rachel described her experience:

> Most of the times I didn't really say yes. I was high or I was drunk and I wasn't really awake or anything. And I would do it and I would like leave right away 'cause I wouldn't want to be there. I'd say no, and try to push them away but I just kind of went with it because I was scared . . . But rape would be some guy threw me on the ground trying to have sex with me and I would scream like no, and that would be rape.

The young women attempt to distinguish *real* rape from date or acquaintance rape, where for them date and acquaintance rape exist in a murky, gray area that is not really rape. This is not surprising, given that rape myths, culturally widespread and certainly familiar to the teens we interviewed, make the same distinction between date rape and real rape and suggest that rape by an acquaintance or a date must be at least partially the woman's fault. Abstinence-only curricula implicitly make the same connection, faulting young women for wearing provocative clothing or trying to tempt young men.

VIRGINITY AND ILLICIT SEX

Cultural messages and myths about sexual assault are used as vehicles by these teens to articulate and somewhat normalize their experiences. Similarly situated cultural messages and symbols governing sexual agency also help shape many of the teens' understanding of their sexual activity, particularly how they interpret virginity loss. Our interviews suggest that most young women, regardless of whether they are sexually active or not, are keenly aware of the message that teen sex is at best inappropriate and at worst immoral.

Maintaining virginity until marriage is a primary focus of abstinence-only education (Teen Aid 1998; Mast 2001a). Curricula tend to reinforce portrayals of sexually active teen girls as promiscuous and of questionable character and to contribute to the idea that virginity is a precious possession that young women must save rather than squander. The portrayal of sexually active teens as "bad girls," hypersexual and immoral, represents the anti-ideal in abstinence-only education. Given that abstinence-only programs set up sexuality in terms of an either/or (either one is a virgin or not), sexually active girls find themselves defined as the "whore" in the virgin/whore dichotomy. Abstinence-only education teaches girls to jealously guard their virginity, sometimes making use of the conservative Christian notion of "purity" to underscore the illegitimacy of teen sex. Hence when Kim depicts her sexual activity as dirty, dangerous, even "disgusting," her portrayal is in keeping with the notion of sex as illicit and contaminating for young women.

Abstinence-only education may mention the advantages of "secondary virginity," sometimes offering a "personal commitment card" or "contract" where teens promise to either remain a virgin or stop having sex and become a secondary virgin. But Heather makes clear that the burden of secondary virginity lies with the ability to appear sufficiently ashamed of one's past:

> I believe if you've had sex, you're not a virgin anymore, but if you're totally regretful of it and you take some time off of just dating or anything with guys, I believe that you can become kind of like a virgin again. Like you saved

your body for so many years and like you regretted everything you did and ask God for forgiveness, I believe you can become one again in a sense.

The abstinence-only message may apply to those who have had sex, but only if they are willing to apologize and repent for their pasts, again suggesting that there is something amiss, even damaged, about young women once they have had sex.

The curricula's position on teen sex as *illicit sex* mirrors, to some extent, cultural messages about girls' sexuality, and not surprisingly, many girls were quite articulate in representing such a view. Sexually active teens in our interviews expressed mixed feelings about themselves, stating, for example, "I wish I never [lost my virginity]. I felt kinda disgusted with myself." Many teens made the same point, regardless of sexual experience. Lisa, a virgin, asserted, "I think it's disrespecting your body. I think you should wait until you're married, you fall in love with that person, and you save [it] for them so it's a really special thing. But if you keep doing it when you're really young, it's not really that special." Using very similar language, Claudia, who became sexually active and pregnant at age 13, commented, "That's sad because a lot of people have several different sex partners when sex is supposed to be something special and you're supposed to be with one person for the rest of your life, and that's the one person you give it to."

Teen girls repeatedly talked about virginity as if it is a gift that one "saves," "loses," or "gives away." Laura Carpenter found a similar approach to virginity loss among some of the young women she interviewed: "The women and men that I spoke with who drew on this metaphor invariably appraised virginity as a very valuable gift, based on its uniqueness, nonrenewability, symbolic import and status as an extension of the giver's self" (2005, 58).[8] For the young women in our study, the construction of virginity as an irreplaceable and valuable gift suggested that teen girls who possessed virginity were themselves valuable only until it was "lost." Though we cannot ascertain from our interviews if abstinence-only sex education contributed to this interpretation of lost virginity, abstinence-only lessons do underscore the permanent loss experienced by those who have sex before marriage. Tracy describes how she felt after she had sex for the first time at age 15:

> I lost a piece of my self-dignity. . . . I mean every person knows if you lose it before you find the person you love it takes away from you. It's just not right. But then at the same time you've already done it and you just keep doing it. . . . I do see other people who go out there and they get respected even though they haven't had sex and it's just like I wish I could get that back 'cause I lost a piece of me. . . . I just feel different. I don't feel all innocent . . . I have this rough type of story to me now, not so soft as what you'd want.

Tracy spoke to the feelings that many of the teen girls in this study conveyed; it was obvious to her that she had become tainted on some level due to her sexual activity. The taint was social in the sense that she had lost the respect of others and was no longer as "soft" as she should be, and moral, to the extent that she had lost "self-dignity." Similarly Laura, who became sexually active at 11 with a 15 year old, spoke with regret about "losing" her virginity: "I wish I wouldn't have lost my virginity 'cause now, I mean, when I want to be with someone, and I want to give them something special, I don't have anything to give them. And it feels really bad." The concept of virginity as a gift to be given but once serves to limit teens' choices when it comes to engaging in future sexual activity. Once their virginity is gone, teens like Tracy tend to feel they no longer have control over their sexuality. These teens continue to be sexually active in part because they believe they are no longer "pure."

PURITY

Several of the teens we interviewed connected female virginity to purity, and by contrast, sexual activity to purity corrupted. Heather, a 15 year old who has had abstinence-only education in school and in her church youth group, described her understanding of purity within the abstinence-only message: "Purity means not just your body but your mind and just your thoughts, keeping those as pure as possible like lusting and just keeping your heart pure. . . . It says in the Bible not to have any sexual immorality." Purity in the context of abstinence from sex makes little sense without the specific religious connotations that Heather mentioned. And Heather indicated the extent to which purity is gendered: "I think girls and guys as far as purity I think they should both be pure, but I think it's kind of harder for the guys because society brings on that they need to be more controlling over the girl."

By the same token, sexually active teen girls had contaminated their purity. Nicole, a sexually active 18 year old with a 1-year-old child, indicates the extent to which sexual activity can "taint" young women:

> There used to be this boy at church . . . and he really really used to like me before I started seeing Richard [the father of my child] and had sex with him. And if I wouldn't have had sex with Richard, then I could have dated [the boy from church]. And he's a really really nice guy and we would have never had sex but we probably would have had a really good relationship and probably get married some day, but I had to screw it up.
>
> Interviewer: So do you think you can't date him if he's a virgin and you're not?

> Nicole: No, I know I can't because that's what he looks for in girls 'cause he's really really really Christian. . . . [Virgins] are a lot more pure than others. . . . like not touched.

If virgins are "a lot more pure than others," then the sexually active teens are the "others." Sexually active teens are the opposite of virgins, corrupted to the point that they are not marriage material for those who have remained chaste. This lesson, of course, appears quite centrally in such abstinence-only curricula as *SCF* and *Sex Respect,* where teen sex is said to have such consequences as "loss of reputation, limitations in dating/marriage choices, negative effects on sexual adjustment" (Teen Aid 1998, 236).

Though Mary has not had many of the same sexual experiences that Nicole has—Nicole has had 12 partners and Mary has had 1—they share a similar analysis of the construction of sexually active teens and virgins. Mary points out that once a young woman has lost her virginity, she is automatically put in the category of "slut," regardless of her age, sexual experience, or relationship status:

> I was always proud to say I'm the only virgin, and I'm not a slut, like if people called me a slut, I'd be like uh uh, I'm not a slut 'cause I'm still a virgin. . . . So you know, I think it's a good thing to have, especially in an alibi or something you know. But I lost it [virginity], so I can't really speak much anymore. . . . I don't think [sexually active girls] are sluts at all; I just think they're viewed as a slut.

Young women are "spoiled" and become "sluts" by virtue of having had sex, and there seems to be little gray area available for teen women: Either one is a virgin, or one is a slut.

The construction of sexually active young women as tainted—even contaminated—is further demonstrated and strengthened by abstinence-only education's focus on STIs as a probable outcome of sex (see Lichtenstein 2000). Detailed descriptions of STIs command many pages of the abstinence-only curriculum, including symptoms and outcomes associated with gonorrhea, chlamydia, HPV, and others (Mast 2001a; Teen Aid 1998). Kim described her sexual activity: "I kind of feel disgusted with myself because I've had sex with five different men. And you know, with the things that could happen nowadays, you know with STDs and AIDS, HIV, chlamydia, things like that, it's just, I don't want to end up with that. . . . 'Cause I don't want to die real young." The risk of STIs represents an important basis for linking sex with contamination (see Brandt 1987). And it has a certain shaming factor—differentially associated with young men versus young women—that easily relates to young women's fears about the loss of reputation for sexually active girls.

TEEN PARENTHOOD

In addition to dealing with the gender differences associated with sexuality and adolescence, some teens also faced pregnancy and parenthood at young ages. Of the teens interviewed, 14 (44%) were teen parents, 1 teen was pregnant at the time of the interview, and 2 had had miscarriages. Unlike national averages (Centers for Disease Control and Prevention 2007; Luker 1996), the majority of teens (82%) in our sample became pregnant by the age of 15. Roughly half of the teens (53%) were using some type of birth control method—although often sporadically—while the remaining 47 percent were not using any type of birth control when they became pregnant.

Access to, use, and efficacy of birth control methods are but a few among many explanatory factors in teen parenthood rates. Scholars have identified several other reasons that contribute to the variation in teen pregnancy rates over time, such as the deterioration of the traditional nuclear family, cohabitation among unmarried couples, social acceptance of unmarried childbearing, and an earlier age of first intercourse among teens (Bumpass and Lu 2000; Guttmacher Institute 2006a). In this section, we focus primarily on whether teens wanted to become pregnant, and if they did not, what measures they took to avoid pregnancy.

For those teens that did not use birth control, their pregnancy intentions were dramatically at odds with the precautions they took to avoid pregnancy. When discussing whether they wanted to become parents, the majority of teens expressed a lack of intentionality, as well as varying views on what pregnancy and parenthood would be like. Similar to other studies (Frost and Oslak 1999; Henshaw 1997), 12 (80%) of pregnant and parenting teens stated that they did not plan or want to become pregnant. Marisa, for example, used condoms sporadically when she had sex with her boyfriend and became pregnant at 17 (her boyfriend was 19). She explains why she did not use birth control consistently: "I felt like I couldn't get pregnant. Like it couldn't happen to me. Like I couldn't see myself with a baby, or taking care of a baby." Barbara, who has two children, did not use birth control at all before her first pregnancy: "I was like 'Oh, I can't get pregnant, you know, I can't get pregnant.' . . . I was like, in denial of the whole thing. I could have used something, but I didn't. And condoms suck because you can't feel it, you know, as good." Other young women voiced the same belief as an explanation for lack of contraception, essentially hoping that they would not become pregnant. For other teens, fear of parental disapproval or punishment led to their not using birth control.

Other teens reported using contraceptives regularly but became pregnant anyway. Rebecca, for example, became pregnant at 14, though she and her boyfriend were using condoms. She responded to a question about why she did not use any other form of birth control prior to becoming pregnant: "I didn't think I could go in and get it. I thought that they were going to ask me a lot questions . . . 'cause I thought, 'oh you're gonna tell my parents or something.'" Rebecca used condoms rather than the pill or another method with a lower failure rate because she knew that she did not have to get parental approval for condoms.

While a significant majority (80%) of teens interviewed stated clearly that they did not get pregnant intentionally, three teens responded to a question about whether they wanted to get pregnant with an "I didn't care." In their 1999 study of teen mothers, Frost and Oslak found that many women answered the question of intentionality with an "I didn't care" response. In terms of intentionality, the "did not care" category is unclear. Unlike the Frost and Oslak study, we probed these responses with follow up questions asking the young women to explain what "I didn't care" meant.

For these young women, an "I didn't care" response seemed to indicate a feeling of fatalism or a means out of their current situation. When asked "did you intend/want to have a baby?" Cara, a 19-year-old mother of a 3-year-old daughter, described her experience:

> No, not really, but I didn't care either. It could happen, whatever.
>   Interviewer: And what do you mean you didn't care?
>   Cara: I don't know, I was in sort of a funky state of mind, I think. Well he was older and I was having problems with my family and he was an older guy. At first I tried to get him to use something but he was like no, I'm too tired, I can't wear these things. I thought I was in love with him and if I got pregnant he would take care of me and I wouldn't have to bother with this anymore. So I didn't really care.

Yolanda, who is a 17-year-old mother of a 2-year-old son, explained her decision:

> I didn't really care. I didn't mean to have a baby. I was going to the center to get birth control and they had tested me. And they said that I should wait a little bit longer to make sure that I'm not pregnant. And then they said they would check me. And it turned out that I was pregnant, so I couldn't do nothing about it.

For both Cara and Yolanda, to say that they "didn't care" if they got pregnant did not necessarily indicate that they intended to get pregnant, or that they were not actively seeking to keep themselves from getting pregnant. Cara stated that she felt generally "out of control" of her life and "really angry." Her boyfriend's refusal to use condoms underscored her loss of control, but his dominance in the relationship also signaled a pathway out of Cara's contentious home life. Yolanda also had some difficulties at home, which prompted her to run away. Similar to Cara, her boyfriend provided an escape from the unhappiness she was experiencing at home. Yolanda moved in with her boyfriend and shortly thereafter discovered she was pregnant while trying to get birth control. In both of these young women's cases, getting pregnant did not stand out as a clear possibility, and their unintended pregnancies were largely a byproduct of their discontent at home.

From the pregnant and parenting teens interviewed, their stories suggest that unintended pregnancies were symptomatic of other troubling issues facing them. However, in multiple cases pregnancy served as a positive event in a teen's life. Several young women stated that they were heavily using alcohol and drugs—with little ambition of finishing high school—until they become pregnant. Impending motherhood motivated these young women to change their lifestyles; they ceased using drugs and committed themselves to finishing high school. One teen noted, "I've been heavily involved in crank . . . the day I found out [I was pregnant] I quit. I stopped everything."

Although motherhood may propel young women to stop using drugs and remain in high school, the difficulties of teen motherhood cannot be understated. All mothers in this study—with the exception of one—described the difficulties of being a teen parent. Even for mothers receiving both financial and emotional support from their partners or families, the primary burden of motherhood was theirs. Young women were responsible for almost all of the day-to-day care of their children and much of the financial support of their children. Notably, almost all of the young women struggled financially, as did the fathers of their children.

Not surprisingly, for the young women who struggled financially, marriage to the fathers of their babies did not increase their economic stability. Of the 14 teens that had children, 64 percent were still in a relationship with the father of their children. Of those, half were living with the fathers of their children, with all but one married to their partners. The other teens that were still in a relationship with the fathers of their babies lived separately from their boyfriends—with their own parents or extended family members—many because they could not afford to live on their own. Teen fathers, like teen mothers, predominately were working for low wages; most fathers had not completed high school.

Our interviews confirm prior national research that indicates teenage childbearing and poverty are better understood as effects of existent poverty, not causes of indigence. In 1988, 80 percent of teenage births were to young women who were already poor (DeGroat 1997; Luker 1996). More recently, in his review of research on programs to prevent teen pregnancy from 1980 to the present, Douglas Kirby emphasizes that poverty is an antecedent to early teen sexual activity and teen pregnancy (Kirby 2001). Studies using in-depth interviews make a similar point (Frost and Oslak 1999; Harris 1997; Leadbeater and Way 2001).

The difficulties of being a teen parent are likely to continue well after these young women finish high school. Many of the teen parents attended a high school that offered on-site day care facilities, food supplements for pregnant and nursing teens, as well as job counseling. A few teens expressed a desire to attend college after graduation, but the majority believed that after graduating from high school they would be able to obtain "high-paying jobs." The reality of achieving these aspirations is unlikely given the current economy, which does not pay unskilled workers high wages.

Whether or not teen parents would have better financial or career options if they were not parents is impossible to directly ascertain. Several indicators, how-ever, suggest that these teens would be making similar choices even if they were not parents. The most telling indicator is socioeconomic background. Almost all the teenagers interviewed, including those who were not parents, came from work-ing poor or low-income families. Moreover, nonparenting teens did not express a desire to attend college any more than parenting teens. Teens' choices appeared to be shaped by factors other than parenthood, which is not to imply that the added economic and emotional hardship of having children is inconsequential. Rather teen parenthood is simply one factor to consider in the larger spectrum of teen poverty.

ABORTION AND ADOPTION

The notion of personal responsibility (which was the cornerstone of the 1996 welfare reform changes) continually surfaced during the interviews. Many teens—both with children and without—expressed the belief that becoming pregnant was a risk attached to being sexually active. According to these teen women, if a person was responsible enough to have sex, then she was responsible enough to have and parent a child. Kim, a sexually active, nonparenting teen declared, "I believe if you bring a baby into this world, and you have enough guts to have sex, you should raise the kid and be a father or mother to that son or daughter. . . . If you have enough time on your hands to have sex, then you have enough time on your hands to have a baby and raise it on your own." These comments fly in the face of Kim's earlier acknowledgement that she had become pregnant and miscarried, and that she was relieved that she had miscarried, "because I knew if I had a kid I would probably leave it with my Dad or with my Mom . . . because I probably wouldn't have no time with it. I'd probably be going to work, going to school or going to work, then coming home and then dealing with a kid. And then trying to get some sleep." Even for teen parents, who knew firsthand the trials that Kim feared, emphasis on personal responsibility and choice mirrored their nonparenting counterparts. According to Claudia, a 14-year-old mother, "I think that if I take the chance, then I will take the responsibility. I didn't plan on having a baby; I didn't plan on being pregnant. But I think if you are going to take the risk of sex, then you need to take the responsibility that comes with it." Pregnancy and motherhood are perceived as consequences for irresponsible sex.

Many teens also wed their beliefs about responsibility and consequences with their antiabortion beliefs. Of the 12 teens that were parents and answered questions about abortion, 8 did not believe in abortion, and only 3 even considered it as an option. When asked why they did not consider abortion as an option many responded with common anti-abortion rhetoric: "I think it's murder. To me, the baby has a heart beat. It may not be fully developed, but he has a heart beat that's not mine." Another teen parent expressed similar sentiments, "I don't believe in abortion because you're like killing a part of yourself and a part of the man who made the baby."

Teen responses also suggest they have been given misinformation about abortion. Teresa, for example, states, "Abortion, that's really hard because people can die with that, and that would be losing two lives. I wouldn't have an abortion if I were to have a baby. I would rather have adoption. That would be better than to kill this innocent little baby that's just coming to have his own life." Teresa attempts to sort through her beliefs about abortion by drawing on pro-life rhetoric as well as repeating claims that appear in abstinence-only curriculum such as *SCF*, that overstate the physical and emotional danger of abortion.

Similar to other studies, the pregnant or parenting teens expressed a personal disapproval of adoption as well as abortion (Frost and Oslak 1999). Although a slightly larger percent of respondents considered adoption (33%) as an option compared to those who considered abortion, the majority never considered adoption. Like many of the teens, Marisa explained why adoption was not an option for her:

> For me personally, I don't have the strength to give my son away for adoption. I wouldn't be able to do it for any of my kids. Yeah they may be good homes but it's just the fact that knowing there's a kid out there that belongs to me. Knowing that, you know, I'm not taking care of that child, what kind of a person does that make me become? I mean I have to live with that for the rest of my life, and that's something I can't live with . . . 'Cause it's my mistake, I think I should have to pay for it.

Marisa's opposition to adoption is both philosophical ("What kind of person does that make me become?") and punitive ("It's my mistake, I think I should have to pay for it").

Many of the young women we interviewed, like Marisa, wrestle with questions that feel uniquely personal and individual to them. Collectively, the interviews portrayed a mix of awareness and maturity on the one hand, and the lack of control and knowledge over their sexuality on the other hand, which typically guided teens' discussions of sex and sexuality. Most of these teens grapple with a lack of power and information associated with their sexuality.

CHAPTER SUMMARY

To say that teen sexuality is influenced and shaped by a complex set of factors seems a banal response to the insights and experiences of the young women in this study. Yet, this is at the core of the shortcomings and problems associated with abstinence-only curricula. The curricula attempts to overly simplify and silence much of the complexity of teen sexuality reflected in our study. As we suggest, it is impossible to claim that any one source of sexual instruction, including abstinence-only education in the schools, is responsible for this lack of power and information. Indeed, teens have difficulty articulating how their school sex education classes relate to their sexual experiences and their analyses of those experiences. It is just as clear, however, that the content of abstinence-only education underscores some of the most damaging and disempowering cultural norms and beliefs about young women's sexuality.

Chief among those, and key to abstinence-only curricula, is the notion that virginity—particularly girls' virginity—is a precious possession that must be safeguarded. Because virginity is to be "given" but once, when a young woman has sex, she is perceived as having lost something irreplaceable and thereby undermined herself as a valuable or worthwhile person more generally. Though not all teens referred to virginity in this manner, the vast majority did so. Likewise, most teens also spoke to the corollary social construction for nonvirgins that appears centrally in abstinence-only instruction. That is, if virgins are pure, then sexually active, unmarried teens are engaging in an illicit activity—to use the language of abstinence-only education—that defines them as morally questionable at best, and sluts at worst.

Abstinence-only sex education also undermines many teen women by intimating that their struggles to define themselves and make sense of their experiences with pressure, sexual assault, and pregnancy mean that they are not normal, are impure, or are at risk. Despite the stereotypes promulgated about teen pregnancy, and about young, low-income teens of color, the interviews did not convey a picture of teen promiscuity. Rather, the patterns appeared to indicate a picture of teenage sexuality that includes a lack of sex education, difficulty obtaining birth control, early sexualization (which was often a result of force or pressure), beliefs in personal responsibility, and opposition to both abortion and adoption.

The lessons of abstinence-only education in the context of morality policies and gender politics are woven together in the concluding chapter. In light of the content analysis and interviews with teen women, the findings suggest that the specific lessons taught by abstinence-only education accentuate and help to further confirm numerous gendered, heterosexist, and problematic messages about teen women's sexuality that exist within the larger culture. Though sex education courses will never provide the only instruction on sexuality, this collection of teen interviews illustrates the complexity of teen sexuality that should, at the least, be recognized and addressed by any sex education course.

NOTES

1. In describing our research interests and asking for participants to be interviewed, we relied on some combination of the "buddy-researcher role" (Cress and Snow 1996; Snow and Anderson 1993), presenting ourselves as sympathetic to and somewhat knowledgeable about teens' experiences, and the role of "credentialed expert" on welfare reform and the specific aspects of the law that target teens (Cress and Snow 1996, 1094).

2. All interviews but one were recorded and lasted from 60 to 90 minutes. We quote interview responses word for word except to add punctuation, delete repeated words, or at times, delete repeated phrases such as "like" and "you know" for clarity.

3. We also contend that young men are socially constructed in different ways than young women, such that their sexuality has long been viewed through a different lens. A sexual double standard continues to structure gendered understandings of sexuality. Although young men have in many ways experienced greater sexual freedom compared to young women, they nevertheless are restricted by the socially constructed understandings of males, male sexuality, and the prevalent norms structuring and shaping their participation in intimate relationships. In many ways, the politics of socially constructing young men today mirrors that of young women, to the extent that the view is narrow, restrictive, and often constructed in binary and contradictory terms. We discuss young men as they relate to pertinent issues facing young women; however, we more exclusively focus on young women because of the gendered nature of abstinence-only education. A thorough treatment of adolescent men is beyond the scope of this book, which is why they play a secondary role in our analysis of policy, gender, and sexuality.

4. Because this study relies on a relatively small sample size of 32 teenagers, when we use percentages, we also include the raw number. Both numbers and percentages are used to show how many teens that we interviewed had a certain experience and to compare to percentages in the general population.

5. Thanks to anonymous reviews from the *Journal of Women, Politics & Policy* for this insight.

6. The absence of young women's discussion and analysis of lesbian, bisexual, or transgender experience, and the curricula's erasure of homosexuality, limits our discussion as well. We are not able, for example, to examine through teen interviews how compulsive heterosexuality works to silence homosexual teens. We are not able to address the possibility for teens' lesbian sexual experiences to undermine the relentless heterosexism of the

curricula. We also are not able to analyze through teen interviews specific social constructions of gay, lesbian, and transgender adolescents; though they are socially constructed in
ways similar to straight teens, they also grapple with a unique set of socially constructed
identities. And while many lesbian and bisexual young women face the same problems
encountered by their heterosexual counterparts, they also experience a host of distinctive
problems. For example, homosexual youth face multiple problems ranging from increased
levels of depression, lack of acceptance, lack of support from institutions, estrangement
from family and peers, increased risk of being victimized, contracting HIV, and becoming
homeless (Medline Plus 2006).

7. All of the percents from the interviews have been rounded.

8. The respondents in Laura Carpenter's research also defined virginity loss through
other interpretive frames (see Carpenter 2005).

BIBLIOGRAPHY

Abma, Joyce, Anne Driscoll, and Kristin Moore. 1998. "Young Women's Degree of Control over First Intercourse: An Exploratory Analysis." *Family Planning Perspectives* 30
(1): 12–18.

Blake, Susan M., Linda Simkin, Rebecca Ledsky, Cheryl Perkins, and Joseph M. Calabrese.
2001. "Effects of a Parent-Child Communications Intervention on Young Adolescents'
Risk for Early Onset of Sexual Intercourse." *Family Planning Perspectives* 33 (2): 52–61.

Brandt, Allan M. 1987. *No Magic Bullet: A Social History of Venereal Disease in the United
States Since 1880.* New York: Oxford University Press.

Bumpass, Larry L., and Hsien-Hen Lu. 2000. "Trends in Cohabitation and Implications for
Children's Family Contexts in the United States." *Population Studies* 54 (1): 29–41.

Carpenter, Laura M. 2005. *Virginity Lost: Intimate Portrait of First Sexual Experience.* New
York: New York University Press.

Centers for Disease Control and Prevention. 2007. "Adolescent Reproductive Health:
Teen Pregnancy" (June 6). Available at: http://www.cdc.gov/reproductivehealth/
AdolescentReproHealth.

Cress, Daniel M., and David A. Snow. 1996. "Mobilizations at the Margins: Resources,
Benefactors, and the Viability of Homeless Social Movement Organizations." *American Sociological Review* 61 (6): 1089–1109.

DeGroat, Bernie. 1997. "Researchers Examine Predictors of Poverty in Teen Mothers."
The University Record (February 11).

Fields, Jessica. 2005. "'Children Having Children': Race, Innocence, and Sexuality Education." *Social Problems* 52 (4): 549–71.

Fine, Michelle. 1988. "Sexuality, Schooling and Adolescent Females: The Missing Discourse of Desire." *Harvard Educational Review* 58 (1): 29–53.

Finer, Lawrence B. 2007. "Trends in Premarital Sex in the United States, 1954–2003." *The
Guttmacher Institute Public Health Reports* 122: 73–78.

Frost, Jennifer J., and Selene Oslak. 1999. "Teenagers' Pregnancy Intentions and Decisions: A Study of Young Women in California Choosing to Give Birth." *The Alan
Guttmacher Institute Occasional Report No. 2* (December).

Guttmacher Institute. 2006a. "Facts on American Teens' Sexual and Reproductive Health." *Facts in Brief*. Available at: http://www.guttmacher.org/pubs/fb_ATSRH.html.

Guttmacher Institute. 2006b. *U.S. Teenage Pregnancy Statistics: National and State Trends and Trends By Ethnicity*. New York: Guttmacher Institute.

Harris, Kathleen Mullan. 1997. *Teen Mothers and the Revolving Welfare Door*. Philadelphia: Temple University Press.

Henshaw, Stanley K. 1997. "Teenage Abortion and Pregnancy Statistics by State, 1992." *Family Planning Perspectives* 29 (3): 115–26.

Horan, Patricia F., Jennifer Phillips and Nancy E. Hagan. 1998. "The Meaning of Abstinence for College Students." *Journal of HIV/AIDS Prevention & Education for Adolescents & Children* 2 (2): 51–66.

Kaplan, Elaine Bell. 1997. *Not Our Kind of Girl: Unraveling the Myths of Black Teenage Motherhood*. Berkeley: University of California Press.

Kirby, Douglas. 2001. *Emerging Answers: Research Findings on Programs to Reduce Teen Pregnancy*. Washington, D.C.: National Campaign to Prevent Teen Pregnancy.

Leadbeater, Bonnie, and Niobe Way. 2001. *Growing Up Fast: Transitions to Early Adulthood of Inner-City Adolescent Mothers*. Mahwah, NJ: Lawrence Erlbaum Associates.

Lichtenstein, Bronwen. 2000. "Virginity Discourse in the AIDS Era: A Case Analysis of Sexual Initiation Aftershock." *NWSA Journal* 12 (2): 52–69.

Luker, Kristin. 1996. *Dubious Conceptions: The Politics of Teenage Pregnancy*. Cambridge, MA: Harvard University Press.

Martin, Karin A. 1996. *Puberty, Sexuality, and the Self: Boys and Girls at Adolescence*. New York: Routledge.

Mast, Coleen Kelly. 2001a. *Sex Respect: The Option of True Sexual Freedom*, Teacher's Manual. Sex Respect. Bradley, IL: Respect Incorporated.

Mast, Coleen Kelly. 2001b. *Sex Respect: The Option of True Sexual Freedom*, Student Workbook. Sex Respect. Bradley, IL: Respect Incorporated.

McFarlane Deborah R., and Kenneth J. Meier. 2001. *The Politics of Fertility Control*. New York: Chatham House Publishers.

Medline Plus. 2006. "Gay and Lesbian Health." Available at: http://www.nlm.nih.gov/medlineplus/gayandlesbianhealth.html.

Plummer, Ken. 1995. *Telling Sexual Stories: Power, Change and Social Worlds*. New York: Routledge.

Remez, Lisa. 2000. "Oral Sex Among Adolescents: Is It Sex or Is It Abstinence?" *Family Planning Perspectives* 32 (6): 298–304.

Roberts, Dorothy. 1999. *Killing the Black Body: Race, Reproduction, and the Meaning of Liberty*. New York: Vintage Books.

Rose, Susan. 2005. "Going Too Far? Sex, Sin and Social Policy." *Social Forces* 84 (2): 1207–32.

Snow, David A., and Leon Anderson. 1993. *Down on Their Luck: A Study of Homeless Street People*. Berkeley: University of California Press.

Teen Aid. 1998. *Sexuality, Commitment & Family*. Spokane, WA: Teen Aid, Inc.

Tolman, Deborah L. 2002. *Dilemmas of Desire: Teenage Girls Talk About Sexuality*. Cambridge, MA: Harvard University Press.

6

Whom and What Are We "Saving"? Morality, Sexuality, and Abstinence

I know I said that you should wait until you're married, but also at the same time, I just think that if you know that person is the one—I've said this to my mom too—I just think that if you know that person is the one, and you want to stay together for the rest of your life, then I say why not? 'Cause that's something that you want to share with that person [and] you know that you both wouldn't take it for granted. . . . It has me confused all the time. You meet somebody and you think, "Oh my god, this could be the person," and you don't do it, which is a good thing, and then you realize you know they're not that person. But at the same time if you know that person is the one for you, and you're just sure [it is] something really special that you haven't felt, then why not do that [have sex] too? And if you break up, then you break up (Interview with Harmony 2001).

There are about 12 million problems with this [abstinence-only] approach— 12 million being the number of sexually active teens in this country who are 19 or younger. More than 70 percent of teenagers have had sex by the age of 18 and 80 percent by 19. Yes, condoms can break, they can slip off, but they are still the best protection [against pregnancy and sexually transmitted diseases] that we have available. (Jocelyn Elders, former U.S. Surgeon General, quoted in Ivins 2002)

WHAT HAVE WE LEARNED?

The political push to bring abstinence-only-until-marriage messages to unmarried people, with a particular focus on adolescents, became legitimized through the changes to welfare in 1996. State sanctioned abstinence-only curricula and programs ironically started during a time period when teen pregnancy rates and abortion rates already had begun to, and were continuing to, significantly decline (Boonstra 2002). In 2006, about half of high school–aged teens have had sex, which is a decline in sexual activity among this age group compared to the previous generation (Guttmacher Institute 2006).

Prevention and empowerment are two goals similarly shared by most sex education advocates; however, their strategies for defining and achieving these goals vary dramatically. For abstinence-only-until-marriage proponents, empowerment means equipping teens with the ability to say "no" to sexual contact until marriage and fostering a culture that supports virginity. In this vein, empowerment is the key to prevention as well: Abstaining from sexual contact is the best protection for preventing sexually transmitted infections, pregnancies, and other negative consequences from engaging in "risky" sexual behavior.

Throughout this book, we have deconstructed the notion that providing abstinence-only education is a sound proposal for curbing social problems. Similar messages have been promoted at various times as the best strategies for creating a successful society. In contemporary society, the focus on and promise of abstinence-only-until-marriage continues to be misplaced and faulty. Less rigid abstinence messages have routinely been included in sexuality education curricula, but since 1996, the way abstinence is defined and the relative weight given to these messages has changed. Over 35 percent of public schools providing sexuality education use abstinence-only curricula, and abstinence-only continues to be the fastest growing type of curricula across the country (Guttmacher Institute 2002; Landry, Kaeser, and Richards 1999).

Moving beyond the increasingly central role of abstinence in public school curricula is the larger problem of how the abstinence message is linked to other issues throughout the curricula. The curricula under investigation in this study cover an extensive breadth and depth of topics. But as the content analysis and deconstruction of the dominant narratives indicates, these lessons are taught through a prism of conservative and gendered understandings of sexuality. The messages of abstinence-only-until-marriage are contextualized and embedded in colorblind curricula that build on, reinforce, and promote a gendered version of the world, where an individual's role and place in the world is determined by their gender (and compliance with heterosexual norms). Teen women are constructed in a variety of ways; sometimes in terms of their innocence, purity, or vulnerability and other times as risky, experimental, and even dangerous. These social constructions have historical threads and have continued to shape society's understanding of adolescents. Not only do many of the abstinence-only lessons provide inaccurate material, the curricula's overarching messages about virginity intertwine—and collide—with both the realities of teen sexuality and gendered ideas about virginity that already exist in U.S. culture.

At any given time, teens are constructed in simplistic and often contradictory terms that fail to capture the true complexities of adolescence. Modern characterizations of teens are woefully inadequate in accounting for the cultural, institutional, and individual factors that uniquely shape individual teenagers. An abstinence-only education model does little to speak to or prepare young people for the complexities of the modern world and, more to the point, how sexuality exists within this context. Consequently, the abstinence-only curricula are more than merely outdated—they are harmful.

Abstinence-only programs and curricula have been scrutinized by a variety of sources and critiqued for their medical exaggerations, inaccuracies, and sometimes outright incorrect information. We add to this growing body of literature by focusing on what we suggest is the equally problematic and destructive effects of the curricula's teachings on issues of sexuality, which promote a specific cultural, religious, and political view of the world. We found overwhelming evidence that *Sex Respect; Sexuality, Commitment and Family; Choosing the Best Life;* and *Sex Can Wait* do little to challenge long-standing social constructions of teens and popularly held gender myths and belief. Quite the contrary, these curricula build on and legitimize narrow gender constructions and beliefs. Many of the topics discussed in the curricula emphasize the negative physical and emotional consequences of premarital sex, abortion, and contraception use, highlighting consequences that are disproportionately directed toward young women.

At the same time, the curricula promote a positive and overly glamorized view of the nuclear family, a view that in many respects is outdated. Families today often include step parents, step children, half siblings, same sex parents, and single parent households. On another note, the family—while a place for stability, love, and security—is also the social institution where children are the most vulnerable to physical, sexual, and emotional violence. Many teens come from familial backgrounds that do not correspond with the image painted and promoted in the curricula, let alone receive parental guidance and education regarding their sexual health.

Even for teens that are fortunate to be in a loving family, sexuality continues to be a topic that is shrouded in secrecy and generally avoided within the household. Research continues to extol the importance of parent–child communication in shaping teens' sexual decision making and ultimately their sexual health, but very few parents talk openly to their children about sex. The majority of teens do not talk to their parents about sex or their intentions to become sexually active, and this silence extends to other adults who could play a positive role, such as health care providers. Teens also lament the lack of preparedness they feel after receiving sexuality education in the classroom. Many feel sexuality education did not equip them with the tools to effectively communicate about sex with their parents or with their partners (Kaiser Family Foundation 2002).

The disjuncture between the curricula's version of the family versus the reality of many families is only one illustration of the general disconnect between the curricula and reality. The curricula are replete with other examples ranging from the lessons about relationships, to gender and sexual agency, to discussions about sexual coercion and violence. Throughout chapter 4 we investigated four leading curricula to examine what lessons were contained in their pages. We documented the multiple ways in which the curricula build on, prescribe, and legitimize gendered understandings of the world (particularly the sexual world) while deliberately erasing differences based on race, ethnicity, class, and sexual orientation that very much exist in society.

These differences that are excluded from the curricula are readily apparent when talking to teen women who have been marked as potential welfare recipients and are at the heart of the original abstinence-only education policy. Through these interviews, the goal was not to show direct causality between the curricula and behavior, because we do not support a view that there is a simplistic relationship between sexual health and teen decision making that is influenced by a single factor. Rather, the intent was to demonstrate how the lessons of sex education are interpreted and folded into young women's individual understandings of their sexuality. In this vein, abstinence-only curricula are part and parcel of the multiple and mixed messages that teens absorb from various cultural, institutional, and familial influences.

Our interviews exemplify many aspects of sexuality that disproportionately burden young and particularly low-income women of color, yet either are addressed inadequately or completely ignored in abstinence-only curricula. Two of the most destructive and common themes that routinely surfaced in the interviews were the lack of sexual agency and lack of information available to young women. Many teens articulated various forms of disempowerment stemming from sexual double standards, lack of access to information and contraception, sexual ambivalence, sexual pressure and coercion, and sexual assault.

Adolescents' sexual agency is hampered by the restrictive construction of teens, particularly in terms of gender and sexuality. These culturally imposed identities in turn shape the understandings these women have of themselves and each other, which play out in a variety of contexts. Several young women recounted their experiences with sexual violence but many of them did not identify these experiences as sexual assault. Instead their interpretations of the violence often drew on popularly held rape myths, cultural stereotypes, and biological beliefs about male sexuality, all of which are confirmed in a variety of ways in the abstinence-only curricula. Two young women believed they had a "choice" in their assault and could have prevented it if they fought harder. Many teens described situations where they unwillingly had sex while intoxicated, under the influence of drugs, or while they were passed out. Nevertheless, they did not identify these instances of unwanted, unwilling, coerced, or forced sex as assault.

Other studies have documented American teens' proclivity toward believing rape myths. Rose (2005) interviewed roughly 100 Danish teens and 300 American teens and found substantial differences between their respective discourses on sexuality and relationships. One significant difference emerged when Danish and American teens defined what it *really* means when a person says "no" to sexual activity. Danish teens were asked when "no means no." There was little ambiguity in their answers among both men and women: "when someone says no that means no" (Rose 2005, 1219). Both Danish males and females discussed saying no in gender neutral terms, which they articulated as a legitimate right for a young man or woman. "Their language did not assume that the male was the predator and the female the prey who was the one pressured into having sex" (Rose 2005, 1219).

On the other hand, the American teenagers in Rose's study struggled with their definition and understanding of deciding when "no means no." Saying "no" was described in gendered terms (it was the responsibility of the woman and in turn her fault when "no" wasn't clear). It was often qualified by whether or not the young woman "was clear in her own mind, whether she really meant no when she said no, how forcefully or frequently she said no, whether she was giving double messages either verbally or non-verbally, what the girl was wearing, and how she was acting when she said no" (Rose 2005, 1219). American teens—both males and females—squarely placed blame for sexual "miscommunication" on young women. Many of the teens interviewed in the study invoked common rape myths including victim blaming: "You can't blame the guy," "I have known girls who tease men," or "[girls] say no when they mean yes" (Rose 2005, 1220). Teens also explained sexual assault as a product of the biological urges inherent in men, explaining that, "If the girl teases a guy, then she has to be ready to get what she gets," and "After a certain point, you can't expect a guy to just stop" (Rose 2005, 1220).

The interviews in this study uncovered a similar pattern of teens ascribing to the rape myths that the women's movement has been trying to debunk for decades. Many of the young women interviewed used rape myths to help explain, justify, and normalize their own victimization. For the teens that were sexualized through coercion or assault, they had no control over their sexual "choices." Yet, much research demonstrates that this is the group of youth who are most vulnerable to future sexual assault. Boyer and Fine (1992) sampled 535 young women in Washington state, and found that among the young women who became pregnant as teens, two-thirds had been sexually assaulted: 55 percent had been molested, 44 percent had been raped, and 42 percent were victims of attempted rape. For these victims, the likelihood of future high-risk behavior increases, including drug and alcohol use, domestic violence, or exchanging sex for money (Boyer and Fine 1992).

The young women we interviewed reported similar experiences. Many of them described overlaying and overlapping issues—early sexual initiation through pressure, coercion, or assault; drug and alcohol abuse; pregnancy and parenthood; as well as ongoing conflicts resulting from power differentials in their relationships. Abstinence-only curricula have little to nothing to offer these young victims of sexual violence in terms of helping them with their pasts or empowering them for a different future. Their life experiences and the multifaceted issues they are grappling with do not lend themselves to simplistic answers. While sexual initiation by force is not the same as initiation by choice, the focus on virginity is nonetheless an empty message to these teens as well as teens that are already sexually active by choice. Even for young women who are virgins, the portrayal of virginity as a precious gift to be saved until marriage is disempowering.

Young people interpret virginity and virginity loss in a variety of ways, ranging from viewing it as a gift, to a stigma, to part of the life cycle process (Carpenter 2002). Through her in-depth interviews with 61 diverse people, including both heterosexual and homosexual men and women, Carpenter discovered that these individuals interpret their experiences of virginity loss through all of these lenses, sometimes borrowing certain elements from each interpretive frame. A person can view virginity loss as part of growing up but also feel burdened by the stigma associated with being a virgin (Carpenter 2002). Men and women experienced all of the interpretive frames; however, a clear gender component emerged in terms of understanding virginity as a gift. Women were much more likely (three-fifths) to interpret virginity as a gift compared to men who were much more likely to see virginity as a stigma.

In the gift giving perspective, which is commonly found in the abstinence-only curricula, virginity becomes a one-time gift that you give to a person you love (in the context of the curricula, your husband). But after the nonrenewable gift is given, what does a woman have left? What if the "gift" was not received in the same manner it was given (i.e., not received as a special gift whose giving was delayed until the "right" person was found)? Under this construct, virginity again becomes more about gifting female sexuality and agency to her partner. It is in keeping with the focus of male pleasure and the downplaying of female sexual pleasure and agency.

The ritual of gift giving is constructed in different ways in the larger social context. Gift giving is generally understood as a voluntary ritual, but at times there is an obligatory component involved (i.e., gift giving to family members on birthdays and holidays). Those women who understand gift giving as a voluntary exchange were sorely disappointed to be pressured by their partners, who focused on the obligatory aspect of gift giving (i.e., "If you loved me you would have sex with me"). Virginity loss in this context can create a lasting negative situation when reciprocity is expected (keeping with the ritual of gift giving) but not returned. For these young women, the relinquishment and subsequent disappointment can be disempowering for years to come (Carpenter 2002). Similarly, many of the young women we interviewed discussed virginity in terms of a gift and mirrored similar feelings following sexual intercourse including loss, guilt, and self-loathing for "giving" their gift to the wrong person.

The young women we interviewed did not have an outlet for discussing and making sense of their emotions. Less than 25 percent of these young women reported having adequate information about sexual health and meaningful conversations with adults, namely parents, concerning their sexual health. Ironically, in a world where information is in abundance, when it comes to sexuality, sexual health, and sexual decision making, information is scarce. Most teens complained about the lack of information about sex and the lack of access to contraception, and what seemed to trouble them the most was the absence of information regarding intimate relationships. Young women wanted to talk about their feelings and had myriad questions about their experiences with past relationships and current relationships. They also voiced their desires to feel better prepared for future relationships. In short, the teens interviewed for this research were not afraid to talk; rather they expressed frustration about the shortage of *adults* who were willing to listen and talk with, rather than to, them.

The "veil of secrecy" surrounding sexuality and relationships did not deter these young women from either engaging in sexual activity or entering into intimate relationships; however, it has forced them to seek inappropriate outlets for advice and feedback, mainly from their peers and media. Although our interviews were not conducted with a large, random sample, there is much corroborating evidence to suggest that the lack of information, candid discussions, and communication with adults characterizes many teens' experiences (Kaiser Family Foundation 2002, 2003a; Rose 2005).

These are but a few examples that illustrate the shortcomings of abstinence-only curricula and how they coalesce with and help shape teens' understandings of themselves and others. Abstinence-only education takes a narrow, gendered view of sexuality and presents socially constructed ideas as uncontested, and often biological, facts about human sexuality. Abstaining from sexual activity and ascribing to conservative gender roles is explicitly and implicitly taught as the path to safety, security, love, and protection from many problems (obviously including problems resulting from unsafe sexual practices). On the surface, advocating abstinence is not an inherently poor or malevolent idea; however, the simplistic and unrealistic way it is taught does little to equip teens to negotiate their way through sexual decision making.

THE SEEDS OF CHANGE?

Despite the growing popularity and resources dedicated to abstinence-only programs, pockets of opposition against the curricula are growing as well. Studies continue to find problems with the curricula, ranging from medical inaccuracies, to using fear-based messages, to fostering gender stereotyping. The National Education Association (NEA), the NEA's Health Information Network, and the Sexuality Information and Education Council of the United States recently held their fourth annual "Back to School" briefing where they reviewed three more abstinence-only-until-marriage curricula (*Why kNOw, WAIT Training*, and *Heritage Keepers*). "These curricula are taught in federally-funded abstinence-only-until-marriage programs located in more than a dozen states across the nation, including, Arizona, Colorado, Florida, Georgia, Maine, Missouri, Ohio, Pennsylvania, Rhode Island, South Carolina, and Tennessee among others. Since FY 2001, the programs that use these curricula have received more then $6 million" (SIECUS 2006b).

Although the curricula vary, the reviews concluded that all three are "riddled with messages of fear and shame, gender stereotypes, and medical misinformation that put young people at risk" (SIECUS 2006a). Like the curricula examined in this research, all three curricula enlist gender stereotyping and make use of rape myths to teach adolescents about male and female sexuality. *Why kNOw* discusses the marital tradition of the groom unveiling the bride to underscore and reinforce gender roles. Students are taught "the groom [is] the only man allowed to 'uncover the bride,'" thus the veiling is an outward symbol of the bride's purity, virginity, and acceptance of her role. The curriculum goes on to explain that unveiling demonstrates "her respect for him by illustrating that she [has] not allowed any other man to lay claim to her" (*Why kNOw?*, 60, quoted in SIECUS 2006a).

Likewise, *Heritage Keepers* capitalizes on existing rape myths, particularly blaming the victim, to warn young women about their potential to incite young men, and it also reminds young men that they are biologically incapable of controlling their sexual urges. "Males are more sight orientated whereas females are more touch orientated. This is why girls need to be careful with what they wear, because males are looking! The girl might be thinking fashion, while the boy is thinking sex. For this reason, girls have a responsibility to wear modest clothing that doesn't invite lustful thoughts" (*Heritage Keepers*, Student Manual, 46, quoted in SIECUS 2006a).

Educational associations and groups are not the only ones opposing the problem-laden curricula. Concerned parents are also organizing to oppose the use of abstinence-only curricula in their children's classrooms. In 2004, a parents' group (Georgia Parents for Responsible Health Education) formed to prevent the use of *Choosing the Best* curriculum at Shamrock Middle School in DeKalb County, Georgia. Parents presented their case to the school board and prevailed (SIECUS 2005). Opposition to abstinence-only-until-marriage is not isolated to Georgia. States, nonprofit organizations, concerned parents, and individuals are challenging the wisdom and contesting the use of the curricula in growing numbers (SIECUS 2005). In 2001, organizations launched the *No New Money* campaign to curb federal funding for abstinence-only programs (SIECUS 2006b). By 2006, the *No More Money* campaign to end federal funding for abstinence-only-until-marriage programs was relaunched, and the number of organizations involved in this campaign doubled to 200 compared to the previous campaign (SIECUS 2006b).

Even though opposition to abstinence-only education is growing, and more studies are adding to the accumulating evidence confirming the problematic—even harmful—effects of the curricula, it is unlikely to disappear in the near future. Abstinence-only-until-marriage is a morality policy that fuels and is being fueled by socially constructed notions of youth, gender, and sexuality. As such, it has followed a similar trajectory of other morality policies. Examining this policy has also uncovered the complex dynamics involved in co-opting, prescribing, and implementing a moral vision as a stealth morality policy.

THE POLITICS OF SEX AND VALUES

Although sexual health advocates share common ground concerning the desired outcomes of sexual education—improving teens' sexual health—they radically depart in terms of how to produce the desired outcomes. The discourse surrounding sexual health is contentious because much of the discourse is grounded in advocates' respective value systems. Abstinence-only education is in many respects a classic case of a morality policy. The emergence of the "problem," the framing process, and the level of conflict surrounding this policy follow an expected pattern.

Complex and overlapping social issues are framed in simplistic terms that lend themselves to easy and "right" solutions because they are "moral" solutions. The problem and solution definition processes involved with morality politics fosters greater citizen participation because when morals are being touted as a solution to social problems, everyone with a sense of "right" morals is encouraged to participate and see themselves as experts on the issues. The role of experts is discounted or even dismissed in this process. This has been the case with abstinence-only education. Abstinence-only programs unabashedly advance a particular set of morals and values that are based on conservative, Christian teachings. This is reflected in the content of the curricula and illustrated by the reliance on "moral" authorities to author the curricula rather than education or health experts. Keeping with the typical pattern of morality politics, over time, conservative groups have amassed "evidence" supporting the efficacy of abstinence-only education; however, the "evidence" has not been supported or replicated by studies that rely on the scientific method of inquiry, nor does it appear in rigorous, peer reviewed publications.

Abstinence-only education developed from a concern about the moral and sexual health of adolescents. It emerged on the scene at a time when teen pregnancy, birth, and abortion rates were steadily declining. While abstinence-only education in many regards mirrors the expected development of a morality policy, it presents two new insights into them. First, morality politics are an attempt to restructure social and cultural values; however, the target group is usually specific, so the reach of these policies is fairly limited. The inclusion of abstinence-only-until-marriage provisions as part of the 1996 welfare reform package is a unique and innovative mechanism for widening the scope of morality policies. Although abstinence-only was initially included in reform efforts under the guise of preventing teen pregnancy and subsequent welfare use, the span of the policy is much greater. As we have attempted to demonstrate, abstinence-only education is not only concerned with potential welfare users. Rather, as we have argued, in many ways it is equally if not more concerned with the values and morals of the middle class.

To enhance our understanding as to how the scope of this morality policy was extended well beyond current and potential welfare recipients, we have examined the interplay between social construction theory and morality politics. Morality politics are advanced from a particular worldview, which generally structures the world in binary terms of what is "right" and what is "wrong." Ascribing to a dichotomous worldview necessitates that individuals in society are viewed in similar terms. The target group (or groups) of a morality policy are constructed as "wrong," which is why the policy exists—to impose the "right" values upon them.

Policy scholars have argued that understanding the politics of social construction can aid in understanding policy agendas and formulation (Schneider and

Ingram 1993). Elected officials initiate policies in response to a problem that has been identified. While articulating the problem, politicians have to identify the group that is exhibiting the behavior that the policy intends to correct. Thus, policy is shaped with a specific group of people (or target population) in mind. The criteria used to identify the target population may or may not be value-based.

Within the purview of morality policies, officials and other relevant political actors use value-based criteria to identify shared characteristics of the target population. These shared traits, which define the target group, are socially constructed and arrived at through the process of characterizing groups of people based on cultural symbols, popular images, political status, and power. Groups are assigned either positive or negative attributes that subsequently are sustained through metaphors, symbolic language, and stories.

The social construction of a group helps shape what types of policies are designed for them. Populations that are positively constructed are more likely to be the recipients of advantageous policies, whereas negatively constructed populations are more likely to receive policy measures that are punitive and coercive. Positive and negative characterizations of a target population are intimately tied to the amount of power a group possesses. Schneider and Ingram (1993) organize target populations into four groups based on the intersection of the group's social construction (positive or negative) and their political power (strong or weak).

Public officials pay attention to how the politics of social construction play out for reelection purposes. They are sensitive to how the target population—as well as other groups—will react to the policies they advocate because of the potential payoff (or conversely, backlash) the official may receive when up for reelection. Populations falling into the positive and strong category (e.g., the elderly and corporate interests) tend to be advantaged by politicians because these groups can assist in their bid for reelection. Groups who are negatively constructed and politically weak (e.g., drug addicts and criminals) will often be the recipients of punitive policies and find themselves on the political agenda because politicians do not fear retribution from these groups. Consequently, policies designed for the negatively constructed, politically weak are often illogical in terms of policy effectiveness (Schneider and Ingram 1993).

Adolescents are politically weak; they are both visible and invisible in society, depending on what aspects of teen lives, choices, and experiences are deliberated. When issues such as juvenile crime, teen pregnancy, or teen sexuality are being debated, teens become very visible. Beyond their "deviance," teens are largely invisible. Teens also oscillate between negative and positive social constructions, and they are frequently constructed in oppositional terms at the same time.

Advocates for abstinence-only education view adolescents in dichotomous terms: sexually active or sexually pure. Teens that have had sex (or are sexually active) are constructed as moral deviants who need to be brought back within the umbrella of acceptable Christian values. Alternatively, teens that have not had sex are defined as morally sound individuals whose moral resolve needs to be supported. In both cases, abstinence-only policy is only possible to the extent that the policy capitalizes on socially constructed understandings of adolescence, sexuality, and gender.

In turn, morality policies reinforce, legitimize, and perpetuate socially constructed definitions and understandings of the recipients of the policy. To better understand the enduring nature of many morality policies, we have argued that we need to more thoroughly examine the intersection of social construction and morality policies. Advancing morality policy is a discursive process because it plays on existing social constructions of a group, while helping to create and shape those constructions.

Many morality policies persist despite evidence demonstrating their ineffectiveness. We see this dynamic with abstinence-only education, which also speaks to the second insight gleaned from this study—the power of stealth morality policies. To date there is an absence of credible evidence demonstrating the efficacy of abstinence-only curricula, and public opinion is not supportive of it; however, it has grown significantly in terms of resources and implementation in the states. Examining the role of social construction in morality politics and tracing the origin of abstinence-only instruction may go a long way to account for this paradox. Using stealth tactics, advocates for abstinence-only education devised a strategy to include this weakly supported provision into a complex welfare reform bill, without any congressional floor debate or vote. By the time this stealth tactic was popularly discovered, the policy was already signed into law. Within this nexus— a negative and politically weak target group and a stealth policy—morality policies may easily exceed their originally intended audience.

Reversing this policy will take much more effort than was necessary to initiate it. And as long as morality policies build from existing social constructions and in turn perpetuate them, they will continue to exist regardless of contrary evidence. Even without popular public or political support for abstinence-only education, the invisibility of teens will aid in the continuation of this policy.

TOWARD A DIFFERENT VISION OF SEX EDUCATION

The dynamic between the social construction of teens and the policies that have been aimed at improving their sexual health continue to fail American youth on multiple levels. The United States has one of the highest teen pregnancy rates, childbearing rates, abortion rates, and sexually transmitted infection rates in the developed world, but American teens do not appreciably differ in terms of their sexual activity compared to other countries (Guttmacher Institute 2001, 2006). Much evidence also exists demonstrating American teens' limited understanding of sexuality, which is expressed in sexual discourses such as their beliefs about gender roles in sexual relationships and their struggle with rejecting rape myths.

Curricula alone do not shape and influence teens. Teenagers' knowledge, interpretation, and understanding of social norms and structures are molded by multiple individual, familial, cultural and political factors. American teenagers have less access to family planning information and services compared to teens in other developed countries, which helps account for American teens' higher levels of pregnancies, childbearing, abortions, and sexually transmitted diseases (Guttmacher Institute 2002). The role of economic, familial, and social disadvantage also must be considered; disadvantaged teens in the United States, Canada, Sweden, France, England, and Wales are more likely than their advantaged peers to experience riskier sexual behavior and higher levels of childbearing during adolescence (Guttmacher Institute 2002). Disadvantage partially accounts for teens' poorer performance on sexual health indicators in the United States because, relative to the other countries, it has the highest percentage of its population living in poverty.

Poverty alone, however, is not the only factor shaping access—and the subsequent consequences resulting from limited access—to family planning services. Political rhetoric in the United States emphasizes the role of individual responsibility, and this extends down to adolescents. "Personal responsibility" is reflected in teen anti-pregnancy campaigns that use slogans such as "You play, you pay," as well as codified into policies governing the conditions in which parenting teens are eligible for public assistance. Americans' general attitudes toward adolescent sexuality are very different from those found in other countries where teen sexuality and sexual activity is viewed in terms of part of the maturation process and transition from adolescence to young adulthood (Guttmacher Institute 2002).

The view of adolescents in the United States is quite opposite to this view, where *sexual activity* among teens is perceived as the problem. Religious conservatives have been very successful in promoting policies that align with their particular view of the world. Their world view includes a preservation and reclamation of patriarchy, parental order, heterosexuality, and Christianity (Rose 2005, 1224). Within this world view, "In the battle over sexuality and choice, it's girls' and women's bodies, lives, and livelihoods that are all too often sacrificed—blamed, marginalized and held accountable for creating the problem of teen pregnancy" (Rose 2005, 1224).

Teens are socially constructed in both positive and negative terms, neither of which allows them to participate and interact in society with any appreciable degree of autonomy. If they are "deviant" they need to be controlled, and if they are "innocent" they are in need of protection. Both views are stunting and limiting in terms of the choices teens' can make and the outlets they can turn to for support. As Valerie Lehr (2006) notes, there is a price associated with these understandings of teens:

> It is also clear that there are costs to maintaining the construction that young people are dependent, and under the control of parents or schools, until they become independent and able to be self-supporting. One cost is that this construction assumes a clear transition to adulthood that increasingly is not reflective of actual young people's lives. (Lehr 2006, 15)

In other words, a healthier understanding of adolescents would require society to see them as interdependent: capable of exercising sexual agency, making decisions, *and* seeking guidance from trusted adults. "If the ideal decision-maker is, rather, a person who consults with others to weight alternatives and make decisions that will have an impact on both self and others, there is quite good evidence that young people do this from a relatively early age, particularly when they are in contexts where they are encouraged to develop their capacities and supported in their decisions" (Lehr 2006, 15–16). Many teens already follow a decision-making process and model that is similar to the model used by adults. Regarding sexual health, this understanding of youth would translate into a more thorough treatment of sexuality in sex education curricula, one that includes information not solely about sexual health but also about healthy relationships and the role of intimacy and sexual activity within them.

BIBLIOGRAPHY

Boonstra, Heather. 2002. "Teen Pregnancy: Trends and Lessons Learned." *The Guttmacher Report on Public Policy* 5 (1): 7–10.

Boyer, Debra, and David Fine. 1992. "Sexual Abuse as a Factor in Adolescent Pregnancy and Child Maltreatment." *Family Planning Perspectives* 24 (1): 4–11, 19.

Butler, Judith. 1990. *Gender Trouble: Feminism and the Subversion of Identity*. New York: Routledge.

Carpenter, Laura M. 2002. "Gender and the Meaning and Experience of Virginity Loss in the Contemporary United States." *Gender and Society* 16 (3): 345–65.

Ferree, Myra Marx, Judith Lorber, and Beth B. Hess. 1999. *Revisioning Gender*. Thousand Oaks: Sage Publications.

Guttmacher Institute. 2002. "Sexuality Education." *Facts in Brief*. Available at: http://www.guttmacher.org/pubs/Factsheet_121399.html.

Guttmacher Institute. 2001. "Teenagers Sexual and Reproductive Health: Developed Countries." *Facts in Brief*. Available at: http://www.guttmacher.org/pubs/fb_teens.html.

Guttmacher Institute. 2006. "Facts on American Teens' Sexual and Reproductive Health." *Facts in Brief*. Available at: http://www.guttmacher.org/pubs/fb_ATSRH.html.

Ivins, Molly. 2002. "Dr. Laura's Later Cause." *No Comment: Rethinking Schools On-Line* 16 (4). Available at: http://www.rethinkingschools.org/archive/16_04/Ncom164.shtml.

Kaiser Family Foundation Publication. 2002. "Communication." SexSmarts: A Public Information Partnership #3240 (July). Available at: http://www.kff.org/youthhivstds/3240-index.cfm.

Kaiser Family Foundation Publication. 2003a. "National Survey of Adolescents and Young Adults: Sexual Health Knowledge, Attitudes and Experiences." Available at: http://www.kff.org/youthhivestds/3218-index.cfm.

Kaiser Family Foundation Publication. 2003b. "Virginity and the First Time." SexSmarts: A Public Information Partnership #3368 (October). Available at: http://www.kff.org/entpartnerships/3368-index.cfm.

Landry, David, Lisa Kaeser, and Cory L. Richards. 1999. "Abstinence Promotion and the Provision of Information About Contraception in Public School District Sexuality Education Policies." *Family Planning Perspectives* 31 (6): 280–86.

Lehr, Valerie. 2006. "Sexual Agency in Risk Society." Conference paper delivered at the Annual Meeting of the Midwest Political Science Association, Chicago, April.

Lorber, Judith. 1994. *Paradoxes of Gender*. New Haven, CT: Yale University Press.

Rose, Susan. 2005. "Going Too Far? Sex, Sin and Social Policy." *Social Forces* 84 (2): 1207–32.

Schneider, Anne, and Helen Ingram. 1993. "Social Construction of Target Populations: Implications for Politics and Policy." *The American Political Science Review* 87 (2): 334–47.

SIECUS. 2005. "Sexuality Education and Abstinence-Only-Until-Marriage Programs in the States: An Overview." *Policy and Advocacy*. Available at: http://www.siecus.org/policy/states/2006/analysis.html.

SIECUS. 2006a. "How Medical Inaccuracies, Fear, and Shame in Federally Funded Abstinence-Only-Until-Marriage Programs Put our Youth at Risk." *Press Release* (October 4). Available at: http://www.siecus.org/media/press/press0133.html.

SIECUS. 2006b. "200 Organizations Launch Nationwide Campaign to Stem Funding for Abstinence-Only-Until-Marriage Programs." *Press Release* (June 6). Available at: http://www.siecus.org/media/press/press0125.html.

Vergari, Sandra. 2001. "Morality Politics and the Implementation of Abstinence-Only Sex Education: A Case of Policy Compromise." In *The Public Clash of Private Values*, ed. Christopher Z. Mooney, 201–12. New York: Chatham House Publishers.

Selected Annotated Bibliography

Carpenter, Laura M. 2005. *Virginity Lost: An Intimate Portrait of First Sexual Experiences*. New York: New York University Press.

Carpenter examines the cultural meanings and lived experiences of virginity loss through interviews with gay, bisexual, and straight young women and men. In the context of her analysis of virginity loss, Carpenter evaluates abstinence-only sex education, showing that the abstinence-only model of sex education teaches teens to view virginity as a gift, to be "given" in the context of heterosexual marriage.

Irvine, Janice M. 2002. *Talk about Sex: The Battles over Sex Education in the United States*. Berkeley: University of California Press.

Talk about Sex investigates the impact of the Christian Right on the politics of sexuality and sex education at both the local and national levels. Irvine describes the political, cultural, and rhetorical conflicts over sex education that began in the late 1960s with the early mobilization of the Christian Right. She shows that Christian conservatives have long recognized the effectiveness of the issue of sexuality—and sex education—as a tool for political mobilization.

Luker, Kristin. 2006. *When Sex Goes to School: Warring Views on Sex—And Sex Education—Since the Sixties*. New York: W.W. Norton & Company.

Luker analyzes the theoretical underpinnings of conservative and liberal views on sexuality, mining the personal experiences and belief systems of parents, students, and activists to shed light on the sex education debate. *When Sex Goes to School* explores the history of sex education and related conflicts, suggesting that arguments about sex education are related to questions about the place of marriage in society and disputes about how to define and interpret gender and sexuality.

McFarlane, Deborah R., and Kenneth J. Meier. 2001. *The Politics of Fertility Control: Policies in the American States.* New York: Chatham House Publishers.
McFarlane and Meier take a thorough look at the past 30 years of fertility control policies in the United States. They implement a morality politics framework to help understand the genesis of these policies. McFarlane and Meier argue that the current practice of approaching fertility policies as morality policies is ineffective and creates an unnecessarily conflictual and complex environment. The authors conclude that current policies are woefully inadequate for solving unintended pregnancies and actually add to the high pregnancy rate found in the United States. *The Politics of Fertility Control* ultimately presses for implementing an alternative policy design to create more sound policy in the future.

Mooney, Christopher Z., Ed. 2001. *The Public Clash of Private Values: The Politics of Morality Policy.* New York: Chatham House Publishers.
In this edited collection, Mooney pulls together the scholarship on morality politics to develop a cohesive framework for examining morality policies. These are unique policies that are concerned with moral, rather than material, policy issues. Within this morality politics framework, various scholars investigate issues such as pornography, physician-assisted suicide, sex education, and abortion. The common thread between these disparate policies is their concern with contentious moral issues that continue to face policymakers and the public in contemporary society.

Sanford F. Schram, Joe Soss, and Richard C. Fording, Eds. 2003. *Race and the Politics of Welfare Reform.* Ann Arbor: The University of Michigan Press.
Race and the Politics of Welfare Reform is a collection of essays addressing the centrality of race, both historically and currently, in U.S. welfare policy. The authors examine numerous aspects of poverty and welfare policy, including public opinion, the role of the media, policy implementation, and social constructions of race, class, and gender. *Race and the Politics of Welfare Reform* puts the 1996 welfare reforms into historical and cultural perspective, arguing that race, racism, and racial stereotypes have been integral to and significantly shaped welfare policy in the United States.

Sharp, Elaine B. 2005. *Morality Politics in American Cities.* Lawrence: University Press of Kansas.
Morality Politics in American Cities takes a look at many of the most contentious morality issues in contemporary America: abortion, gambling, pornography, and gay rights to name a few. Instead of focusing on the national dimensions of these debates, Sharp conducts an innovative study that investigates how these morality issues and politics play out in local, urban communities. Through her research, Sharp shows how local morality politics are connected to national politics and how important urban centers are to understanding morality politics more generally.

Tolman, Deborah L. 2002. *Dilemmas of Desire: Teenage Girls Talk about Sexuality.* Cambridge, MA: Harvard University Press.

Dilemmas of Desire is a study of adolescent sexuality and girls' sexual desire through interviews with young women. Tolman deconstructs the notion that girls and women do not have strong sexual desires as compared to men, showing how the absence of culturally available "discourses of desire" associated with women affects young women's sexuality and social development. Tolman calls for a transformation of constructions of gendered adolescent sexuality, toward enabling young women to fully express their sexualities and to develop sexual agency.

Index

About the Authors

ALESHA E. DOAN is Assistant Professor of Political Science at the University of Kansas. She is the author of *Opposition and Intimidation: The Abortion Wars and Strategies of Political Harassment*.

JEAN CALTERONE WILLIAMS is Associate Professor of Political Science and Department Chair at California Polytechnic State University. She is the author of *"A Roof Over My Head": Homeless Women and the Shelter Industry*.